W9-BGV-006

Sun Rise

SUN RISE

SUNCOR, THE OIL SANDS AND THE FUTURE OF ENERGY

RICK GEORGE

Former Suncor President and CEO

with JOHN LAWRENCE REYNOLDS

HarperCollins Publishers Ltd

Sun Rise

Copyright © 2012 by Rick George.
All rights reserved.

Published by HarperCollins Publishers Ltd

First edition

HarperCollins books may be purchased for educational, business,
or sales promotional use through our Special Markets Department.

HarperCollins Publishers Ltd
2 Bloor Street East, 20th Floor
Toronto, Ontario, Canada
M4W 1A8

www.harpercollins.ca

Library and Archives Canada Cataloguing in Publication
information is available upon request.

ISBN 978-1-44340-892-9

Printed and bound in the United States

RRD 9 8 7 6 5 4 3 2 1

CONTENTS

1. STEPPING INTO CORPORATE QUICKSAND 1

2. A BUSINESS OF BIG BETS. 13

3. MY CAREER PATH: FROM PICK-UP TRUCKS TO WHITE ELEPHANTS 27

4. SUNCOR BECOMES PROFITABLE . . . AND CANADIAN 43

5. CLEANING UP AFTER MOTHER NATURE 65

6. MOVING WEST: RELOCATING CLOSER TO THE ACTION 77

7. THE PETRO-CANADA SAGA. 89

8. BLENDING CULTURES AND VALUES AT THE NEW SUNCOR 111

9. FUN AND PROFIT: THE SECRETS BEHIND SUNCOR SUCCESS 125

10. THE IMPORTANCE OF A SECOND MARKET FOR CANADA'S OIL. 137

11. MEETING FIRST NATIONS OBLIGATIONS 151

12. HOW TO STEADY A THREE-LEGGED STOOL 161

13. THE ALWAYS PRESENT (AND FREQUENTLY FRUSTRATING) POLITCS OF
    PETROLEUM. 175

14. THE CHALLENGE OF GLOBAL WARMING 189

15. THE LEGENDARY TWO-JAWED FISH 205

16. THE PROMISE OF ALTERNATIVE FUELS 221

17. EMPHASIZING DEEDS OVER WORDS 239

18. A GREEN AND PLEASANT FUTURE 249

ACKNOWLEDGEMENTS 263

NOTES 265

INDEX. 272

1. Stepping into Corporate Quicksand

In early 1991 I stood on a platform just north of Fort McMurray, Alberta, and surveyed what I suspected would mark the end of my career in the petroleum industry.

I was staring at an essentially malfunctioning industrial plant located in a stretch of northern boreal forest extending as far as the eye could see in every direction. The wilderness had a kind of majestic beauty often associated with the North, and it served as home to a few thousand First Nations residents, along with black bear, moose, beaver and various predators. The land had been carved and irrigated for millions of years by the Athabasca River, which originates in the Columbia Icefield within the Canadian Rockies straddling the continental divide and meanders north, eventually joining the Mackenzie River on its way to the Arctic Ocean.

The landscape was gently rolling, almost flat. There is a magnificence about such vast open country, even when it lacks dramatic landmarks, but this area appeared destined to remain unknown and unexplored, save for the bands of First Nations who have survived its harsh climate for a millennium or two. Lacking both mineral resources and tourist appeal, the land had little to offer the world beyond a habitat for those First Nations people and the fish and wildlife that sustained them. With one enormous exception.

Beneath the surface was an estimated 1.8 trillion barrels of crude oil, making it the largest resource of its kind in the world.

Unlike virtually all the other sources of petroleum tapped throughout the globe since the first commercial oil well was drilled in 1853, this did not await discovery and drainage like some massive subterranean swimming pool. The petroleum is suspended for the most part in a blend of sand, clay and water below ground and beneath a covering layer of shale. And it's not even petroleum as we know it. It looks nothing like the amber-coloured, easily flowing oil that you may see being poured into your car's engine, or even the "black gold" spewing from the gusher oil wells depicted in movies.

In fact, it's not oil. It's bitumen, a sticky black substance with the characteristics of thick, cold molasses. The nearest you're likely to get to bitumen in its raw form is when you drive on asphalt roads; asphalt is composed of bitumen that has been heated and mixed with fine gravel.

First Nations people encountered bitumen seeping out of the ground in various locations throughout this section of northern Alberta at least a thousand years ago, and they made practical use of it, applying the more fluid sources to the seams of their canoes to seal them from water. They also discovered that burning the substance in pots created a smudge to ward off the hordes of black flies and mosquitoes that clouded the skies.

These massive reserves of bitumen make up Canada's oil sands,[*] and while they may be unique in size, they are not unique in the world. A deposit almost as large as Alberta's can be found in Venezuela, and smaller bitumen reserves are located in the United States,

---

* Many people use the term *tar sands*, a description that not only suggests negative qualities but is also factually incorrect. Tar has no relation to petroleum; it is a synthetic substance derived from wood, primarily pine. The region I'm speaking of is rich in petroleum-based material and should be referred to as *oil sands*.

Russia, Africa and the Middle East. The dream of recovering oil from Alberta bitumen on a commercial basis was born in the 1900s, when John D. Rockefeller was building Standard Oil into the giant that we now know primarily as ExxonMobil. (Standard Oil was broken into several companies in 1911.) The most appealing feature of the oil sands was the fact that they were there to be taken. Instead of cruising the world in search of oil hidden beneath ground and drilling ten dry wells for every one that proved successful, why not focus on the largest known source of oil?

A lot of minds went to work on the idea over the years. A lot of money was spent to make it happen and a lot of companies invested millions of dollars in the dream. One of them was my employer at the time, Sun Oil, which began processing bitumen from the oil sands in 1967. After more than twenty years of unproductive effort, Sun recruited me to make the oil sands work where those before me had failed, although that's not how my assignment was viewed by others. Failure had been so deeply ingrained in the company over the years that many employees suspected I had been tapped to shut down the project entirely and cut Sun's losses.

I could have turned down the job. In fact, there were times during my first few years in Canada when I wondered why I *hadn't* turned it down.

I had already achieved more than I envisioned for a guy from Brush, Colorado, population around five thousand people with maybe an equal number of cattle and horses. When the job offer arrived I was living in London, England, with my family—wife, Julie; sons Zachary and Matt, thirteen and ten, respectively; and five-year-old daughter, Emily. We had been in Britain, moving between London and Aberdeen, Scotland, for ten years and, after something of a cultural adjustment, enjoying it. I was in charge of Sun Oil's international operations on the upstream side, which included exploring for oil, developing reserves, producing the oil and transporting it to the customer. My responsibilities included operations in the North Sea, the Middle East and a few other regions beyond North America.

I enjoyed my work. At age forty I had spent my entire working life, including high school summer jobs, in the petroleum industry. Living in London with a young family, relatively free to make major decisions far from the interference of head office back in Philadelphia, I was satisfied with both my life and my career. Julie and I took our children for vacations in Europe, where we treated them to sights, cultures and experiences that enriched their lives as much as they did ours. London remained one of the world's great vibrant cities, and the international petroleum industry was growing more dynamic in its range and challenges with every passing year. Alberta was not only far away geographically; it was far from my mind as well.

Yet as much as I find satisfaction in my work, I also enjoy tackling new challenges. In my position in London, these were as small as making a personnel change and as massive and complex as supervising the design and installation of the world's first purpose-built floating production vessel to tap North Sea oil, a project that proved exceptionally successful and earned me the position of running Sun's international operations.

When Tom Thomson, CEO of Suncor, Sun Oil's Canadian arm, asked me to consider coming to Canada as his appointed successor, I had one reason—I was comfortable and settled—for saying no. I had two reasons for at least giving it consideration. One was Tom himself, a cultured man with high integrity and admirable values, whom I liked personally. His request was even more persuasive because I knew Tom was suffering from terminal cancer, and my selection would probably be his last major management decision.

The other reason was my inclination to look for new challenges. Taking over the reins at Suncor would mean making its oil sands operations profitable, something no one had managed to do so far. I suspected it would be the most demanding task I had ever assumed, and my optimistic outlook made me believe I could succeed.

I'm no Pollyanna, but whenever I'm faced with a problem, I tend to focus on the positive side rather than evaluating all the things that may go wrong. On the scale of the old "Is the glass half empty or half full?" cliché, I tend to consider the glass completely full. This has inspired a lot of kidding from my children, who say I'm the most optimistic person they've ever known.

They may be right. I don't know where it comes from, but I always find myself avoiding the prospect of failure, of any kind. I honestly wake up every morning thinking that the world is an amazing place and that by the end of the day I will have learned something new that I don't know about yet.

The combination of affection and concern for my friend Tom Thomson, curiosity in a fresh challenge and my innate optimism persuaded me to accept the position and move with my family from London to Toronto. I did this with the realization that I would be working on a project with weak prospects for success, an operation famous for the number of problems it had to cope with and the number of years it had failed to meet both production and profit expectations. As if I needed another disincentive, I learned the company had undergone a major labour dispute in 1986 that lasted almost six months. Was it any surprise that the firm had been tagged with the title "Canada's unluckiest oil company"? It occurred to me that this might not just be oil sands. Maybe it was corporate quicksand.

Sun Oil had been founded in Pennsylvania more than a hundred years earlier and, like most other petroleum companies in the United States, it grew in rough proportion to the automobile industry.* On its hundredth anniversary, Sun ranked number twenty on the Fortune 500 list of American corporations, employing almost 40,000 people and investing $1.5 billion in capital spending each year. It had opened Sun Company of Canada as a subsidiary in 1919, incorporating it as Sun Oil Company in the 1920s, and operated a chain of Sunoco service stations across much of the eastern area of the country, fed by a refinery in Sarnia, Ontario.

The Canadian arm began to develop the oil sands soon after the Second World War, and Sun became the majority shareholder in the Great Canadian Oil Sands, or GCOS, in 1967. Within a few years, GCOS was rolled into Sun Oil Canada, or Suncor, with the entire oil sands development managed from Dallas, Texas.

Things didn't go well from the beginning. Between production costs that floated near or above market prices and an apparently endless cycle of fires and freeze-ups, the oil sands operation was costing Sun Oil about $100 million each year. Desperate to stem the flow of red ink, the company began selling many of its Sunoco service stations in Canada, using the revenue to buoy up its oil sands operation. Just to complicate things a little more, 25 percent of Suncor had been sold to the province of Ontario in the 1980s, driven in part by a nationalistic fervour dictating that Canadians, whose petroleum industry was dominated by foreign giants, should own at least part of a foreign-owned company that was exploiting its natural resource.

---

* The corporate history becomes rather convoluted as the name changed several times over the years. The parent company got its start in life as the People's Natural Gas Company in Pittsburgh in 1886 but soon became the Sun Oil Company and took on variations of the name Sun Oil and Sun Company before eventually becoming Sunoco in 1998. On the Canadian side, after a brief stint as Sun Company of Canada from 1919 to 1923, the company was known as Sun Oil until 1979, when it became Suncor, and ultimately Suncor Energy in 1997. I use Sun, Sun Oil, and Sun Company interchangeably to refer to all the incarnations of the American parent.

The Ontario investment was based on politics, not economics. Canada's federal government had launched an integrated oil producer and marketer, Petro-Canada, as a Crown corporation a few years earlier. Petro-Canada, it was trumpeted, would provide the country with a window on the domestic petroleum industry during a period of international unrest and sporadic global gasoline shortages. As Canada's biggest consumer of petroleum products, Ontario demanded its own window, which is how the provincial politicians justified their investment of public money in a private company. In fact, their motives were more ambitious. The terms of the agreement committed Suncor to transfer majority ownership and control of the company to Canadians "as quickly as possible," and if it did not achieve this goal by the end of 1984, the province would retain the right to negotiate the purchase of an additional 26 percent of Suncor common shares.

This was no marriage made in heaven. Sun's head office people in Philadelphia were growing more and more impatient with the oil sands investment, meaning the Canadian operations generally. The sale of one-quarter of the company to the province of Ontario brought the Americans some cash, but they neither benefited from nor welcomed the participation of Canadian politicians and their staff in the decision-making process. One solution could have been for Sun Oil to take Suncor public entirely; creating a 100 percent Canadian-owned company would have left it free to pocket the cash and someone else to deal with the oil sands. This might have worked if the price of oil had remained high, but by the mid-1980s prices were drifting below $7 per barrel. No one wanted to buy into an historically money-losing oil operation, especially one associated with fires, labour problems and high production costs. And, facing its own financial problems in the United States, parent Sun Oil wasn't interested in advancing yet more money into Canadian Suncor. It was stuck with a losing hand.

In 1985, Sun Oil enticed Tom Thomson from Esso (Exxon's Canadian subsidiary) to run Suncor. It would be difficult to find two more contrasting corporate personalities than Suncor and Exxon. Exxon's approach to management has always been tightly disciplined, following strict guidelines. In comparison, Sun's approach at the time, especially where the oil sands were concerned, consisted for the most part of flying by the seat of its pants.

Tom and Suncor were not a good fit. He disliked the oil sands, disliked the near-constant interference from Philadelphia and disliked the rather loose method of management he encountered at Suncor. The folks at head office didn't appear interested in helping him. Meanwhile, the directors representing Ontario's interests were not at all happy with the performance of the province's investment.

This was the scene I walked into in early 1991 when I accepted Tom's invitation to fill the post first as Suncor COO and later, with the knowledge and understanding of Tom's medical condition, as CEO. I was aware of the internal strife at Suncor, its dismal performance and the complex ownership arrangement. I was not aware of the extent of the oil sands operation and the depth of the problems to be overcome if the oil sands were to cease being a drag on the company's fortunes and begin building a decent return on its investment.

That first visit to the Suncor facility near Fort McMurray opened my eyes to the scope of the challenge, which is when I began asking myself if my move from London represented the first step toward the end of my career. Subsequent visits and an opportunity to look deeply into the history of failures launched a new perspective. The constant inability of Suncor to generate reasonable profits was linked to ongoing production problems at the oil sands, creating a doomsday mentality among Suncor people. Gossip in the company's coffee rooms often centred on when—not if—the company would be sold or shut down. When profits dropped in Suncor's conventional oil and gas business, including the operation of its chain of Sunoco service stations, the response of head office had been to terminate employees. Even the exploration side was underperforming; its failures at finding new sources of crude oil and natural gas consistently placed the company in the bottom quartile within the industry. All of this, when I arrived in Toronto and later travelled to Fort McMurray, was happening in the midst of a highly competitive market and a nasty global recession.

In fact, the only thing lower than the company's prospects was the morale of its employees. Things were so bad that it took a telephone and letter-writing campaign by management to urge attendance at the annual Christmas party. Communication between divisions within the company was practically non-existent, and when I looked around for a corporate culture I found . . . nothing. It didn't exist, either written or in the minds of Suncor people.

Some people within Suncor suggested the oil sands would be a millstone around my neck, an insoluble problem that would drag the company and me ever downward, just as it had my predecessors. But the more I thought about the potential of the oil sands, and the more I reflected on the basic production problems that had been apparent to me from my first exposure to the site, the more I reconsidered the analogy. If I could implement some ideas that occurred to me during that first visit, I could transform the site's historically negative cash flow into a long-term profitable venture. The company needed hope as much as anything. As soon as Suncor employees began to see that the company was capable of producing profits, they would respond to the creation of a corporate culture and a strategy based on achieving success. And once we erased the red ink from the books, I could free myself and the company from excessive head office interference, start attracting new talent and turn a losing mentality into a winning attitude.

I was uncertain how much time it would take to achieve these goals, and I was definitely unaware of the obstacles I would encounter along the way. And although a voice inside me kept insisting, through the first few weeks of my experience with the oil sands, that I should turn around and head back to London, I remained for more than twenty years.

Over that period I discovered more about petroleum technology, about the energy industry, about the concerns of environmentalists, about the First Nations people of the North and about myself than I ever expected to know. I needed that knowledge to tackle the many unexpected responsibilities of being Suncor's CEO, including assuming stewardship of the wilderness environment in which we operated, employing new technology to lead the industry to higher levels of efficiency, stressing the importance of community within and beyond the corporation, and managing enormous levels of growth in a controlled manner that benefits a variety of participants, many of them opposed to our corporate existence.

Apparently it worked. In the twenty-one years from 1991 to 2012, Suncor grew from a primarily U.S.-owned company valued at less than $1 billion to a wholly Canadian corporation with a capitalization of more than $50 billion.

It was gratifying, and it was often fun. Not always, of course. I met with my share of disappointments, let-downs and lessons.

Anyway, they are all here in as much detail as I dare reveal. And whether you believe Suncor and the oil sands represent one of the great business stories of our generation or a threat to the future of mankind, you will find much on the following pages to answer questions and stimulate reflection. And maybe some controversy as well. That's fine with me. Few things in the twenty-first century are more controversial than the impact of Canada's oil sands and their means of satisfying the world's future energy needs.

The one thing I hope you will keep in mind through the rest of this book is my sincerity in telling the story, my insistence on dealing with facts over fancy.

Who needs fancy when the facts are so fascinating on their own?

2. A Business of Big Bets

Most people encounter the oil industry in one of two ways. Both tend to leave a negative impression.

One occurs when they are filling up the fuel tanks of their cars or trucks and discover that gasoline costs more per litre or per gallon than it did last week, last month or last year. The fact that lower prices for gasoline (yes, they happen now and then) are rarely noticed, and that prices seem to jump on summer weekends when motorists are buying more gasoline, adds to the impression that giant oil companies are ripping off consumers.

The other encounter occurs when they read in newspapers or see on TV the supposedly terrible effects of the petroleum industry on our air, water, health and the general well-being of the world. Is oil really the biggest risk to humanity since the Black Plague? Based on news reports and statements by some environmental groups, it's easy to believe this is true.

I'm not dismissing these perceptions of the industry in which I have invested all of my adult life. They are held, for the most part, by people sincere in their beliefs, and I respect their point of view. I grow frustrated only when that point of view reflects either a hidden agenda or total ignorance of the truth. Many facts easily located and confirmed tend to be overlooked or simply ignored by critics, yet they explain much that is right and, yes, a few things that are wrong about the petroleum industry.

Here is the first essential fact: gasoline, and most other products derived from crude oil, is a commodity. By definition, commodities vary by price rather than by any substantial difference in their qualities. Your family car, for example, will run as well on gasoline refined from Saudi Arabian crude oil as it will on the same grade of fuel refined from petroleum that originated in Nigeria, Venezuela or the Alberta oil sands. The only real contrasting properties are price and supply, which occupy opposite ends of the same teeter-totter—lower the supply and you raise the price; raise the supply and you lower the price. Pretty basic stuff.

It follows that whoever controls the supply controls the price, and for the last half-century the controls have been in the hands of the Organization of Petroleum Exporting Countries, or OPEC. Algeria, Angola, Ecuador, Iran, Iraq, Kuwait, Libya, Nigeria, Qatar, Saudi Arabia, the United Arab Emirates and Venezuela are the member states. While production figures vary from week to week, about half of the 80 million-plus barrels of oil consumed around the world each day are produced and marketed by OPEC members. Among those twelve members, however, true power rests in the hands of just one: Saudi Arabia. With the world's largest conventional oil reserves and a highly developed and sophisticated production system, the Saudis have dominated global oil production for more than half a century. At least a third of all production from OPEC countries originates in Saudi Arabia.

Unlike other OPEC members, the Saudis neither need nor choose to maximize their oil production. Instead, they regulate it. By increasing or decreasing their production rates, the Saudis control international oil prices as effectively as you change the speed of your car by pressing or releasing the accelerator pedal. The only factor that influences the price of petroleum products, especially gasoline, more directly than the Saudis and their OPEC partners is the taxes imposed by state and federal governments. As a result, Saudi Arabia plays a swing role in oil production. Every other OPEC member keeps its petroleum pedal to the metal for maximum production, leaving it to the Saudis to stimulate either consumption or price, according to the cartel's goals.

The power this provides Saudi Arabia is enormous, as you might expect, and it extends well beyond producing and pricing oil. For example, during the Arab Spring of 2011, citizens in countries throughout the Middle East demanded greater individual rights, wider democratic freedoms and less oppression from their government leaders. The demands led to widespread upheavals. Egypt placed its former dictator on trial, Libya descended into a civil war that resulted in the death of its own dictator, Muammar Gaddafi, and Syria launched a brutal crackdown that saw demonstrators shot dead in the streets. Elsewhere, peaceful protests brought varying degrees of response from national leaders: protestors in Tunisia, Algeria, Morocco and Yemen obtained concessions ranging from the ouster of prime ministers and other senior government members to the release of political prisoners and the promise of free elections. How many of these promises will be fulfilled and made permanent has yet to be determined, but at least the protestors generated a response.

Curiously, almost nothing was heard from Saudi Arabia, a country that historically ranks among the most repressive in the world where human rights are concerned. The Saudis boast that the incidence of crime in their kingdom is low compared with other countries, and they attribute this to a policy of punishment that includes beheading, stoning, amputation and lashing, much of it conducted in public. That's a disturbing price to pay for a low crime rate, and it includes near-total dominance of everyday life by the ruling Saud family. Ordinary citizens lack any vestige of political power, and even the most peaceful protest usually results in jail sentences for participants.

The ban on demonstrations in Saudi Arabia is similar to those in other Middle Eastern countries, yet citizens almost everywhere else chose to ignore threats of violence and arrest. Why not in Saudi Arabia? Because in the Arab Spring, King Abdullah transferred large sums of money generated from oil sales to the two hundred or so princes who wield local control over the country. The princes, it was understood, could use the money to tighten authority or bribe citizen groups and their leaders to avoid demonstrations. However they were achieved, stability and unbending support of the status quo were uppermost. Only the enormous amount of cash in the Saudi Arabian treasury could make this possible.

The Middle East and the rest of the world may be shuffling at various speeds toward greater individual freedom and justice, but few people expect Saudi Arabia to join the movement for at least a few generations. In the fall of 2011, King Saud announced that for the first time in the country's history, women would be permitted to vote in municipal elections. No elections are held at higher levels, however, and all senior posts will continue to be filled by members of the Saud family.

Despite the Arab Spring, OPEC countries are unlikely to mould themselves in the foreseeable future into stable democracies according to Western standards. Saudi Arabia is merely the most prominent OPEC member where limited freedom and human rights abuses are concerned. Of the remaining eleven, only one country—Ecuador—qualifies as a stable democratic state, and its production capacity represents perhaps 1.5 percent of OPEC output. Middle East oil and democratic freedoms are, if not mutually exclusive, a rare combination.

Things don't get much better outside of OPEC. Countries such as Oman, Kazakhstan, Indonesia, Sudan and a host of other petroleum-producing regions are more noted for their repressive or unstable governments than for their contribution to international oil supplies. With much of the world's oil reserves located in countries that are not among the most democratic and tolerant regimes, oil often becomes either a great leveller or a handy blindfold, depending on your point of view.

Of all known oil reserves, only 20 percent are located within countries that can safely be defined as stable democracies, where private petroleum companies are free to operate. Like it or not, much of the petroleum consumed on a global basis is controlled by governments that neither share the West's value systems nor, unlike most democratic countries, channel the funds earned from their petroleum reserves into improving the lives of their citizens.

Everyone familiar with the dynamics of the petroleum industry is aware of OPEC and its power. The organization has proven very effective at achieving its goals over the past forty years, but cartels do not last forever. I expect we will witness a significant change in the power and cohesiveness of OPEC over the next decade. We should be prepared for a rough ride. Worldwide change is never a smooth event, and the demise of OPEC's influence is likely to produce wide volatility in the price of petroleum and perhaps other energy sources as well.

While OPEC's influence remains, countering its economic and political power is neither easy nor effective. The International Energy Agency (IEA) was created in 1974 to "promote diversity, efficiency and flexibility within the energy sectors of the IEA member countries," to "remain prepared collectively to respond to energy emergencies" and to "expand international co-operation with all global players in the energy markets." Its members are Australia, Austria, Belgium, Canada, the Czech Republic, Denmark, Finland, France, Germany, Greece, Hungary, Ireland, Italy, Japan, Luxembourg, the Netherlands, New Zealand, Norway, Poland, Portugal, Slovakia, South Korea,

Spain, Sweden, Switzerland, Turkey, the United Kingdom and the United States. In reality, the IEA was created as a means of balancing the power of OPEC to some degree, as can be read between the lines in its promise to "ensure the stable supply of energy to IEA member countries and promote free markets in order to foster economic growth" and eliminate energy poverty. [1]

IEA's balancing act is more illusion than reality. A good example occurred in June 2011 when, in response to the loss of production due to strife in Libya, the IEA announced it would release 60 million barrels of crude oil from its strategic reserves onto the open market. Only about 40 million barrels were actually released. Still, the move generated a good deal of reaction. It sounded like a lot of oil and it was, until seen against the global consumption level.

Each and every day of the year, the world consumes more than 80 million barrels of oil. On that basis, the headline-grabbing news that IEA was "flooding" the market with 60 million barrels of crude oil actually meant it was replacing less than three-quarters of a single day's use globally. Or half a day in reality. IEA may attempt to level the playing field between OPEC and the rest of the world, but its influence is severely limited.

Oil is found in other regions of the world beyond the OPEC countries, and the process of discovering it continues, with some success. Brazil's production is growing, and shale oil deposits in North America's Bakken formation, an area that stretches from North Dakota and Montana into Saskatchewan, are estimated as high as 20 billion barrels. Geologists and engineers keep looking for new deposits of oil in every region of the world, investing hundreds of millions of dollars on conducting surveys, negotiating land leases and drilling wells—with the average success rate of finding new oil floating around 10 percent.[2]

In the midst of all this activity, a chorus of criticism can be heard from sources ranging from former U.S. president George W.

Bush ("America is addicted to oil") to members of the Sierra Club and similar environmental advocates who, if they could, would snap their collective fingers and in an instant end the use of petroleum products everywhere in the world.

Whatever their motives, these critics are wrong in my opinion. America, or more correctly the industrialized world, is not addicted to oil any more than you and I are addicted to oxygen. Change "oil" to "energy" and things become clearer.

The world needs energy. It needs energy to make life for every human on the planet, seven billion of us and counting, more secure and comfortable. It needs energy to help educate us, transport us, feed us, unite us and cure us when we suffer injury and disease. Yes, we can always walk, ride bicycles, paddle canoes and entertain ourselves without radio, TV or movies. But the things that define so much of our lives in the twenty-first century and make us better educated and healthier than our grandparents demand energy.

By severely restricting the production and the use of petroleum products, we reduce the energy options available. This is clearly counter-productive as long as we do not have a means of substituting that lost energy source with something as cheap, as effective, as secure, as widely available and as environmentally acceptable as petroleum. And we haven't. Not yet.

Like it or not, the energy derived from petroleum has become essential to the lives of most people. What's more, it may become essential to providing food, comfort and health benefits for those people in sub-Saharan Africa and elsewhere in the world who badly need all three. Petroleum as a source of energy can help provide them.

Someone calculated the total volume of oil the world consumes each year as one cubic mile.[3] You may want to stop and imagine that for a minute. A pool of oil a mile in each direction and a mile deep. That's how much we pull out of the ground to meet the world's petroleum needs every year, and the need is growing year after year. That's not our total energy needs, by the way. To replace all the other sources of energy used around the world, including coal, wood, hydroelectricity, nuclear, solar and wind, would require another two cubic miles of petroleum, since only a third of our energy needs currently come from oil. Of these other sources, coal and wood represent by far the largest volume.

You can argue that the world can and must be weaned from oil to at least some degree, but let's consider the time needed to switch energy sources in the past. In 1700, the world depended on wood almost exclusively for its energy needs, which consisted of heating and cooking. It took two hundred years for coal to replace wood as the primary source of energy. In the mid-1800s, while coal was becoming the leading fuel source, petroleum-derived kerosene began growing as a substitute. Kerosene was eventually displaced by natural gas and, with the advent of motor vehicles, by gasoline and diesel fuel. Each stage in the process took at least fifty years. How long will it take us to move from petroleum to some new energy source? And what will that source be? Wind turbines? Solar panels? Nuclear power? I suspect the period between serious implementation of these technologies and their ability to meet a significant percentage of demand on a worldwide scale will take a century.

The changeover from global reliance on petroleum to renewable energy sources is not going to be easy. Change on such a massive scale rarely is. But we should not stop innovating just because the challenge is difficult. We need to continue working on new energy technologies and new ways of delivering energy to consumers.

Some day the rising tide of technological advance will cross the declining line of oil reserves, and an energy revolution will occur. But suggesting that a global effort to halt or at least seriously limit the consumption of petroleum in the next few decades of this century is simply out of the question. The proof can be demonstrated with one word: China.

China recently surpassed the United States in the number of new motor vehicles sold in one year.[4] If it hasn't already, China will soon exceed the States not just in the sales figures but also in annual production of motor vehicles. The country turned out an estimated 20 million cars and trucks in 2011, all but a few of them intended for domestic consumption and the vast majority powered by gasoline or diesel fuel. While China claims to be as adamant about clean-burning fuel-efficient cars and trucks as any country, its plans for electric-powered vehicles have a goal of reaching just 5 percent of new cars in the foreseeable future.[5]

With a burgeoning middle class and more than a billion people, China's thirst for oil will parallel an expected demand for motor vehicles that are as modern and comfortable as those in the rest of the industrialized world. The demand will be almost matched by similar growth in India and Brazil, two populous countries whose economies rival China's in fast-paced expansion. China and India together represent one-third of the world's population and eight times more than the population of the United States, yet in total they currently consume less energy.* What happens when their population, enjoying new levels of prosperity, seeks similar levels of comfort to those of Americans, Canadians and most Europeans? Who will tell them to tone down their expectations and ride more bicycles, take fewer airplane trips and abandon many middle-class comforts that the West has benefited from for a hundred years?

Meanwhile, voices in the industrialized West calling for severe limits to petroleum consumption grow more strident. Unfortunately, people in China, India, Brazil and elsewhere tend not to agree. They

---

* According to the U.S. Energy Information Administration, February 2012, total primary energy consumption in 2010, in trillions of BTUs, was as follows: China, 77,807; India, 19,093; and the United States, 101,553.

have watched for several generations while advanced countries built their economies and lifestyles on easy access to low-cost petroleum and enjoyed swift travel on autobahns, freeways and turnpikes. Now that their countries' economies are opening the doors to similar opportunities, people in the West are beginning to preach the promised benefits of a petroleum-free society.

They are not likely to listen. Can we blame them?

The International Energy Agency, headquartered in Paris and considered by many the most reliable non-aligned source of energy consumption data and forecasts, estimates that oil will continue to be the dominant fuel in the primary energy mix through at least 2035. The agency also confirms that China doubled its consumption of energy from 2000 to 2009, when it overtook the United States to become the world's largest importer of energy.[6]

So just how much oil will be needed over the next few decades? The people who calculated that the world uses a cubic mile of petroleum annually projected that, by the middle of this century, the expanding global population and the growing middle class in China, India and Brazil will require the energy equivalent of six to nine cubic miles of petroleum every year.[7] The lesson seems pretty clear to me: we need to expand the energy choices available to us, not restrict them.

While the developing and newly industrialized world enters an era of high oil consumption, demand for petroleum in the West will increase steadily for at least the next generation. This raises a moral dilemma. As I write this, four out of every five barrels of petroleum consumed around the world are under the control of governments and administrations that we do not trust entirely, and with whom we often disagree when it comes to basic human rights and dignity. And guess what? It's becoming difficult to find oil elsewhere. Response to the growing need for oil involves exploring for new petroleum reserves in locations such as deep ocean water or the

Arctic that grow more demanding of our technological abilities. Even if production from these sources proves substantial, we in the West have few chances to displace producers such as Saudi Arabia when it comes to both production volumes and cost.

Another fact worth noting is the unique nature of the petroleum business. Its extent is global and its impact may be massive, but in many ways it is a small industry. I have met the top executives of most major western oil companies, and we could all gather for a meeting in a space not much larger than the average living room. This is a business of big capital and big bets more than big crowds of people. In the summer of 2010, Suncor Energy (as the company became known in 1997) was the second largest company in Canada based on capitalized value. Only Royal Bank was larger by that measure, and the difference between us was very small. To achieve that scale, Royal Bank required about 80,000 employees. We needed just 12,000 to work in the oil sands as well as at our retail outlets.* If our production were derived entirely from established oil fields and we were not engaged in the downstream end of the business—the service stations and other retail operations—we could have almost the same capitalization value with 6,000 employees or fewer.

It's also a very competitive industry. Next to professional sports, I don't know of any other business more driven to succeed. And, as in many sports, the oil industry is no longer strictly a male domain. Workforce and executive positions in the petroleum business reflect the diversity of society generally, and women are assuming key roles in both operations and management positions.

The ambition in the petroleum industry reflects the massive amounts of money risked at every step along the way, from exploration to production and refining. This is no mom-and-pop

---

* We rely on a large number of contractors outside the corporation, but the capitalization/employee measure remains valid.

business. Major moves are measured in billions of dollars, meaning you need both nerve and deep pockets to play in this league.

As I noted earlier, it's also a commodity business. Despite advertising claims by gasoline companies regarding the nature of the fuel they pump into your car's gas tank, the products are essentially identical grade to grade. On that basis, we can't outpace the company running the oil field next to us on the quality of the crude oil we're pumping or, for the most part, on aspects of the fuel processed by our own refinery. We can win only by working harder and more efficiently than the other guy, and we'll take every opportunity available to us.

This fierce competition drives all aspects of the business. I'm always amused whenever someone suggests that collusion exists between the large oil companies. We may be a small group, and we may know what each of the others is planning or developing, but nothing in the oil business hints of collusion. It's essentially cutthroat competition, where all players believe they can beat everybody else, and sometimes they do whatever it takes to prove it.

These facts are important not because they are new but because they form the background against which the oil sands, the world's second largest petroleum reserves, should be assessed. The existence of these reserves is proven, they are located within one of the world's most admired democracies and they represent the largest source of crude oil directly available to the North American market. By 2015 the Alberta oil sands will be producing about three million barrels of crude oil each day. At that rate, and with the current level of technology to remove the bitumen from the ground and convert it to oil suitable for refinement, the reserves should last more than 170 years.

This was one of the reasons I reassessed my first reactions to the oil sands and the challenge of making them productive and profitable. The oil sands represent the best long-term secure source of oil for

North America and other regions of the world, and the manner in which they were turned from a generally money-losing venture into an efficient operation is revealing and instructive.

But my reasons for sharing the story now extend beyond the purely business end of things. I believe it is important for both sides of the dialogue on energy production generally, and the oil sands in particular, to be heard. Whenever I've discussed these topics in detail with those who condemn production at the oil sands, we discover with some surprise that our views are not as far apart as we initially believed. I'm not suggesting that one side swings the other around to its point of view, but far more is achieved through dialogue than through one-sided statements in the media. One of my reasons for writing this book has been to cover the Suncor side as openly and honestly as I can.

There may be some surprises along the way. In fact, I'll do my best to provide them.

3. MY CAREER PATH: FROM PICK-UP TRUCKS TO WHITE ELEPHANTS

The seeds of my career in the petroleum industry were planted during a summer job after graduating from high school. I was working for a company that maintained oil feeder lines and equipment in northeast Colorado. Nothing in my family or personal background was even remotely connected to oil, and while I planned to pursue an engineering degree at college, it hadn't occurred to me that I could find employment in the petroleum industry. But a lot of things about the business attracted me to it over that summer.

The first was the industry itself. Working in the oil patch was serious business. It meant locating, pumping, refining and distributing oil products to be used in cars, homes, aircraft and industries. This struck me as having more importance in the grand scheme of things than many other engineering applications. It was also a global business, another attraction to a kid who had rarely travelled beyond the state of Colorado and had never flown on an airplane. Maybe an oil patch job would enable me to see the world.

To be honest, however, my eighteen-year-old view of the world was coloured most of all by the fact that every man in the industry appeared to be driving a shiny new car or pickup truck. I liked that. What small-town Colorado kid wouldn't? A job in the business seemed to promise enough income to buy a car right out of the showroom. If someone wants to claim that Rick George based at least some of his career decisions on the appeal of earning money, I'll admit it's true.

I enrolled in engineering at Colorado State with the long-range plan to work in the oil business. These were the late 1960s, and I need to say something about another decision I made. My years at CSU were spent during the height of the Vietnam War. Half a million Americans were fighting in that country, and thousands of them were coming home in body bags or terribly wounded, mentally and physically. Young men of my age were subject to the military draft. Their eligibility for service was based on the draft number they were assigned: the lower the number, the greater the likelihood of being called up. I drew 68, a fairly low number. My older brother Phil had drawn a much higher number a few years earlier, but although the likelihood of his being drafted was lower than mine, he chose to enlist, and served four years in the Air Force. He was not sent to Vietnam, but he fulfilled his duty.

My draft number came up early in my fourth year of studies. It was 1972, and the war no longer had much support among Americans. In fact it was winding down, and no one believed it would end with an American victory, yet the chance of my being drafted and shipped to Vietnam was very real. As long as I remained a student, my draft eligibility would be passed over. Graduation would eliminate my exemption. Whatever the outcome in Vietnam, I was not convinced that investing two years of my life in the military would help anyone, or the fading war effort. On top of all of this, Julie and I were planning to marry soon.

My engineering studies covered four years. Colorado State offered a five-year program if your grades were good enough, and mine met the test. I may not have set new academic records, but I consistently scored As and Bs, which qualified me for an extra year of study and another year of exemption from the draft, so I chose the five-year program. By the time I graduated the draft had ended, and everyone was impatient to bring our military home.

I don't regret the decision. Others either chose to serve or had little choice. I have thought about my actions over the years since and, based on everything I knew then and much that I know now, I believe it was the correct decision for me.

I had done well enough at university to attract job offers from a number of petroleum companies when I graduated. In retrospect, my timing couldn't have been better. A few months earlier, an Arab oil embargo had followed Egypt's invasion of Israel. The result was near panic at gas stations around the world, a jump in oil prices from $2 or $3 a barrel to almost $20 and a sudden demand among oil companies for engineering graduates with petroleum experience. The best way to counter a future embargo by the Middle Eastern oil countries was to locate and produce oil from other regions of the world. The industry desperately needed qualified people to get the job done, and there I was—a freshly minted graduate looking for work with an oil company.

The offers poured in, many with airline tickets attached for some distant city and a head office interview. I had never boarded an airplane before, but over a few months I flew at the oil companies' expense to locations all around the United States, a guy just out of his teens being treated like a genuine VIP. I remember thinking how cool it was to be flying five miles above the ground. Now, forty years later, I often wish I'd never seen the inside of an airplane.

After considering all the companies that offered me a position, I chose Texaco. Their headquarters were located in Houston, the centre of the U.S. oil patch, and my first assignment was to join a project group assigned to design and build refineries and other complex installations. Julie and I had married during my last year at Colorado State, and soon after moving to Houston she found a position teaching at an inner-city high school, a job she enjoyed immensely. So there we were: a young married couple pursuing meaningful careers in the centre of the U.S. oil industry.

During the first few months it was fun. I was earning what at the time was an impressive salary and planning multimillion-dollar developments in an industry buzzing with new ideas and growth prospects. The euphoria began to evaporate one day while I was working on a new refinery project in Port Arthur, Texas, when I realized that I was one of about five hundred engineers assigned to the same type of job. I got to know another engineer on my team, a very capable guy who had been doing the same thing for twenty years. I enjoyed my work, but the prospect of keeping essentially the same job for the next two decades or more didn't sound all that exciting. That's what engineers in the oil business did, and it's what I had been trained to do over five years of study. This didn't work for me. I needed wider horizons, and I began to consider what I could add to my training that would open new doors yet keep me in the centre of things.

Much of the oil industry's work extended well beyond drilling rigs, refineries and service stations and into the offices where leases and contracts were negotiated. Engineers weren't involved in this activity. It took people with a legal background to draft and interpret complex contracts and agreements, and it seemed to me that lawyers trained in contract law who also knew a good deal about the practical aspects of locating and producing oil would be highly valued in the petroleum business. Just as important, they would face different challenges from project to project and wouldn't be looking back at some point at twenty or thirty years of repetitive work. Within a year of joining Texaco I enrolled at the University of Houston Law School, determined to add a law degree to my engineering credentials. For most of the next four years I fulfilled my duties in Texaco's engineering sector by day and attended law classes at night. Texaco was impressed enough to permit me to take full-time studies during my final two semesters.

The experience proved valuable in ways I hadn't expected, many of them beyond both law and engineering. My engineering studies, by definition, had focused on finding answers via formulas and mathematics. This was the only meaningful goal, so there was little incentive for engineers to spend time on liberal arts. Shakespeare, after all, can't help you measure napthene levels or plan a thermohydraulic installation. This focus on mathematics left me handicapped when it came to assessing situations in the real world, the one without charts and calculations.

Engineering is precise and involves universally acknowledged facts that are easily confirmed. Solutions are based on black-and-white results; something either performs to standard or it doesn't. In contrast, the study of law is based to a large extent on recognizing the existence and significance of grey areas in order to reach a fair decision. That's what the law school professors were looking for. If you were unable to evaluate the points on both sides of the dispute, you weren't getting the job done. Law taught me I had to accept that I could not predict 100 percent accuracy in any foreseeable circumstance, so I had to make decisions weighted on my own judgments and understanding of the facts.

This was a huge change for me. In law school I dealt with problems whose answers were equivocal and subjective, and during my first semester I learned just how ill-prepared I was in comparison with my classmates. Studying law also involved an enormous amount of reading, far more than I had done to earn my engineering credentials. The result of my law training was to yank me from the fixed-in-stone precision of engineering and teach me to express myself not with infallible formulae but with written and verbal discussion.

I never practised law, nor did I ever intend to, but my law education affected my personality and changed my career in ways I could not have imagined at the time. It broadened my capabilities by opening up a whole different approach to solving problems. At the same time, I had to learn how to avoid some aspects of law that would have saddled me with problems as a manager. For instance, lawyers must become adept at deciding what can go wrong in a given situation, and that's always a benefit. But you can spend so much time checking out the negatives that you lose focus on the reason you're making the move in the first place. Engineers approach a project from a different angle, thinking, "If I apply this pressure at that temperature in these conditions, I know what the result will be." That kind of predictability makes you optimistic, whereas law makes you cautious. If I were asked to pinpoint the single best move I made in preparing for my career, it would be learning how to blend the fixed and positive attitude of an engineer with the nuanced approach of a lawyer.

Within a month of passing the Texas state bar exam, I was transferred out of the engineering division in Houston to Texaco's head office in White Plains, New York. Soon I was jetting off to various locations around the world, drafting and modifying contracts with governments and multinational companies. Instead of spending my days at refinery sites or in a work cubicle, I was seated in boardrooms, prepared to negotiate the best oil lease terms for my employer. At twenty-seven, I had an advantage shared by few, if any, of the other people at the table, who were either oil executives or lawyers and were generally much older than I was. The oil people across from me knew little about contract law, and the lawyers with them often knew even less about the mechanics of the petroleum business. I was comfortable with both sides, which gave me a head start when negotiating on behalf of Texaco.

THE ways of the world, and the economic and political power of oil, came into sharp focus for me during those early years with Texaco.

The echoes of the oil crisis of 1973 continued to resonate, and the importance of oil and its limited long-term supply were openly discussed as strategic elements for countries around the world. I'm surprised that more wars haven't been fought over oil—who owns it and who has the right to produce it. We've come close on more than one occasion, including an incident that involved me and might have led to an armed skirmish, although I was fortunate enough not to be on site when it (almost) happened.

It was 1978, and Texaco was drilling an exploration well in the Mediterranean. The project was one that I had helped negotiate under a production licence from Malta. We were perhaps halfway to the depth where we expected to find the oil deposit when a submarine suddenly surfaced near the rig and a few heavily armed crew members began rowing a dinghy to the drilling platform. The sub belonged to the Libyan navy, and one of the sailors handed the foreman a note that said he and his crew had twenty-four hours to leave the site or the submarine would blow them off it.

I flew from New York to Malta while another Texaco representative went to Tripoli to talk to the Libyans, and the whole thing became a minor international incident with diplomatic communications flying back and forth. Eventually the case landed in the International Court of Justice, where it took a decade to resolve. In the end, none of it mattered very much; the well proved to be a dry hole.

I liked the work at Texaco and I learned a lot from visiting foreign countries, but all the travel meant I was away from home a good deal. By this time Julie and I had two children and were living in Connecticut, far from our roots in Colorado. Julie is a wonderful mother, but having her husband out of the country one week out of two throughout the year was a lot to ask, so I began giving serious thought to my family's needs as well as to my career future, which didn't appear to be with Texaco. As much as I liked my work, the company had an antiquated policy that said you could not move up from one job level to another until you had put in a certain number of years at your current grade.

I was too impatient and my family was too important for me to accept spending so much time away from them for the next ten or fifteen years. I began looking for a position with another oil company, and that's how and why I made the move to Sun Oil in 1980. My initial posting was with the international upstream group in Dallas, and it included developing a strategic plan to deal with Sun's $400 million portion of a $700 million project to produce oil from the Balmoral field in the North Sea. My presentation to the board proposed that we invest in a purpose-built floating production vessel for the well, a heady thing for a guy just thirty years old.

Floating production vessels for offshore wells weren't new, but until then they had all been adaptations of existing ship designs. The result was inevitably a compromise of sorts, and I wanted the company to consider building a vessel exclusively for one purpose. When the board approved the idea, I was appointed to supervise the project, including overseeing the commercial negotiations, approving the final stages of construction in Gothenburg, Sweden, and directing the offshore installation and operation. This meant spending several years in Britain. With my family I moved first to London and then to Aberdeen for a time before returning to London.

The custom-built floating vessel proved enormously successful despite skepticism from some quarters of the company. Construction was completed six months earlier than planned, the project came in within the budget and the platform was put in place and into production without major hitches. As a bit of icing on the cake, oil prices, which had been depressed for some time, began rising just as the first barrels of crude flowed out of the platform and into the marketplace. It all made me look heroic. Never underestimate the value of good luck.

My success in Britain marked me as the guy who might, just might, be able to turn the oil sands around, and so at Tom Thomson's request we once again gave up London, this time for Toronto and eventually Calgary.

After living in one of the most bustling cities in Europe I found myself looking out over the Alberta oil sands, absorbing all the activity of Suncor's open-pit mine. Actually, I was watching the *inactivity* of the mine. A lot of the equipment appeared to be under repair, leaving the extraction plant, where the bitumen was separated from the sand and water, sitting idle. I asked one of the production staff nearby if this happened very often. "All the time," he said, shrugging his shoulders, and I began to understand why the facility had never turned a reasonable profit and why, unless massive change was made, it never would.

I knew almost nothing about the Alberta oil sands before agreeing to join Suncor. It may have been mentioned during my university studies and I was aware, while working with Sun Oil in Europe, that the company's Canadian subsidiary was actively involved in producing crude oil from the site, but that was it. Later, I learned that Sun had pioneered the process on a large scale back in 1967, almost a quarter-century before I arrived.

More than forty years before that, some early attempts at recovering the oil had been made on a small scale using hot water to liquefy and separate the bitumen, but this had been research and development, not full-scale production. Although a few barrels were shipped out of the area year by year, most of the activity around Fort McMurray involved fighting fires created by sloppy maintenance policies. One of the fires destroyed the first serious commercial plant, which had been established during the Second World War. There might have been a lot of promise in the oil sands, but there had been little success.

One company that appeared to have made progress was Great Canadian Oil Sands; it launched operations in 1953 using a patented version of the hot water process pioneered in the 1920s. Sun Oil bought into GCOS in 1963, eventually acquiring 81 percent of the company. The deal involved agreeing to build a plant costing $240 million and capable of producing 45,000 barrels of crude oil per day. With oil selling around $2.50 per barrel at the time, and the separation process being far more energy- and labour-intensive than today, this was not a get-rich-quick scheme. Besides, the demand was low. The enormous oil reserves in Saudi Arabia and across the Middle East were reaching capacity, and oil was still gushing from fields in Texas, Oklahoma and California. Closer to home, Imperial Oil had tapped the big Leduc oil field just outside of Edmonton, and the region promised other deposits of oil free of sand and water.

So why bother with the oil sands? I looked back on some company records and found two statements made by J. Howard Pew, whose father had been one of the founders of Sun Oil in 1886. All these years later, it's interesting to review his rationale.

In 1949, Pew foresaw a shortage of crude oil for all of North America and worried about "the vulnerable dependency on offshore sources that a shortage would imply." The oil sands, he believed, could prevent such a crisis, and Pew took the first step in committing Sun to develop them and avoid such a shortage. Many years later, the same man justified Sun's investment in the $250 million GCOS plant when he said,

> This is a great challenge to the imagination, skill and technological know-how of our scientists and engineers. . . .

Unless projects of this kind can be periodically challenged and solved, our organization will become soft and eventually useless. I am convinced that this venture will succeed, and that it will be the means of opening up reserves that will meet the needs of the North American continent for generations to come.

In 1967, when the Great Canadian Oil Sands plant was completed and officially opened with great fanfare, Pew was among the many guest speakers. At eighty-five years old he represented the early believers in the promise of the oil sands, and he made a prediction about the oil sands' value and success:

The best minds in the oil industry estimate that by 1985, less than twenty years hence, the world requirements for petroleum will be two and a half times what they are today. For the North American continent they estimate that, by 1985, the demand will be twice the present consumption. It is the considered opinion of our group that if the North American continent is to produce the oil to meet its requirements in the years ahead, oil from the Athabasca area must, of necessity, play an important role. No nation can be long secure in this . . . age unless it is amply supplied with petroleum.

I admire Pew's vision. His words are every bit as valid today as when he spoke them. Unfortunately, there were a couple of flies in that particular barrel of ointment. The plant was not yet operating when he made his speech, a fact that diluted the impact of his grandiose prediction. This may also have prevented him from discussing the prospects of the operation turning a profit. And while his logic and vision were admirable, his timing was less so.

Shortly after Sun effectively acquired GCOS with a commitment to fund the new production facility, a consortium of producers created a new company, Syncrude, to develop the oil sands. Syncrude did not commit itself to a full-fledged production facility on its leased lands until 1973, and it took another five years before crude oil flowed from it in commercial quantities. Sun remained the sole high-volume producer during that period.

For twenty-five years, the GCOS oil sands project had all the appearance and performance of a massive white elephant. By 1990 the brilliant vision of J. Howard Pew had deteriorated into an apparently bottomless pit of losses resulting from production costs that often exceeded the market price of the oil.

Problem after problem arose, each setback made more complex and costly by the remoteness of the location and the challenge of the climate. Northern Alberta is resource-rich, wonderfully expansive and often very beautiful, but between November and May it is no place for the faint of heart. Winters are long and cold; overnight temperatures of minus 40 degrees Celsius are common from December to March. These extreme temperatures place heavy stresses on operating equipment that is not specially designed to deal with them. The challenge of the cold weather affects every aspect; even grease for the equipment freezes solid at these temperatures, and when the impact of these conditions was not totally accounted for, disaster struck.

In January 1968, just a few months after start-up, all three boilers at the GCOS plant broke down in the middle of one of the coldest months on record. The boilers were relied on to generate the massive volumes of hot water needed to strip the bitumen from sand. The lack of heat not only halted production but also caused the offices and employee residences heated by the same boilers to freeze. The boilers also powered the electricity generators, and like tumbling dominoes, a series of catastrophes followed. Water pipes throughout the facility froze and burst, creating floods a metre deep that soon froze into solid ice. It took months, not days or weeks, before the ice could be removed, the damage repaired and the plant put back into production.

Between events like that one and lesser crises, the plant struggled along for seven years before showing a small profit of $4 million in 1974, followed by another period of annual losses.

It's amazing to me that the people running Sun Oil out of Philadelphia did not throw up their hands and sell the entire operation to the highest bidder, assuming they could find one. They couldn't be happy with the plant's operations, or with the provincial and federal governments' refusal to provide assistance through tax breaks for many years. The province of Alberta, for example, insisted on levelling royalty payments based on crude oil produced by the plant and not on the bitumen. This meant that a producer drawing a barrel of oil out of the Leduc oil field south of Edmonton, a procedure that involved little more than drilling simple wells and opening valves, paid the province the same amount as GCOS paid after mining, crushing, mixing, heating and purifying almost five tonnes of earth to yield the same barrel of oil. Meanwhile, the federal government controlled the selling price of crude oil produced from the oil sands and levied an export tax on every barrel shipped outside Canada.

Things improved over the years through small steps. By 1979 the plant was making a small profit, thanks in part to the federal government's permitting the company to set international prices on its oil. Productivity improved little by little, based on experience acquired by workers and management alike. The progress wasn't the result of discovering new ways to boost production and reduce costs as much as learning how to avoid disasters such as the boiler failure and freeze-up of many years earlier. Still, the future appeared bright enough for Sun Oil to assume complete control of the oil sands project, dissolving its relationship with GCOS and hanging a new name on the corporate door: Suncor.

Unfortunately, the new name didn't change the old record very much. Depressed market prices, constant equipment breakdowns and the impact of the National Energy Program (NEP) in 1980 all worked against the company's ability to turn the corner and generate a reasonable profit for its U.S. parent.

The NEP, a clumsy attempt by the federal government to regulate a very complex industry and impose Canadian ownership on much of it, prompted the Ontario provincial government to enter the industry with its own Canadianization program. A year after the introduction of the NEP, Ontario Premier William Davis announced that his government had agreed to purchase 25 percent of Suncor, giving provincial residents their "window on the oil industry." By the time the negotiations were completed international oil prices had risen dramatically, driving the calculated price of the 25 percent share well above the original estimate to almost $650 million. Ontario would pay half in cash and cover the balance in a ten-year note, payable to the parent, Sun Company, at an annual interest rate of 14.357 percent.

Neither the somewhat inflated price, based on current oil prices, nor the high interest rate, reflecting the inflationary period, appeared to concern Ontario's politicians. They called the deal a good investment for Ontario, and expected an annual return of 15 percent. It also marked, the government claimed, a first step in the total Canadianization of Suncor. The terms included an incentive for Ontario to raise its ownership to 51 percent within five years.

Reviewing the company's performance over the next few years, however, Ontario chose not to exercise its option. Based on the results of the provincial election following the purchase of the Suncor shares, Ontario voters chose not to exercise their option either. Having watched public funds poured into a private company in a distant province, they voted the Progressive Conservatives out of office, ending more than forty years of the party's dominance in that province.

Ten years after the imposition of the NEP and Ontario's investment in Suncor, little had changed. When I landed at Fort McMurray in 1991, I realized I would be managing a company that spent much of its time repairing equipment and extinguishing fires, that was one-quarter owned by a distant provincial government, that had barely covered its operating costs each year for the past decade, and that was controlled by a number of impatient men in far-off Philadelphia who appeared to be perpetually on the verge of selling the business to whoever appeared interested.

I could hardly wait to get started.

4. Suncor Becomes Profitable . . . and Canadian

Optimism is a great asset, but fear is a wonderful motivator. For the first few weeks after I grew familiar with the Suncor oil sands operation, I began to fear that the problems it faced were insurmountable. I had wrenched my family out of life in one of the world's great cities, living on the doorstep of all the culture and wonders of Europe, to settle in Toronto and focus my efforts on a perpetually underperforming investment a few thousand kilometres farther west.

A quick glance at the Suncor books in that first year revealed the true scope of the problem. It was costing us about $20 to produce a barrel of crude oil that was often selling for as low as $12 to $15. We could either pray for prices to rise well above the $20 mark and remain that high, or we could go to work and reduce the per barrel cost to a level that would ensure a profit.

To be sure, Suncor was more than the oil sands facility. In addition to being an upstream exploration and production company, its downstream assets included a refinery in Sarnia, Ontario, and a string of retail service stations under the Sunoco name located throughout Ontario and Quebec. I didn't regard these retail assets as either the most urgent problem or the key to the company's overall success. My primary interests were in the upstream part of the business, where the oil is located and delivered to refineries. I decided the oil sands represented the core of the company, despite the fact that the U.S. parent Sun Company considered them a disaster.

The oil sands were a unique resource. We needed to find a way to tap them economically while making the smallest possible impact on the environment. Most important of all, this vast reserve of potential oil was sitting on our doorstep, eliminating the need to make enormous investments searching for new undiscovered deposits.

This was a crucial factor in my decision to focus almost exclusively on making the oil sands productive and efficient. I had seen dozens of oil companies go broke searching for deposits worth developing. After spending millions of dollars to locate an underground reservoir, they would spend millions more developing it and setting up the infrastructure to move the crude oil to markets, hoping they could recover enough to make their investment worthwhile. Thanks to the oil sands, we could skip the front end of that effort. It was the back end—converting the bitumen into oil that would flow to distant refineries—that represented the major challenge.

In the middle of evaluating how to turn the Suncor operation around, I realized that the difference between the oil sands and traditional production wells held the key to the solution. Once oil has been located the process becomes one of getting it from its underground source to refineries, which means production is essentially a transportation issue: bringing the oil up to the surface and moving it across land and water to its destination. At the oil sands, transportation was only the second stage of the process. First we had to produce the bitumen, then convert it into oil suitable for use by the refineries. This sounded more like manufacturing than transportation. Our oil sands operation had more in common with a pulp and paper plant than with the oil fields in Saudi Arabia or the North Sea, and seeing it in that light would become a guide to many management decisions I made over the next two decades. But producer or manufacturer, nothing mattered if we didn't get volumes up and costs down.

The biggest source of pressure on the job didn't come from Sun Company in Philadelphia; it came from me. Failure in the oil sands wouldn't mark me as incompetent, because none of the CEOs who preceded me had been successful either. Some aspects of business are insoluble, and the oil sands were being tagged with that label. So what made me stick around?

I was driven by the classic fear of failure experienced by anyone dropped into a new and challenging job. Balancing this was an intuitive sense that success was within reach if the correct changes were made, and that success in the oil sands would resonate across Canada and throughout the entire industry. If I were wrong, I would have to restart my career with some other company, probably somewhere else in the world. With all the upheaval my family had just gone through, I wasn't about to let that happen.

The more I looked into the situation, the more I began to identify two core barriers to success that appeared surmountable: one cultural and the other mechanical.

You can't make a wise decision in any business, I believe, without talking things over with the people on the front line, because they're the ones who know first-hand what's happening. On my second visit to the oil sands, I sat down with Mike Supple, the man who had operated our plant for several years and surely knew as much as anyone about making it work. "Mike, we need to get our costs down here," I said. "What's the best we can do, in your opinion?"

Mike was a transplanted Brit who wore a tie even when walking around the plant. He was the grizzled veteran, the guy who kept things running from the spring black fly season through the hot summer and into winter, when the temperature often failed to rise above minus 17 degrees Celsius for weeks. I was the young guy just in from London, working out of a corner office in far-off Toronto, looking for answers I didn't have. Mike was determined to set me straight. I encouraged his total honesty. In fact, I insisted on it.

"Listen, Rick," Mike lectured me in response to my question. "If we work really hard for the next couple of years, I figure we can drop fifty cents a barrel out of the cost structure."

I felt stiff-armed. Mike, the man with the clearest view of the operation, was telling me that we would never make Suncor profitable, no matter what we did. He left no room for debate.

His attitude wasn't a total surprise. Mike was a seasoned field manager with lots of experience at handling corporate office types, and he wanted to set the new guy straight. Hey, I'd been to that rodeo. I'd stood around with grease on my coveralls while somebody in a Brooks Brothers suit told me he had answers to questions I'd never considered. It wasn't Mike's skepticism of me that was disturbing. It was his inability to see the scope of the changes we would have to make if the company were to survive.

Mike's response convinced me that I wasn't dealing with just a technical problem. If his vision reflected the company's view where the oil sands were concerned, it wasn't going to work. Everyone in the organization recognized that we needed to cut our production costs by at least $5 a barrel if the oil sands venture was to achieve financial success and ensure its future. Now Mike was telling me that two years of hard work, along with a bit of luck, might earn us an improvement amounting to one-tenth of our goal. He knew we had to do much better than that. He just didn't seem to believe we could.

By this time Syncrude had established itself in the oil sands as a competitor and was struggling with many of the same challenges we were facing. Fortunately for Syncrude, it had received a boost from both Ottawa and Alberta. Oil sands operations were new and marginally viable economically, and each operator negotiated its own deal with the federal and provincial governments, meaning no two deals were alike. A move by both governments in the mid-1970s had reduced the taxes and royalty rates imposed on Syncrude, permitting the company to survive economically. Shipping its first barrel of oil in 1978, ten years after the Suncor plant began operations, Syncrude had been created as a consortium of petroleum companies, each of which saw promise in the oil sands but chose to hedge its bets by sharing the risk with others.*

Neither company was achieving much success because both lacked the funds and the motivation to explore and pay for technical innovation. There wasn't even a competitive attitude between the two companies that might stimulate the kind of technical breakthrough the venture needed. Instead, both Suncor and Syncrude appeared to be lurching forward in incremental steps, searching for ways to increase production volumes and lowering costs just to survive. Under those conditions Mike's attitude was understandable.

I'm a patient guy, but this wasn't acceptable. We needed fresh energy to produce rapid change. We also needed a major leap in productivity more than we needed a bunch of small improvements that amounted to nothing much. Otherwise both my career and those of a lot of other Suncor people would be hanging in the balance. Nobody seemed to know where or what the major advance might be, even though they were dealing directly with the biggest barrier to success every day.

I didn't bring oil sands experience with me, but I brought a fresh eye. The opportunity to take that leap in production and profit

---

* It continues to operate as a consortium. In 2011 the joint venture partners were Canadian Oil Sands (36.75 percent), Imperial Oil Resources (25 percent), Mocal Energy (5 percent), Murphy Oil (5 percent), Nexen (7.25 percent), Sinopec (9 percent) and Suncor (12 percent).

occurred to me while watching machines removing oil-bearing sands from an open mining area. The problem, I realized, could be traced back to a decision made more than twenty years earlier about how to remove the bitumen-bearing sands and transfer them to processing facilities.

In any business venture it's logical to pick the low-hanging fruit first. At the oil sands, this meant recovering the bitumen closest to the surface, employing the same techniques used in open-pit mining. Whether the resource you're after is iron ore, coal, gold, silver or any other material, the process is similar: strip away the overburden, access the resource and cart it off for enriching and refining. It's not a pretty sight, but many industrial activities aren't. Like everyone else, I would rather look at a grove of trees than at a line of steel plants, or a trout stream instead of a gravel pit. Like it or not, however, steel and gravel and a hundred other materials are essential to modern life. The challenge is not to do without them but to operate them efficiently and ensure that they are as environmentally neutral as possible. Then, when their productive lives are over, you need to restore the site to close to its original condition. The first stages of oil sands development, launched twenty-five years before I arrived, involved the simple process of first exposing, then removing, the most accessible oil-bearing soil and carting it away for processing.

This has led to one of the most widely spread and erroneous criticisms of the oil sands: that half of northern Alberta will be excavated to obtain the bitumen. It won't. Of the trillion or so barrels of oil locked into the earth, only about 10 percent will be recovered through pit mining. The remainder will be accessed via a technique that will disturb the land no more than the traditional method of drilling wells to access petroleum reservoirs elsewhere in the world. It's the sight of the mining pits that produces a negative reaction from most people, but those pits will not extend all across Alberta nor remain forever. When the excavated pits have been completed, they will be filled in and planted with the same northern boreal forest that has grown in the area for millions of years. My goal is that your grandchildren and mine will not be able to tell a restored mining site in the oil sands from an area untouched by machinery. That's more than either a promise or a goal; it's a legal prerequisite that we have already begun to fulfil. For the moment, however, mining remains the most visually disturbing aspect of the oil sands to many people. Back in 1991, it was also the biggest barrier to success.

THE people most experienced at moving earth from place to place aren't oil workers; they're miners. So in the mid-1960s, when Suncor first geared up for large-scale production at the oil sands with open-pit mining, it relied on mining expertise when it came to choosing machinery to excavate and transfer the soil. To the miners Suncor consulted, this meant bucket wheels: huge, complex machines consisting of a massive wheel feeding a series of conveyor belts, the entire contraption mounted on treads.

Picture a carnival Ferris wheel. Now replace the seats with buckets about the size of a dumpster. Equip the buckets with a set of teeth at their front end, then push the wheel against the ground and begin to turn it. When the wheel turns, the buckets fill themselves with ore and are carried to the top of the wheel. As they rotate down the back end of the wheel, they swivel upside down and deposit their load onto a moving conveyor belt. The wheel itself can be lowered to dig into the earth below grade, or raised to reach material above the machine. It can also be pivoted from side to side on a vertical axis. The entire contraption moves like an arthritic dinosaur, pulling conveyor belts, some stretching a kilometre or more, behind it.

Bucket wheels had been used in European open-pit mines,

usually those producing soft coal, for decades. Some are among the largest mobile machines ever created, standing 96 metres high, 225 metres long and weighing more than 12,700 tonnes. For a project as vast as the oil sands, they appeared ideal to the miners who were consulted. But in the oil sands they were a total disaster, a realization that hit me only after I approved the purchase of a new bucket wheel head—the portion of the machine that digs into the earth—for $5 million in my first few weeks on the job; the part soon became redundant.*

Bucket wheels, and in particular Suncor bucket wheels, were ideal proof of a rule that every engineer understands instinctively: the more complex a piece of mechanical equipment, the greater the probability of its breaking down. In addition to their complexity, they were handling material harder than the soft coal they had been designed for, especially in winter, when the bitumen-bearing sands froze as solid as concrete. The sand in the Athabasca basin is primarily quartz, a hard, crystalline material that wore out teeth on the buckets after as little as twenty-four hours of operation. Add to that the problem of maintaining equipment in below-freezing temperatures for as much as eight months of the year and the amount of downtime for the machines—averaging almost 50 percent annually—was no surprise.

Three bucket wheels were being used to access the bitumen-bearing soil at Suncor when I arrived, and usually at least one of them was out of service at any given time. The original downtime was bad enough, but the remote location meant either maintaining a large inventory of spare parts to repair the machines or waiting weeks for delivery from the European supplier. Losing a third of

---

* Syncrude's operations at the time used draglines as well as bucket wheels. Draglines—basically large buckets pulled through and along the ground on the end of a cable by an oversized crane—are awkward and limited in their ability to reach all layers of a site.

productivity when one piece of outdated equipment broke down was illogical; losing two-thirds when a second piece of equipment proved unavailable was ludicrous. Yet that's what had been going on for years. Instead of recognizing the folly of basing so much of the plant's productivity on a flawed link in the chain, the only solution had been to keep more spare parts on hand and schedule downtime when the bucket wheels were expected to be out of service.

I was convinced that replacing the bucket wheels with a more reliable system would produce an immediate leap in productivity. I also knew that buying the new equipment would require a major and unbudgeted capital investment, necessitating approval from a head office that considered spending money on the oil sands like tossing cash into a deep, dark hole.

I'm no fan of consultants, but before I visited Sun in Philadelphia with my hand extended, waiting for someone to place a few million dollars in it, I wanted some allies. So we hired a consultancy firm to examine the bucket wheel technology, research more efficient ways of doing the same thing in similar operations around the world and hand me a convincing report with firm recommendations.

The report confirmed my opinion. Our costs were way out of line compared with similar operations mining copper, gold and iron ore. The bucket wheels were old technology, far too complex to be relied upon, and even with the best of maintenance in ideal working environments they were prone to an unacceptable rate of breakdowns. In northern Alberta winters, breakdowns were inevitable. The solution? Replace the three clunky behemoths with a system of several large power shovels and a fleet of trucks to carry the sands to the processing plant. Total estimated capital cost: $120 million.*

---

* When the people at Syncrude realized how effective our solution was they followed our lead, banishing the bucket wheels and draglines and cutting their costs accordingly.

Trucks and shovels did not sound exactly high-tech to me, but the operational logic of the idea was obvious. When one bucket wheel was out of service, we lost 33 percent of our productivity. If we replaced the three bucket wheels with ten power shovels, and one shovel was inoperable at any given time, we would lose only 10 percent productivity. The power shovels were also far simpler to operate and much easier to service than the bucket wheels, making them less likely to break down and cheaper and faster to bring back into service when they did. The same advantage could be obtained with a fleet of 50 heavy trucks doing the work of the kilometre-long conveyor belts; losing a truck to mechanical problems meant losing a maximum 2 percent of productivity, not 30 or 50 percent. Based on the consultants' estimates, eliminating the downtime and maintenance associated with the bucket wheels would save us about $5 a barrel.

The consultant's report made it easy to recommend scrapping the bucket wheels and replacing them with trucks and power shovels, plus crushing the ore near the mine, making transportation and handling easier. The decision may have been easy, but finding the money would be a challenge. The $120 million was more than an entire year's cash flow from Suncor. What's more, our total capital budget was set at $50 million annually, and I was proposing that we spend over twice that much to employ technology that had never been tried in mining the oil sands. After all those years of losses and disappointments, the Sun directors at the U.S. headquarters were in no mood to open the company chequebook.

I took the consultants' report to Tom Thomson, who appreciated the wisdom of its advice but was reluctant to lead the charge to Philadelphia. Part of the reason was his rapidly declining health. At heart, however, he had little faith in the chance of success where the oil sands were concerned. Whatever confidence he may have had when he became CEO five years earlier had faded when all his efforts and experience failed to turn things around. So it was up to me to sell Sun Company's board on the idea of giving us access to $120 million through a line of credit that would permit us to replace the notoriously unreliable bucket wheels with trucks and power shovels.

I have probably never worked harder to make a sale than I did on those visits to Philadelphia, but I have also never been more confident that the benefits would be certain and substantial. When we received approval from the board to purchase the trucks and shovels, I knew we were on our way, although it took two more years before the equipment was in place.

Another decision was even more difficult. The abandonment of bucket wheels and organizational changes within the company meant laying off hundreds of employees, which is one of the hardest decisions any CEO can make. It was especially difficult in this case because the layoffs were not the result of anything the employees had done or not done but of a necessary change in technology. Whatever the reason—a sale of assets, a shift in strategy, a need to reduce costs—I never made decisions that resulted in lay-offs without a good deal of soul searching and an awareness of the impact they would have on employees and their families. Ultimately, of course, the decision saved the company and created thousands of new jobs, but at the time it was hard for me to implement and even harder for the workers to accept.

The change in equipment launched a similar change in key personnel to make the new system work, and I began counting on three key managers who shared my vision of Suncor's future and were prepared to help me realize it. I brought in two brilliant people from outside the company, hoping their fresh perspective would be free of the pessimism that all those years of failure had created among existing personnel: Dee Parkinson-Marcoux, whom I placed in charge of the oil sands operation; and Barry Stewart, recruited from Petro-Canada to handle the exploration and production (E&P) side of things.

I also began relying on Mike O'Brien, whom I had met in London a year or two earlier, when he came through town searching for European financial support for the oil sands. He had spent some time in Fort McMurray during a period when the cash costs to produce a barrel of crude from the oil sands were $28 and the oil sold for $25, and when half the expenditures on the site went to cover equipment repairs.

Things at the oil sands had grown so desperate in the late 1980s that Sun Company had instructed Mike to offer 50 percent of the operation to Imperial Oil for $125 million. Had the offer gone through, Sun would have been very pleased to turn a portion of its holdings into cash, Imperial would have acquired the bargain of the millennium, and my family and I might have remained in London. Imperial turned the offer down.

So Mike knew the oil sands situation in detail, and his position as vice-president of finance and planning meant I would be relying on him to help find the financing we needed. It wasn't just Mike's background and experience that impressed me. He beamed self-confidence and a what-the-hell demeanour, which made him just the guy to counterbalance the atmosphere of doom and gloom. He remains both a close personal friend and an important member of the Suncor board to this day.

MIKE and I agreed that we could build Suncor into a petroleum company like no other. Some of this uniqueness was based on regarding the oil sands as our primary source of crude oil. As I mentioned earlier, unlike other oil companies we didn't have to cruise the world looking for oil deposits—they were right under our feet. We also recognized potential benefits based on some technical aspects of the oil we would be shipping south. When our oil sands facility was processing bitumen in sufficient quantity, we began tailoring its component mixture to meet the needs of each refinery buyer. The end product of crude oil—specifically gasoline—may be more or less identical from marketer to marketer, but the oil that is processed to produce the gasoline can differ markedly in viscosity and impurities. Refineries are set up to reach optimum performance based on the nature of the oil they receive, and we were able to deliver certain qualities in the oil that improved the overall profitability of the refineries operated by our key customers.

We were ready to launch other innovations as well, but it became clear that we would be hamstrung if every new idea was subject to prior approval from the board of the U.S. parent, Sun Company. And they were. The people in Philadelphia were understandably doubtful about the oil sands ever becoming the success they hoped for, and they watched over our every move. "If we had access to our own cash flow," Mike O'Brien suggested one day, "we could really get things done here. What we need to do is go public on our own, get the U.S. to sell their shares, and cut us free."

It made sense financially, and it also reflected the original goal of selling shares to Ontario a decade earlier. It also made sense in another measure.

"Those guys in Philadelphia," Mike added, "they just don't like us!"

He was right, but it wasn't personal. Sun Company received no credit on its balance sheet for Suncor's efforts where the oil sands were concerned, and someone suggested that whenever Suncor was mentioned in the media everyone in the business, including the Sun Company directors, assumed we'd had a new setback at Fort McMurray. Another complication began looming on the horizon: the government of Ontario, having generated little more than headlines from its investment in Suncor years earlier, was making it clear that it wanted Sun Company to buy back the province's shares.

The rumours complicated our relationship with our U.S. parent, which was not great on a number of levels. If Philadelphia was not pleased with our performance in Canada, I was just as unhappy with the board's actions when it came down to making decisions.

Suncor board meetings were held four times annually, usually in Toronto. About three weeks before each meeting, I would meet with Bob Campbell, Sun Company chairman and CEO, to review the latest operations and financial results, show him my plans, explain the strategy and generally get his approval before presenting it to the Suncor board. Too often, usually late on the night before the meeting, I would receive a telephone call from Bob, who would explain that something had been screwed up, and many of the things I had asked approval for were going to get a rough ride from the board. As a result, the board meetings became a waste of time and a major source of frustration.

Mike translated this into evidence of widespread animosity toward Suncor by Sun Company board members. Whether true or not, it added impetus to his suggestion about persuading Philadelphia to consider selling its shares. If we really wanted to make the oil sands work, we would have to run our own show.

We began planting the idea of going public in the minds of financial executives at Sun Company, bypassing the board when possible. Mike had a good relationship with one of the top financial people in Philadelphia, and he provided at least tacit encouragement. Among other benefits, going public would be a way to satisfy Ontario's intention to get out of the petroleum business, where they shouldn't have been in the first place. Sun Company had little interest in buying back the Ontario-owned shares. Why not offer them in an IPO? With encouragement from Mike's contacts at head office, we began pressing that idea.

Eventually, we won them over. Sun Company agreed to combine 20 percent of total shares with the 25 percent held by the province of Ontario. The bundle would be sold via public offering, leaving the parent company with a controlling 55 percent ownership. With this decision agreed upon, our next step was to settle on a share price, and we contacted a number of investment bankers to help us establish a target. Mike O'Brien and I took our show on the road, visiting bankers across Canada, in the northern United States and over in Europe, explaining Suncor's operations and prospects as a means of fixing a share price that the market would accept.

Naturally, potential investors wanted to know what was happening with our oil sands operations. For years they had been hearing nothing but bad news out of Fort McMurray, and we wanted to share our plans for turning the operation around. To this day Mike and I still laugh about a luncheon meeting we set up in New York City with fifty financial heavyweights, most of whom knew only that the Suncor oil sands development was a problem-plagued venture that had barely broken even for years.

As you might expect, nobody is more hard-nosed than the Wall Street banking crowd when faced with people looking for their money. After lunch Mike set up my pitch by explaining that we were about to launch an innovative new method of accessing oil-laden sand for processing, a technique that promised to reduce our overall production costs by as much as $5 a barrel. It was sure to guarantee future profits and make our IPO irresistible to investors. I could see the bankers respond with interest, since this promised to turn a lot of red ink into solid profits. As I rose to speak, they were almost on the edge of their chairs, eager to hear how we were going to change twenty-five years of an underperforming investment into a northern money machine. So I told them.

"We're going to dig the sand out of the ground with power shovels," I said, "and load it into trucks that will carry it to the processor."

I suspect they were prepared for news about some space-age technology, a breakthrough that would send them running back to their offices with handfuls of *Buy!* orders. Or maybe we just oversold them. But when they learned our breakthrough consisted of equipment similar to the machines they could see at work anywhere in Manhattan, digging foundations for the newest skyscraper, I saw a lot of eye rolling and blank expressions. Big trucks and big shovels? This was a breakthrough? They had every right to be skeptical. Looking back, I think I would have felt the same in their place, based on the history of Suncor.

A few years later, when the same bankers saw our P&L (profit and loss) statements and understood the true impact of the changeover, the skepticism vanished. Nothing improves a company's credibility in the eyes of its shareholders more effectively than positive financial results.

ELSEWHERE, estimates for the IPO price were all over the map. One banker suggested $30 a share, which made the Sun Company board smile. Another went to $26, a third estimated $25 and a fourth quoted $18 a share. Who was right?

The U.S. parent and the Ontario government liked the sound of a $25 share price and on that basis agreed to the offering with CIBC Wood Gundy and RBC Dominion Securities as the lead underwriters. Two months later, after the market absorbed the news and the skeptics began to be heard, reality set in and $25 was no longer viable. The target price, the market said, was closer to $18 a share.

Mike O'Brien and I had just taken off on an Air Canada flight from Toronto to Calgary on the day our underwriters hit us with that news, and we knew it would not go down well with either the board in Philadelphia or the Ontario cabinet in Toronto. The two of us spent the entire trip speaking on in-flight phones with the underwriters, Sun Company's CFO, and a deputy minister representing the province of Ontario. Sun's CFO had assured his board

that the sale would bring in $25 per share, and he was not look-
ing forward to informing them that they would have to take a 25
percent haircut. In fact, his reply couldn't have been more direct:
"We're not going to sell!" The deputy minister followed his lead,
saying if Sun wouldn't sell at that price neither would the province. He knew the provincial government was on the hook for
a loss covered by taxpayer money, and he didn't want to rack up
an even bigger loss than the American parent would suffer. Things
were beginning to fall apart and suddenly everything was up in the
air in more ways than one.

By this time, my relationship with Sun Company chairman
Bob Campbell had deteriorated badly. Mike O'Brien had a better
relationship with the CFO, so I left much of the back-and-forth
discussion to them. Somehow we had to convince Sun Company
to take the price being offered by the underwriter. If Sun would
go along with it, Ontario would follow and dispose of its shares. If
Sun refused the deal, we had spent several months accomplishing
nothing, and I was not optimistic about future dealings with the
U.S. people.

Mike and I spent almost the entire flight to Calgary negotiating
with four different sources: the two shareholders looking to maximize their return and our two lead underwriting investment bankers, looking for some way to rationalize the vast difference between
the earlier price and the latest one. As well as explaining to both
Philadelphia and Toronto that they had to accept a lower price, we
had to persuade Dick Falconer at Wood Gundy and Mike Norris at
RBC Capital to fix a suitable figure. It was a tough sell, and it didn't
become any easier when the bankers pointed out that even $18
could be optimistic, suggesting we might have to settle as low as $15
if we delayed the IPO. This prompted Sun Company to propose
dropping the whole deal until they could get an acceptable price
sometime in the future, to which Mike responded, "You only get

to walk down the aisle once. If we back off, we can't return three months from now and try to do it again. We have to do it *now*."

I give Mike O'Brien a lot of credit for sticking with the negotiations despite all the gloomy talk. Finally, somewhere over Saskatchewan, the bankers agreed to $18.25 per share. They saw their "order book" for anything higher than $18 per share as very weak. We chose $19 per share as the public offering price. Faced with the possibility of having to settle for an even lower price, Sun Company and Ontario agreed, and I breathed a sigh of relief as we were about to land in Calgary. This was the birth of the public Suncor, the first step in converting it from a U.S. subsidiary to a Canadian entity— and the beginning of a remarkable success story.

WE may have settled the price while in the air, but we had more work to do on the ground. Suncor's history of problems in the oil sands was well known in the investment industry, and it coloured the media's response to news of the offering. One financial columnist predicted, "Suncor's earnings will eventually peter out, along with its oil sands plant and its refinery."[1] And a securities analyst published a report titled *Suncor Inc. New Issue—Avoid*.[2] At least part of the pessimism was due to depressed world prices for crude oil at the time.

Comments like these are not helpful in any sales situation, and our offering was no exception. To sweeten the deal, the shares were sold in two tranches. Investors would be required to pay only $9.50, or half the share price, at the outset, with another $9.50 due a year later. Meanwhile, they would be entitled to 100 percent of dividends paid for the year in which they acquired the shares. Even with this carrot dangling in front of the market, fewer than half the shares in the original package were made available at the kick-off. The rest were held back in anticipation of higher crude oil prices.

The government of Ontario sold the remainder of its shares in April 1993, just over a year after the initial IPO, for $25.25 a share.

Over the next two years, things changed significantly. Thanks to higher world oil prices and the positive impact of our decision to replace the breakdown-prone bucket wheels with power shovels and trucks, news of the impending offering of Sun Company's remaining 55 percent ownership of Suncor in 1995 was greeted with banners and brass bands. "It's a great deal—I'll be a buyer!" declared one energy analyst, and another added, "It's the favourite stock pick among Canadian integrateds." With reviews like that, how could we lose? When the $1.2 billion issue was released in late May 1995, it sold out within minutes, proving that nothing succeeds like success.

Now that we were out from under the presence of Sun Company, I felt free to implement changes to Suncor that I believed would help us reach new levels of growth and success. One of them dealt with our chain of retail Sunoco service stations.

In the petroleum industry, service stations represent the downstream, or retail, side of the business, the brand that buyers look for when filling the fuel tanks of their vehicles. Obviously an important link in the chain, retail operations depend on intangibles like branding, advertising, marketing and promotion. Petroleum fuels and lubricants, for the most part, are commodities, and since it's more or less impossible for consumers to distinguish one commodity from another, you do it with "feel good" factors.

I have difficulty with intangibles. My academic training and business background are based on managing the upstream side, which involves solving specific problems, not choosing clever slogans or approving service station designs. Having come up through engineering, I found the downstream side of the business was not my primary interest. Most oil companies reflect the same attitude, focusing on either upstream or downstream operations. On the upstream side you discover, develop and transport crude oil and gas. On the downstream side you refine the oil and sell products made from the crude oil to end users. I was an upstream guy, and I believed that maximizing our investments in production would prove best for Suncor. I had experience with refining, but I didn't know a whole lot about marketing, and frankly it didn't interest me very much. Nor did I believe this would make a major impact on our corporate bottom line. Despite public perception, the profit margin on retail gasoline is less than five cents per litre, and the return on our capital investment in the Sunoco chain of service stations was not impressive. I grew convinced we could make better use of our money and energy by focusing on the upstream side.

This was my position when we began selling off Sunoco service stations. In Quebec, all the stations we owned were swapped with Ultramar for their stations in Ontario. We had a refinery in Ontario, and our wholesale and retail business in that province was strong. Ultramar boasted a similarly strong presence in Quebec, so both sides benefited from the deal. In some instances we closed a number of low-volume Sunoco stations in Ontario or sold them to off-brand marketers.

The entire process was done with one goal in mind: to strengthen Suncor's position on the upstream side. This would enable us to focus the lion's share of our efforts on streamlining our oil sands operations and prepare us to tackle the economic and environmental challenges we faced.

THE tale of taking Suncor public comes with a couple of lessons. One is that individual investors should read stories from analysts and columnists with a skeptical eye, prepared to separate fact from opinion. The facts about depressed oil prices at the time of the first offering and Suncor's history of problems were unfortunately true. The suggestion that these were insurmountable was merely opinion based on the limited information available. I prefer optimism and hard work over opinions. If you have enough of the former you can eventually change the latter, surprising lots of people with the things you accomplish.

Another lesson addresses the folly of investing in private companies as a purely political tactic. In 1982 Ontario's Conservative government under Bill Davis paid $650 million (plus annual interest chages of almost 15 percent) at the top of the market for 25 percent of Suncor in order to have its "window on the petroleum industry." Ten years later the NDP government led by Bob Rae sold the same shares during an economic recession and wrote off more than $400 million of its investment. It was the classic "buy high, sell low" error of amateur investors on a large scale. In addition to costing Ontario taxpayers a substantial loss, the pricey venture was one of the factors that cost the Conservative party its legislative majority in 1985.

There is a third side to the story worth mentioning, one that I try not to feel smug about. When Sun Company decided to wash its hands of Suncor by selling its remaining shares, members of the Sun board probably felt good about divesting themselves of both an anchor and a headache. Whatever their feelings, the second sale of shares to Canadians freed us from oversight and second-guessing by the people in Philadelphia, made Suncor a wholly Canadian corporation and provided us with the freedom to build the oil sands operation into the powerhouse I always thought it could be.

Here's the side of the story that I suspect shook up the Sun board members who had been anxious to dump its unloved progeny: within three years, the capital market value of Suncor exceeded that of its former parent, Sun Company.

5. CLEANING UP AFTER MOTHER NATURE

If industry analysts had fully understood the impact of our change-over from bucket wheels to trucks and shovels and acknowledged the cyclical quality of world oil prices, they might have tempered their pessimistic view of Suncor's future in 1992. That's old news, I admit, but it parallels an even bigger problem we face today.

It's difficult to think of businesses that receive more criticism from more corners of society than Suncor and the other companies tapping the oil sands. The criticism extends well beyond shouts of "Clean up your act!" It includes demands that the entire oil sands operation be shut down, and that not one additional barrel of oil be recovered to meet the needs of the global market. And these demands are made for the most part not by individual citizens but by highly placed government officials such as Nancy Pelosi, the former speaker of the U.S. House of Representatives, and prominent activist organizations like Greenpeace and the Sierra Club.

I meet as often as I can with groups and individuals who want to see activity at the oil sands halted. Not all of them take an extreme view. Many are pragmatic advocates whose concern for the environment is genuine and whose approach to the problem is rational. They include people such as Rob McIntosh, one of the founders of the Pembina Institute; Steven Guilbeault, formerly of Greenpeace and now co-founder and deputy executive director of Équiterre;

Ken Ogilvie, former executive director of Pollution Probe; Gerald Butts at World Wildlife Fund Canada; and several others. They appreciate the complexity of the issue and help look for ways to satisfy the interests of both sides.

Others are less flexible. Meetings with them often begin in an adversarial mood. After an hour or so, however, things tend to settle into a relaxed dialogue. At some point during the exchange I begin to morph in their eyes from a satanic plunderer into a reasonable guy searching for a way to run a business while making as little environmental impact as possible. I'm not sure any minds are changed during the meetings, but I believe understanding improves on both sides, which counts as progress in my book. More important, the meetings tend to end with some degree of mutual respect.

I'm nonetheless surprised at the lack of understanding among people from all interests—consumers, environmentalists, investors and much of the media—regarding the oil sands and what they represent. Critics of the oil sands are free to denounce the world's reliance on petroleum, but expecting to replace it with another source of energy within a week, a year or even an entire generation is more than impractical; it's unrealistic. I know, because at Suncor we have been exploring and investing in a range of alternative sources of energy for several years. If I honestly believed we could meet the expectations and needs of our customers, employees and shareholders and the general public by switching from petroleum to solar, wind, biochemical or any other energy source, we would be out of the oil sands tomorrow. It's not going to happen, however, and I would like people to understand the true role of the oil sands in meeting a vital need before they insist that the world would be a better place without them.

To understand fully what Suncor and other companies are doing at the oil sands, it's necessary to grasp the unique aspects and challenges they present. I'm not being cynical when I say that firms engaged in oil sands production are cleaning up nature's biggest oil spill. Every company in the oil sands region is engaged in the same activity. Reduced to basic steps, it involves removing bitumen-soaked sand from its location, stripping the sand of bitumen, and returning the cleaner sand to its approximate original location. The only real differences between an industrial oil spill and oil sands recovery are size, location and intent. The size of the oil sands area exceeds any imaginable petroleum spill, and the location is about as remote as you can get in North America. The intent is to produce petroleum to satisfy a market demand; the clean-up aspect is a by-product.

Bitumen has soaked more than 140,000 square kilometres of northeastern Alberta and a portion of Saskatchewan for millions of years. That's a lot of land, but it represents less than 5 percent of Canada's boreal forest. After more than forty years of petroleum production from the oil sands, only about 0.02 percent of the country's boreal forest has been disturbed by open mining, and every site will be restored to near-original condition. Anyone who claims that oil sands activity is destroying Canada's boreal wilderness is engaging in wild exaggeration.

The bitumen trapped within the oil sands resulted from the same material and process that produced crude oil reserves in Saudi Arabia, Texas, the North Sea and almost every region of the world. The process involves applying heat and pressure to thick layers of algae and other organisms over untold millennia. The result in most regions is natural gas and crude oil. In the Athabasca region of Alberta, the ancient life forms escaped the extended and intense pressure and temperatures that created free-flowing crude oil in other parts of the world and instead produced bitumen.

People have been using bitumen for thousands of years. It has been found on the tools of Neanderthals in Syria dating back 40,000 years or more. As I mentioned earlier, bitumen sealed the seams of canoes and kayaks used by First Nations people long before the arrival of Europeans. It was also used by ancient Egyptians in their practice of preserving corpses as mummies. In fact, the word *mummy* derives from *mumiyyah,* a Latin borrowing of the Arabic word for bitumen.

The amount of bitumen in the oil sands is staggering. Those 1.75 trillion barrels represent 75 percent of total North American oil reserves. Not all of the oil is recoverable, admittedly, but if it were easy-flowing crude oil instead of thick, cold-molasses bitumen, and it were located in one massive subterranean pool instead of mixed with sand and water, it would be the world's largest source of petroleum energy, and Canada would easily be the wealthiest country in the world. And while many environmentalists would continue to condemn the effect of carbon emissions from global use of petroleum, few people would be upset by the drilling and pumping rigs needed to move the "conventional" oil to market.

Unfortunately, nature didn't hand Alberta a massive pool of easily flowing light oil, so before the bitumen can be used to power cars, heat homes and factories and serve as raw material for various petroleum-based products, it needs to be separated from sand and water. Two very different technologies have proved effective. Surface mining involves transporting bitumen-soaked soil to processing plants; this is the system employing trucks and power shovels, similar to mining ore. The other process is to separate the materials beneath the surface and remove heated bitumen from the ground relatively free of soil and water, a method known as *in situ* production.

Surface mining accounts for only a small proportion of the oil sands to be processed. Most of the bitumen is being and will be recovered in situ through steam-assisted gravity drainage, or SAGD, eliminating surface excavation and tailings ponds.

The concept of SAGD is fairly simple, but the technology is complex. Two horizontal wells are drilled through the bitumen layer, one positioned about five metres above the other. Steam injected into the upper well heats the bitumen and lowers its viscosity until it flows down to the lower well. From there, the easy-flowing bitumen is pumped to the surface for further processing, eliminating the use of power shovels and trucks and avoiding the large excavations associated with open-pit mining. More than 80 percent of the bitumen to be recovered from the oil sands will be removed in situ, and less than 5 percent of the surface will be temporarily disturbed. The process also permits the water used to be recycled easily, reducing our need to draw water from the Athabasca River.

The system that attracts most of the critical press on the oil sands is surface mining, and it's not difficult to understand why. Encountering an open-pit mine in the middle of wilderness is a shock because it looks like a massive opening in the earth. Open-pit mining is hardly exclusive to the oil sands. The process occurs in hundreds of places around the world as a way to get access to various raw materials. We need to ensure that this form of mining occurs with as little impact as possible on the surrounding environment and that when the mining activity ends the site is returned to its original state. Those have both been prime goals for Suncor for many years, and our practices are legislated and monitored by the province of Alberta.

Open-pit mining is not the most sophisticated industrial process in the world, no matter what resource is being sought, and the oil sands activity is no exception. The bitumen accessible by mining lies in layers from forty to sixty metres thick and within seventy-five metres of the surface, sandwiched between an overburden of muskeg above and flat limestone rock below. The overburden is removed and used as dams and embankments during the mining process. With the overburden gone, the power shovels transfer the bitumen-laden sand into trucks that carry it to the processing plant. When the mining site is exhausted of bitumen, the overburden is replaced as part of the restoration process.

At the plant, hot water and agitation become the primary means of separating the sand and bitumen, creating a frothy slurry. Much of the sand falls away from the slurry into giant settling vessels and, after further processing to remove residual sand and water, thick crude oil remains. The heavy crude must either be diluted with lighter oil or partially refined before it can be transported through pipelines to refineries across North America.

The partial refinement, or upgrading, of the oil provides a couple of important benefits. First, it enables the oil to flow more easily through pipelines to refineries, where it will be processed into gasoline, diesel fuel and other products. The distance the oil travels is enormous. For years almost half of the Suncor oil produced from the oil sands flowed east to a Sunoco refinery in Sarnia, Ontario, almost three thousand kilometres away.

The second benefit is more subtle but almost as important. To most people all crude oil appears essentially the same: a thick, gooey liquid that looks like molasses and sometimes smells like rotten eggs. It's the job of refineries to convert the oil they receive into specific product categories according to the markets they serve. Refineries perform this function in different ways, depending on the kind of equipment they use and the technology they employ, and this provides an opportunity for oil sands producers.

As I noted earlier, when upgrading the bitumen from the oil sands into crude oil for use by refineries, we can change the composition of the synthetic crude according to the needs of the refinery. Within limits, the crude sent to refinery A may differ from that sent to refinery B, providing each with the optimum, or near optimum, raw material and improving their respective efficiency levels. Depending on the nature of the change, we can save money at our end or at the refinery end. Either way it's a plus.

♦

IT takes almost two tonnes of oil sands to produce a barrel of synthetic crude oil, which will comprise about 90 percent of the oil
encased in the sand. This is substantially more than could be recovered when the industry was launched. Back then, squeezing 75 percent of the oil from the bitumen was an acceptable standard. With
the bitumen removed, the leftover material is called tailings, and
over the years we have introduced a number of enhancements to
remove residual oil from tailings.

Stripped of bitumen, the tailings—sand, silt, fine clay particles
and water, along with a very small volume of unrecoverable bitumen—are fed into ponds where the solids are permitted to settle
out. This can take years, and tailings ponds are not the most attractive sights you are likely to encounter in your lifetime. They also
represent a risk to wildlife, especially aquatic birds. Sound cannons
are used to warn the birds away, a technique that's normally very
effective. It's rarely necessary, however, because migrating waterfowl
are normally clever enough to avoid landing on the ponds. But
Murphy's Law applies in the oil sands as often as anywhere else. The
unfortunate death of 1,600 ducks at a Syncrude tailings pond in
April 2008 occurred when freak weather forced the ducks to look
for an immediate landing area and the sound cannons, as it happened, were not in operation that day. In the twenty years I've been
associated with the oil sands, nothing similar has occurred.

Once the solid material has settled sufficiently from the tailings
pond, and water has been removed for processing in a closed-loop
system, the pond and original excavation site are filled and restored.
We and every other company involved in producing bitumen from
the oil sands are required by law to reclaim disturbed land.

Much has been made of the amount of water drawn from the
Athabasca River and the presence of bitumen in the river as a result

of oil sands production activity. Currently, about 1 percent of the Athabasca's flow is used by oil sands producers. Total allocation of water from the river, including municipal and other industrial uses, is about 3.2 percent of its flow.* It's worth comparing this figure with the proportions of flow drawn from the North Saskatchewan River by the city of Edmonton (37 percent); from the Oldman River in southern Alberta (60 percent); and by the city of Calgary and other users from the Bow River (65 percent).

It's true that bitumen can be detected in the waters of the Athabasca, but the material has been leaking into the river unaided by human activity for millions of years, and nothing suggests that the bitumen levels are measurably higher now than in the past. The province of Alberta monitors in great detail the amount of water drawn from the Athabasca, as well as the quantity and quality of process water returned to the river, and reports its findings publicly.

It doesn't stop there. A team composed of representatives from the government of Alberta, the federal government of Canada, the environmental community and the petroleum industry is working to establish a world-class monitoring system that will represent a major upgrade from current facilities. This is important to all parties concerned about both petroleum production and water quality because they need access to the best data available, gathered and interpreted according to an agreed-upon formula. It's the only way possible to avoid clashes of different data sets leading to conflicting assessments. And it underlines how seriously everyone is taking the question of water quality.

---

* The parallel admittedly is not perfect, but it's interesting to note that from 50 to 75 percent of the water in the Niagara River is diverted away from Niagara Falls to produce electrical energy. For people who enjoy witnessing the might of nature, Niagara Falls is clearly not what it used to be. With that in mind, the 1 to 2 percent of the Athabasca flow used by oil sands producers can be seen in a new perspective.

The extent of the efforts to restore open-mining sites to their original state may be surprising to some people. Before the overburden is stripped away, for example, botanists remove seed samples from existing vegetation. Landscape nurseries in Edmonton and elsewhere receive the seeds and use them to propagate seedlings. When the site is ready for restoration the seedlings are returned to the site, where they are planted and cared for until they mature. In this manner every restored site provides a home for precisely the same kind of plant life that existed there before the land was disturbed. By 2011 Suncor and other oil sands operators had planted more than 7.5 million seedlings in fulfilling their land reclamation obligations.

Instead of acting in opposition, nature frequently assists us in the process. We have learned, for example, that inserting dead trees firmly into the ground on reclaimed mine sites attracts nesting pairs of hawks, eagles and other predatory birds. The birds begin producing chicks, which they feed from the large population of mice, voles, rabbits and other prey flourishing among the shrubs and maturing trees. Wildlife in the oil sands even persuades us to adapt our approach to meet its preferences. On one occasion, work on a section of reclaimed mine pit was halted for a few weeks, leaving an exposed cliff face. When teams arrived to finish filling the area, they discovered the cliff face had been claimed by dozens of nesting swallows. Instead of disturbing the birds, the teams relocated the filler material originally intended for the cliff. I understand the swallow population has expanded enormously, kept busy and well fed, no doubt, by more mosquitoes.

The process of recovering and upgrading the bitumen trapped in the oil sands is immensely complicated and expensive, even without following all the stringent rules involved in meeting environmental standards and land restoration. Most but not all of these standards are set and monitored by government statutes. I take special pride in the fact that Suncor has consistently set environmental standards and goals exceeding those required by government regulators. Admittedly, part of this strategy has been based on the consciousness that society expects stringent monitoring where the environment is concerned and it is in our interests to stay ahead of that particular curve.

A substantial portion of our efforts, however, has been driven by the Suncor value system. It is important to our employees and all of our stakeholders, and important to me personally, that Suncor be recognized not for maintaining standards that are "good enough" but for setting the pace for everybody else—including, on more than one occasion, the regulators themselves.

THE cost incurred in producing hundreds of thousands of barrels of oil each day from the oil sands is substantial, calculated in capital investment as well as labour and maintenance. Billions of dollars are spent year after year, much of it directed toward finding answers to a long list of questions. Can we increase the proportion of oil recovered from 90 percent to 93 or 94 percent? Is it possible to extend by a few days the time between maintenance periods of the 400-ton dump trucks (costing $5 million each)? Are we maximizing the amount of water we recycle and minimizing the volume of effluents from our operations? The industry keeps searching for answers to these questions, with encouraging results.

High processing costs in the oil sands are offset to some extent by the fact that we don't have to invest much money to locate the oil. Exploration expenses vary widely, with no guarantee of success, and an oil company can spend millions upon millions of dollars without expanding its reserves by a single barrel. In the oil sands, the field costs are fixed and calculable, making it easy to set a bottom price line that determines whether investments and efforts are going to pay off or not. As of mid-2012 Suncor needed a world price on crude oil of $40 per barrel to cover its production costs and sustaining capital and $60 per barrel to return a reasonable profit. The majority of this profit, by the way, is reinvested to grow the company, improve its productivity and continue to reduce its environmental impact.

Is it all worth the price, considering the impact these operations make on the land? Would things be improved if we turned off our trucks, power shovels, production facilities and support groups and left the oil sands to the bears, moose and beaver? Wouldn't that encourage the world, or at least one corner of it, to wean itself from petroleum and launch a new crusade for a future free of greenhouse gases and all the problems associated with oil? Can't we begin replacing it with wind power, solar generators, biomass and geothermal sources?

To put it bluntly, no. I know, because Suncor was among the first major oil companies to become actively involved in developing and employing technology based on a number of potential alternative sources of energy. We know these sources well, and while there may be promise in wind and solar power, neither offers the efficiency and reliability needed to replace hydrocarbons.

And walking away from the oil sands would make no impact on the world's consumption of oil, because OPEC producers that were able to do so—most notably Saudi Arabia—would open their taps a little wider to fill the gap. If they chose not to, the price of oil would rise, with a massive negative impact on the global economy.

An oil sands shutdown would also make only a minor dent in the concerns of the environmentalists, especially with respect to greenhouse gases. It would make a substantial impact, however, on the livelihood of tens of thousands of exceptionally talented and dedicated oil sands workers. Among them would be many First Nations and Métis residents in the region, including a few self-made millionaires who operate service companies vitally associated with Suncor and other oil sands–based firms. From the North American point of view, stopping the oil sands production would increase our dependence on oil from distant nations, many of them at odds with Western values and policies and almost none of them as reliable and open as Canada.

The world needs energy. Western civilization is based on it, and has been since the Industrial Revolution. Canada has built a substantial portion of its sovereign income by producing and marketing petroleum, using the money to finance a range of national programs including its health care system. The primary source of energy for transportation, heating and manufacturing throughout the world is petroleum based. The effective operation of the oil sands—in a manner that respects all the environmental aspects—is a reasonable and necessary response to the demand for this energy.

6. MOVING WEST: RELOCATING CLOSER TO THE ACTION

The departure from the scene of the province of Ontario and Sun Company changed the culture of Suncor. We were now a wholly independent Canadian corporation beholden to several thousand shareholders instead of to one distant and domineering parent company. The change, not only among senior executives but among employees at every level, was apparent in a new confidence and positive outlook.

From my angle, it changed my vision of what the company could and should become, and I began searching for ways to sharpen the focus of that vision. Among my first steps was to relocate the head office from Toronto to Calgary. I had questioned the wisdom of running the company out of Toronto from the beginning. Why would an oil company whose largest potential asset was in northern Alberta locate its major decision-making group halfway across the country?

There were two reasons. One was linked to the 25 percent ownership of Suncor by the province of Ontario. The provincial government, having purchased its portion with tax dollars from Ontario residents, would not look kindly upon a decision to move the firm to another province, no matter what impact it had on the company's performance. It just wouldn't look good. Newspaper editorials and political opponents would have castigated the government for permitting a move to Alberta, but when the province bailed out, we were free to go.

The second reason for remaining in Toronto was conformity, of a sort. With the exception of Petro-Canada, the other major oil companies had been headquartered in Toronto for some time. And that included Shell and Imperial Oil, which was 70 percent owned by ExxonMobil. Ontario was the country's largest market for petroleum products, and the presence of the Toronto Stock Exchange was probably another reason for remaining there. But Alberta's rank as the country's largest petroleum producer couldn't be ignored. Shell was the first to break the tradition, moving to Calgary in 1984, and I made a decision for Suncor to follow suit in 1995. Imperial Oil finally departed Toronto for Calgary in 2005.

Tradition wasn't that important in light of all the benefits I saw in relocating, but employee reaction to the news became a concern. Calgary might have become the centre of the oil business in Canada, but Toronto was the centre of almost everything else, striving to fulfil the role of world-class city. All of the country's major financial companies were headquartered there, the city's international film festival was becoming a major event, there was plenty of live theatre and great restaurants, and the lifestyle was about as attractive as you could find in that corner of the world. Julie and I and our children were living in a suburb near Lake Ontario. We liked the town and the availability of good schools nearby, and we liked visiting Toronto for entertainment and dining.

In contrast, Calgary was still referred to as "Cowtown"—usually by people in Toronto. The moniker was not only insulting; it was inaccurate. Almost everyone in the petroleum industry maintained important links with Calgary, which was on the verge of shifting from a town best known for its annual stampede to an urban centre where major business and financial decisions were being made. Despite this, I suspected that we would lose a number of people.

None of this dissuaded me from moving, however, and to reduce the chance of losing valuable people I offered a guarantee: if any employee regretted relocating to Calgary within three years, we would move them back to Toronto at our expense. Of the thirty or so employees who made the move I believe only one or two took up the offer of a free return trip. The others settled in and are pleased to be part of not only of a growing company but also a growing city that is actually rivalling Toronto in many respects. Maybe the choice of restaurants, theatre, art galleries and all those other world-class attractions isn't as plentiful as Toronto's yet, but the Rockies are just an hour's drive away, the year-round sports opportunities are out-standing and there is a unique vibrancy to Calgary.

I have to admit that the head office move wasn't greeted with universal joy, especially by some of Suncor's operating groups in the field. They had been making autonomous decisions, moving quickly to take advantage of changing situations and proving suc-cessful at it. Head office had been 3,500 kilometres away, and now it would be practically just down the street. The impact would be more psychological than practical, but I knew it would generate some unease among the Albertan staffers. In explaining to one business audience at the time why some Suncor field operators did not greet the move from Toronto with unbridled enthusiasm, I asked them to imagine how they would feel at the news that their mother-in-law was moving next door. I think I made the point.

All in all, the discomfort level faded quickly. Making the move to Calgary heightened the changed mood of the company and everyone associated with it. We became closer to the industry both geographically and psychologically. With the oil sands just an hour or so away by air, I felt more comfortable about our decision to gear up our operations and expand production.

♦

"Go big or go home" is more applicable to the petroleum industry than anything else you can name. Exploration, drilling, leasing rights, production equipment and refining costs are often measured in billions of dollars. The payoff may be substantial but so are the risks. The risk begins with the initial search for oil. Years of work can be spent acquiring the acreage and rights, conducting seismic surveys and drilling wells that produce no oil but lots of red ink. Refineries cost hundreds of millions of dollars to build; once in operation they may fall victim to boom-and-bust cycles that leave them producing very thin profit margins. Oil prices rise and fall at a dizzying rate; producers can be facing staggering losses one month and rolling in cash the next. And one error, or more likely a combination of small errors, may result in an oil spill costing untold millions of dollars in clean-up costs, legal settlements and corporate reputation. This is not a business for either shallow pockets or weak hearts. You don't exactly roll the dice with every move, but you sure weigh the odds carefully.

By 1997 we were settled in Calgary, and the move to trucks and shovels at the oil sands, along with the installation of a new vacuum tower to expand our upgrading capacity, was paying dividends. After years of fires, mechanical breakdowns and multiple losses, Suncor was on solid ground financially. I was concerned, however, that we were a single-train operation. We had one mine feeding one extraction plant leading to one upgrader, and all of the product flowed through one pipeline. We had back-up facilities where practical, but the fact remained that if one section of the chain broke the entire complex operation stopped until that link was restored. Shutting down one component for scheduled overhauls and refits meant widespread stoppage, and unexpected failures, while minimal compared with previous years, could still occur. Things were too risky.

The obvious solution was to add a second train of mining, upgrading, processing and transportation. Besides reducing the risk, it would increase our production capacity and our cash flow.

We scoped out a plan to expand an existing production area known as the Steepbank Mine. With the size of the reserves at this location, and assuming a daily production level of 200,000-plus barrels, we calculated a minimum twenty-five-year production life for the mine. The rest of the plan involved adding new extraction and upgrading facilities to handle the increased volume of bitumen, modernizing the existing units to improve capacity and efficiency, and investing in a new pipeline capable of handling 500,000 barrels of crude oil each day. Other equipment to be added or modified included sulphur and hydrogen recovery units, heat exchangers to recover heat energy and reduce fuel consumption and new technology to cut our water usage.

It was a good plan but it came with a heavy price. Incorporating all the features would cost an estimated $2.2 billion, which was about double the capitalized value of the entire company. It would also take years to complete, which meant not a penny would flow back from all that expense and effort for some time. We had two choices. We could remain as we were, trying to anticipate and avoid shutdowns while hoping to minimize our capital costs and maximize our profit margins. That would be the safe route in the short run, but I considered it foolish in the long run. Business is an organic life form that either grows or withers on the vine, and I had no interest in withering.

We had to take the second choice and grow our scale as well as our vision. We were the company, after all, that had proven the viability of the oil sands. Now almost a dozen other companies were moving into oil sands production, each as determined as we were to make a long-term success of their investment. This was neither the time nor the place to be hesitant. Still, it's natural to pause before signing off on a commitment to spend more than $2 billion, and some people have asked if I had any second thoughts before giving a green light to the move, which we christened the Millennium project. My answer was consistent: "Not for a moment."

You can't make any major decision in life or business without being analytical at the outset, and everyone on the project team did his and her homework in this regard. We determined the cost, projected the earnings, calculated the return on capital, checked that our balance sheet could handle the expenditure and confirmed that we could complete the work within the scheduled timeframe. This is textbook planning that, in some ways, is equally necessary whether planning a new production chain or purchasing a new truck.

The chief variable in our case was the price of a barrel of crude oil. We were, after all, engaged in producing and marketing a global commodity. No matter how much effort and investment we put into our product, it would sell at basically the same price as our competitors, whether they were located elsewhere in the oil sands or halfway around the world in the Middle East.

This was definitely Big Bet time. We would be committing our company to billions of dollars in expenditures financed through our own internal cash flow, not equity, and that would not begin to generate revenue for years. I took a lot of heat once the project was launched, especially when the original estimate of $2.2 billion ballooned into a final tab of $3.4 billion. That, combined with the usual fluctuations in price and market demand, made many shareholders and analysts uneasy. Where would oil prices be in the cycle when the expansion was completed? If they were higher, we would win big; profits would rise along with our share price, and life would be sweet. If they were lower, we would be deep in debt with little hope of climbing out in the short term. When it came time to decide whether to go ahead with the project, crude oil was hovering around $12 per barrel, and the prestigious business magazine *The Economist* was forecasting that it would drop to $5 a barrel and stay there for some time.[1] Meanwhile, CEOs all across the Alberta oil patch were giving orders to slash capital budgets and roll back operating expenditures to weather the storm.

At this point, the best analysis in the world won't justify your decision. Either you abandon your plan or you consult your intuition. If your intuition is sufficiently strong and you're brave enough to assume an attitude contrary to the rest of the herd, that's the route you follow.

The herd's opinion to reduce capital expenditures represented a signal for us to launch the Millennium project without hesitation. Why? Because good management is not about the state of things as they are today. It's about the state of things as they will be tomorrow. It's like Wayne Gretzky's explanation of his success as a hockey player. "Don't skate to where the puck is," Gretzky's dad is said to have advised. "Skate to where it's *going* to be." Oil prices, I reasoned, could never stay as low as they were in 1997. By the time Millennium came on stream they would be high enough to easily justify the investment. Our job was to skate to where the market was going to be.

I suspect that for the time being, there was more than a little head shaking around town as oil company executives got together to ask, "Did you hear what those guys over at Suncor are doing? They're spending money—billions of dollars of it!" No one in the business asked me how I could justify committing the company to such high spending when prices were so depressed. If they had, I would have answered: cycles.

Effective planning in the commodities business demands an understanding of cycles in production and prices, combined with many years of experience watching those cycles. By their very name and nature, cycles keep changing. Some are short, some are long, and nothing you see this week or this month will be in the same place next week or next month. Too many people, from top executives to men and women investing for their retirement, stay the course without questioning the speed or direction. When they see stock prices rise they assume it's time to buy. Of course, it's usually the time to sell. If you're running in the middle of the herd, you're behind the cycle. Whenever I see a herd running, I tend to turn in the other direction.

Commodity prices move in cycles because the price is driven by supply and demand. When I looked around before deciding to approve Millennium, I could see that all the fundamentals for a return to higher oil prices were in place. Demand was building and supply had slackened. Prices had nowhere to go but up.

Succeeding in any business demands an honest view of the world and a full understanding of macroeconomics. A lot of people in the petroleum industry are fine at analysing rates of returns and other measures. I value their expertise and opinions, but too many people are weak on the intuitive side, and I believe that's a handicap. If you don't have much intuition, you'd better have lots of nerve, and even with a sharpened intuition you'd better be prepared to make some wrong bets from time to time. Just try not to make them on billion-dollar capital decisions.

The Millennium project was a big bet that paid off almost from the day we announced the program, when our share price jumped about $7. When it finally came on stream, Millennium's impact on our productivity, cash flow, capitalization, employment levels and long-term security for shareholders and employees alike was positive across the board. Rather than sliding to $5 per barrel, crude prices rose sharply and remained well above our production costs. And as I write this the project's final $3.4 billion expenditure, which looked excessive, has generated the highest productivity increase by any oil sands producer since its completion, for the lowest investment.

While I relied on my intuition and somewhat contrary nature to reach the decision about launching Millennium, I also drew upon the wisdom and advice of my management team as well as guidance and counsel from the Suncor board. The Suncor team was, in case I need to say it, first rate and a key part of the company's success. In fact, whenever somebody asks me to define the secret of my success as a CEO, I answer: *I try to hire people who are smarter than me.* And JR Shaw, chair of the Suncor board at the time, was especially supportive and encouraging.

The principle of hiring smarter people than you remains a good strategy, but not an infallible one. Bright people tend to know their superiority in one aspect of business or another, and this can lead to problems. Egos get in the way, individual goals may trump corporate goals and an inability to function as a team player can reduce anyone's capabilities. The benefits tend to exceed the risk, however, and I would still choose to hire the smartest people available than depend on easy-going people who may fail to reach expectations—mine and theirs.

SOMETIMES planning, experience and great teamwork still fail to produce a winner, and as long as I'm talking about the things that worked out well for Suncor, I had better acknowledge at least one thing that did not. Every business management book talks about how you learn more from your failures than from your successes. If that's the case, the Stuart shale oil project was an education in itself.

The Stuart project was associated with Southern Pacific Petroleum, an Australian company with a plan to recover oil trapped in massive shale deposits along the coast of Queensland. The process involved removing the shale using methods similar to our shovel-and-truck technique. The rock would then be crushed in a processor and the oil deposits vaporized in a rotating kiln with an interior temperature of about 500 degrees Celsius. The vapour would be transported to a condenser and would flow out of it as heavy oil similar to the petroleum we were producing from the oil sands, but bypassing the bitumen stage.

There was some resemblance between the Stuart operations and ours. We recover bitumen by washing it from the surface of sand particles; they would recover oil from particles of rock by vaporizing the hydrocarbons attached to the solid particles. The similarity persuaded us to launch a joint venture with Southern Pacific Petroleum in 1997, investing $150 million and assuming the role of project manager. If we wanted to expand our production capabilities beyond the oil sands, the theory went, we should avoid competing with all the other companies combing the globe for undiscovered oil deposits and become leaders in recovering heavy crude from alternative sources.

A pilot plant in Calgary indicated that the process at the Stuart plant was a commercially feasible operation, encouraging us to scale up the technology and install a production facility in Australia. The usual procedure at this stage is to expand the pilot plant's capacity by a factor of ten, using a pure research and development (R&D) approach to assess its performance and its likely success or failure. We wanted to make the process economically feasible from the beginning, so we scaled the Australian unit up by a factor of fifty.

We quickly discovered that something that looks promising on a small scale can be far less effective when sufficiently enlarged. The Stuart plant also defined the differences between our technology in the oil sands and the one used to recover shale oil in Australia. Oil sands technology uses water heated to about 90 degrees Celsius, which easily separates the bitumen from the sand particles. Heating the crushed stone at Stuart to 500 degrees Celsius proved far more difficult. The high temperatures within the kiln broke down the carbonate material in the shale and produced a very fine dust that exited the kiln and proved difficult to control. This was not a good situation. Production peaked at about five thousand barrels per day and stalled there; this level would not have been enough to justify continued operation economically even without complications. We were already sensitive to concerns voiced by various groups about carbon emissions, and both the energy expense and carbon dioxide levels couldn't justify the volume of oil being recovered. Stuart was also operating in close proximity to the Great Barrier Reef, and while we saw no direct impact on that unique natural treasure, as time passed we grew uncomfortable about both the economics and the environmental risk of the project.

After about three years of frustration and concern, made more challenging by the distance between the two countries and our inexperience in dealing with an Australian company, I began to question the wisdom of continuing with Stuart. If we were going to abandon our involvement, however, I wanted everyone who had invested a few years of their working lives on the concept to feel that they were part of that decision, so I gathered about fifteen members of the team together. Then I went around the table, giving everyone an opportunity to talk about the prospects of success and the dangers of maintaining our involvement with the project.

This is a decision-making process that I have always tried to practise. It consists for the most part of listening before deciding. Once the decision was reached, of course, the fallout dropped on my shoulders. That's the way it had to be. But the process did not disempower those who had developed and worked on the project or who opposed shutting it down. I reached a decision knowing that everyone who had been involved in a major capacity would understand how I made up my mind, helping to ensure that they would be more likely to fully support the move.

In this case I heard a good deal about the operating problems, the environmental concerns and the worries about the overall safety of the process. So we threw in the towel, sold our participation and wrote off about $100 million. The Stuart plant went through a couple of other owners before being closed for good in 2005.

We didn't give up on the idea of moving into other energy fields. In fact, we made a decision to change the name of the company to Suncor Energy, marking our investment in wind and biological energy and our commitment to exploring and developing sources other than petroleum.

Shale oil may yet become a large and economically sound source of petroleum, especially in North America. The state of Colorado boasts massive deposits, and a number of companies are hard at work on these sites developing technologies to extract crude. Good luck to them. Through the rest of my tenure at Suncor, however, I was content to focus most of our attention on the oil sands and to leave shale oil to others.

7. The Petro-Canada Saga

How often do you get a chance to merge two companies whose operations blend almost hand in glove, whose cultures differ widely and whose combined assets make it the largest of its kind in history? Obviously not often. And how likely is it that you get two chances ten years apart?

That's how Suncor absorbed Petro-Canada. The deal generated great controversy and changed the face of the petroleum industry in Canada. Yet most of the important decisions on the mechanics were made between four guys in a hotel room, working out the details with no lawyers, accountants, advisers or second guessers anywhere in sight.

From my point of view, the Petro-Canada acquisition marked both a personal achievement and a period of intense sadness. All in all I think it makes a heck of a story, and the details have never been fully revealed until now.

Many challenges grew out of Petro-Canada's legacy. The federal government launched the Crown corporation in 1975 to provide the country with a domestic oil company as a means of balancing domination of the industry by foreign firms, the majority of them American. The idea of a 100 percent Canadian company participating in the oil patch played relatively well everywhere in

Canada except in Alberta, where most of the country's domestic oil reserves were located. Albertans consider themselves more self-reliant than those in other regions, and the news that an Ottawa-inspired public corporation was about to muscle in on the province's most important industry was not well received. Choosing to locate Petro-Canada's head office in Calgary did little to dilute the animosity.

Petro-Canada could never escape its origins as a government-owned firm operating in direct competition with private companies. I'm afraid management didn't help overcome this stigma either, especially in the early years. Without getting into a debate about private versus public corporations, I can say it is clear that Petro-Canada demonstrated an attitude and a behaviour that shareholders of most private companies would never tolerate.

From the day Petro-Canada opened its doors the company went on a buying spree with taxpayers' money, purchasing the Canadian refineries and retail operations of Gulf, BP, Petrofina and Atlantic-Richfield. It became known as much for its extravagance as for its products. The first Petro-Canada chairman and CEO occupied the entire top floor of the company's office tower in Calgary, equipping his executive suite with, among other goodies, a private chef. It was the kind of excess that most privately held companies rejected, and the fact that every penny was underwritten with public funds made things appear even more excessive. Resentment in the Alberta oil patch ran wide and deep. The plaza in front of Petro-Canada's Calgary headquarters was even called Red Square by people who would never forgive Ottawa for creating the company or its employees for working there.

At almost every turn, Petro-Canada appeared to pay premium prices for underperforming assets. "The people's oil company," as it was called in some quarters, seemed to lumber along, buying retail gas stations when the rest of the industry was consolidating theirs and missing opportunities to improve its bottom-line performance. As a result its share price was perpetually depressed compared with competitors, and its image within the industry was abysmal. One oil industry commentator likened it to "the wicked witch of the west."[1]

Even after the federal government decided it shouldn't be in the petroleum business and began divesting itself of Petro-Canada shares in the early 1990s, the company retained its Crown corporation roots. This was no surprise. For twenty years it had to one degree or another been supported by public funds. Expecting its key decision makers to assume the role of entrepreneurs just because the share structure had changed was unrealistic. Many couldn't shake their close association with Ottawa, and they seemed to retain an elitist identity in the same way, I suppose, that sailors serving on board a fleet's flagship see themselves as a privileged group.

From my first days with Suncor, I was keenly aware of Petro-Canada and the fact that its share price appeared perpetually depressed against the true value of its assets. Even though its refineries and retail outlets were doing well, the company would never live up to its full potential as long as it dragged its Crown corporation roots behind it.

I knew and respected Jim Stanford, Petro-Canada's CEO in the 1990s, and in 1998, soon after the Millennium project got underway, I began talking with him about his company's future. During one of our talks, Jim suggested the timing might be good for a merger, with me as CEO of the new, larger company. My response, of course, was immediately positive. Part of the appeal was the Petro-Canada chain of retail service stations whose locations fit neatly into the Sunoco network with limited overlap, and its efficient refinery operations. Some of Petro-Canada's other assets, in my opinion, were not of the quality I wanted to see on Suncor's books, but these were minor points.

The primary attraction of a merger would be the opportunity to immediately scale up Suncor. This wasn't just a matter of growth for its own sake but an issue of self-preservation and future opportunity. The need for growth is a given for any corporation, and in an industry where even run-of-the-mill investments carry billion-dollar price tags, being a large company is far more advantageous than being a small one. Compared to the ExxonMobils and BPs of the world, Suncor and Petro-Canada were small. A merged company would be at least medium-sized, with more clout and a larger and more diversified asset base. As separate entities, Suncor and Petro-Canada would always be also-rans. As a single corporation, they would exert substantial leverage.

I kept weighing the manner in which the two companies would fit together. Suncor was strong in the oil sands, and our well-established refinery operations in Sarnia served as a domestic destination for our crude. Petro-Canada had solid conventional oil and gas assets, and a large retail and marketing arm. As a bonus, the Petro-Canada refinery in Edmonton was relatively close to the oil sands and ideally geared to process the petroleum we produced.

The word *synergy* is tossed freely around whenever corporate mergers are discussed. In this case the term would be fully appropriate because, in a broad sense, the companies looked like two halves of a larger whole.

My major concern was the contrasting corporate cultures. At Suncor we had cultivated a can-do attitude resulting from our pride at turning the oil sands property into a relatively smooth-running, cash-generating operation and our success at breaking free from the dominance of the U.S. parent. At Petro-Canada things were different. The company had perpetually underpriced stock, a reputation for free spending and a decision-making process that often appeared bogged down in bureaucracy.

The Petro-Canada discussions went well, and Jim and I decided that the next move should be to bring in a qualified third party to evaluate the qualities of each company and submit an opinion on the viability of a merger. We chose RBC Capital Markets as the adviser, with Mike Norris, head of its investment banking division, as leader of the team. Mike possessed all the qualities we needed. In addition to his investment experience and MBA, Mike boasted a degree in civil engineering and had launched his career at Mobil Oil and Gulf Canada. He knew the business.

We were so confident in Mike's ability to grasp all the implications of a Suncor and Petro-Canada merger that we initially agreed to have RBC serve both sides, an unusual move to say the least. RBC Capital Markets would conduct its study free of any influence from either company. We also agreed that, should the merger go forward, Mike and his firm would represent one side in the resulting negotiations.

All this preliminary work, of course, had to be carried out in total secrecy. To help ensure that it was, the RBC group assessing the companies occupied rooms in a Toronto airport hotel far from Bay Street, booking them as accommodation for guests at an upcoming family wedding, which seemed appropriate.

RBC's assessment was thorough and conclusive: the proposed merger had substantial strategic merit for both organizations, and negotiations should be launched to measure relative values, perform due diligence, determine the proposed executive team for the new corporation and move toward a target date for completion. This kick-started a flurry of activity over the next few weeks by teams of investment advisers, accountants and lawyers, numbering in the hundreds, all working frantically while wrapped in a cloak of secrecy. Petro-Canada retained Mike Norris and his team at RBC as lead advisers while we opted for the team of CIBC and Morgan Stanley.

Among the key decisions we needed to agree upon was the relative value of each company. Since this would be a share exchange and not a cash buyout, the assessment would determine which side, if any, would be dominant. Would the deal be close to a 50–50 split, essentially rating the two companies as equal in assets, or tilt in one direction or another? Based on valuations from advisers on both sides, we agreed on a 52–48 split, with Suncor representing the larger proportion.

We also recognized the need to find our way around restrictions in the Petro-Canada Act. Written when Petro-Canada had been created as a Crown corporation, the federal Act limited its stock ownership to a maximum of 20 percent by any shareholder. Over the years many Petro-Canada apologists had blamed the company's poor stock performance on these ownership restrictions, an argument I never bought. In any case, some form of exemption from the Act would be required for the deal to succeed, a step we believed could be achieved.

Jim Stanford and I were pleased with the deal. He would stay on as board chairman, and I would fill the CEO role of the new, larger company. Assembling a management team, I chose Mike O'Brien as my CFO, interviewed Petro-Canada managers to determine their roles within the new company, and prepared Sue Lee, our senior vice-president of human resources, for the complex job of merging the staff and reconciling a host of contracts and agreements once the merger was declared official.

The process unfolded smoothly. Too smoothly, as it turned out. By the middle of 1999 the terms had been negotiated, the legal documents were prepared for signature, the press releases were ready for distribution and we believed we were about to make history not only in the petroleum industry but in Canadian business. We were so confident of the benefits of the merger for both groups that we scheduled simultaneous board meetings on a Sunday morning in July. Directors from both boards would sign off on the deal, press releases would be distributed and investors would receive the news before the markets opened on Monday morning. The new executive team was booked to leave early on Monday for a road show on which we would present details of the merger to key press and shareholder groups across Canada and the United States.

With everything in place, the Suncor board and I gathered that summer Sunday morning in the Sun Life building, looking forward to the challenge of merging the two firms into by far the largest Canadian-owned integrated oil company. At the same time, Jim Stanford and his board were meeting at the Petro-Canada building just down the street.

I can't recall if we were ready to pop champagne corks that morning. I only remember the telephone call from Jim Stanford's office. The Petro-Canada board, I was told, would approve the merger only if the split was 50–50, not 52–48. The portions had to be even, they insisted. The decision came as a complete shock to the Suncor board and to me, and contradicted numerous agreed-upon evaluations and decisions made during the previous several weeks. It more than disputed the agreement that both sides had reached in good faith. It was, in my opinion, a betrayal of trust.

I couldn't agree to the demand. Not only did it conflict with the formal documents we were ready to sign, but it would mean going back to square one on key aspects of management, policies, finances and other factors, essentially restarting the entire process. This didn't appear to matter to the other side. It was either 50–50, I was told, or no deal at all. Under those terms it was no deal, and I informed the Suncor board that we would not be going forward with the plan.

For the rest of the day I went through a range of emotions—

anger, frustration, disappointment and confusion. Dozens of professionals had worked for thousands of hours in total secrecy to track down and resolve every conceivable detail of the merger. Jim and I had tied our futures to the project, agreeing on the long-term benefits for employees and shareholders alike. Just a day earlier there had been no hint of a problem. No one from the other side had raised any serious issue. Had something happened overnight?

As I discovered later, that's exactly what had occurred.

Jim Stanford and I, along with our advisers, had agreed on all the broad details and the general merits of the merger. We had also agreed that, where the board and the top executive teams were concerned, we would be totally transparent about the plans. The draft agreement named the new company's executive team and confirmed that a new board of directors would be created, with representation from each existing board. Not every executive or every board member would occupy the same position with the new company, of course. And some people would lose their positions.

On Saturday, the basic plans had been presented to the directors prior to the formal signings slated for the following morning. The directors had been kept fully aware of the progress, so few surprises were expected. One of our advisers described the deal as "baked"— every element had been addressed, examined and resolved. Board approval following such a process is pretty much automatic.

Then the trouble began.

It was a bit of a tradition for Petro-Canada to host a dinner for the directors and the chairman on the evening before a board meeting and to discuss the topics to be covered the next day. At the Saturday night dinner, of course, the only topic was the merger with Suncor to be finalized the next morning. As a result, this particular dinner was viewed as something between a wake and a celebration, I suppose, since it was the last time everyone would gather as board members. In his words to the board, Jim Stanford discussed the senior management positions for the new company and the composition of the newly restructured board. Though the board's specific makeup had yet to be determined, it became clear that some directors would be moving to the new board while others would be dropped, and both the CFO and the CEO of Petro-Canada would be out of the picture, replaced by Mike O'Brien and me. There was nothing Machiavellian about this decision. My role had been established early on in discussions with Jim and later in the reports of the advisers, the ones who recommended the 52–48 split favouring Suncor. This was business, after all, with billions of dollars riding on the line, and decisions had to be made in the general interests of employees and shareholders.

I've been told a few board members grew passionate about the impending demise of Petro-Canada as an independent entity, perhaps fortified by rounds of drinks prior to and during the Saturday night farewell dinner. "This is a jewel, a major Canadian company," was the general tone of the dissenters, who grew louder and more determined as the argument gained momentum. "Why are we selling it out, with all its history, to somebody else? We won't have our CEO or our CFO running things. Is this really such a good deal, giving the company up so easily?" As I understood it, they weren't entirely opposed to selling the company, but they didn't want to sell what had been created as a Canadian icon into a minority position.

The breakaway group apparently proved persuasive because other directors, who perhaps hadn't seriously reconsidered giving their approval to the move, became swept up in waves of nationalism and nostalgia. This is when everything came apart. The animosity remained when the board gathered on Sunday morning for what should have been a quick formality and fuelled the stunning rejection. The move had nothing to do with valuation or reality and everything to do with pride and prejudice. Nobody was going to treat Petro-Canada as a junior partner, the rebels and their allies declared. The only way the merger could go forward was if the terms were adjusted to reflect a 50–50 deal.

This was out of the question. How could a single corporate culture be created when each side believed it had an equal say in matters such as policy, values, objectives and structure? It would be a hopeless task leading, without a doubt in my mind, to vast inefficiencies in the short term and potential dissolution in the long term. The proposal went to the heart of how to run the new company.

In a small manner, I understood the attitude behind this gambit. Crown corporations, I suspect the thinking went on that Saturday night, are not supposed to be absorbed by private companies. They were the ones to do the absorbing, as Petro-Canada had done when it was established. Crown corporations such as CNR and Air Canada had been privatized in the past without serious objections, but they had emerged as independent privatized entities, not minority partners within a larger firm. With that kind of thinking, the 4 percent difference in relative value between Suncor and Petro-Canada was too much to swallow.

Regardless of the merits of that argument—and I didn't accept any—we were dealing with matters of trust. The directors who insisted on revising the 52–48 split had known of the formula for weeks and had access to the rationale behind it. Yet they didn't voice any concerns until the eleventh hour, tossing enormous amounts of work and expense aside with a demand that could only be rejected by the Suncor board.

Every disappointment brings a lesson with it, and the lesson I learned from this debacle was never to assume that your counterpart CEO in a business deal has the same relationship with his or her board as you do. I've used the word *trust* often in describing the failed merger but it still fits: the core of the matter was not accounting or culture or historical precedent, but maintaining an agreement.

The Petro-Canada experience also caused me to consider the true role of corporate board directors. I have sat on a number of boards, all of them associated with first-rate companies, and have been honoured to do so. Too often, however, I have been surprised and disappointed to see some board members vote or try to influence the votes of others based on their own personal interests rather than those of the shareholders they have been chosen to represent. One way to avoid this kind of conflict is to choose members who do not view their compensation for sitting on the board as a major contribution to their standard of living.

I am not at all suggesting this was a factor in the Petro-Canada board decision, only that board members should be focused on the interests of the corporation and its shareholders, not on their own biases or benefits.

I'VE never believed in dwelling on failures, and I didn't dwell on this one. We had other goals to reach and other challenges to face, although I must admit that I wondered from time to time what might have been if the deal had gone ahead as planned. The road show was scrapped, the press releases were destroyed, and the consultants and advisers were paid and moved on to other projects. Life went on.

Jim Stanford chose to retire as CEO some time later, and was replaced by Ron Brenneman. I came to know Ron fairly well. In fact we've gone fly-fishing together, and for several years we held annual CEO and chair golf tournaments. I and John Ferguson, the chairman of our board, would play against Ron and his chairman, Brian MacNeill. John had joined the board in 1997 and was elected chairman a few years later when JR Shaw retired.

John and I connected quickly, perhaps because we shared similar origins. Both of us came from working-class backgrounds where

the value of a dollar was well respected and you never took anything for granted. More than that, he performed as a great chairman and helped the entire team to grow Suncor successfully. John
was an outstanding entrepreneur, and thanks to his experience he
understood the process of taking calculated risks to achieve results.
Through our years of working together I relied on him for many
things, especially advice. Sometimes the things that he said were
not what I wanted to hear, but it was worth listening because he
was both honest and wise. John is also a keen golfer, and whenever
he and I teamed together in a tournament we usually walked away
with the best score of the day.

Golf, of course, leads to discussions, and around 2007 or so
the discussions began that would lead to fresh consideration of a
merger with Petro-Canada. The more John and I kicked the idea
around, the more it became apparent to both of us that if the merger
planned ten years earlier been completed it would have benefited
both sides.

For a while it was just casual talk, but things grew more pressing
within Petro-Canada. The company had made some international
plays and moved into oil sands development as well. Their cash flow
was strong, and their properties in the North Sea and along the east
coast of Canada were good producers, as were their refinery operations. But the company's execution was not reflected in its stock
price, and various activist shareholder groups, including the massive
Ontario Teachers Pension Plan, began openly expressing dissatisfac-
tion with the stock performance.

Petro-Canada's shares were habitually underpriced for a number of reasons besides its Crown corporation heritage. One was
the difference between its size and its global ambitions. The firm
was attempting to become a flagship corporation, establishing
Canada's presence in the global oil business. It may have been a
noble goal, but Petro-Canada lacked the size and the impact to be

taken seriously, even when it made strategic purchases of foreign assets. Its purchase of Lundin Oil in 2001 and the German-based company VEBA in 2002 brought the firm oil field rights in places like Libya, Syria, the North Sea and the Caribbean, and made it Canada's largest integrated oil and gas company. On the surface these were good moves, especially when, shortly after the deals were finalized, oil prices swung onto the rising curve of their cycle. Yet the acquisitions failed to drive the price of Petro-Canada shares into line with the value they might have been expected to earn. Once again, the market appeared to undervalue both the strategy and the shares.

When nothing appeared to boost the company's share price to the level that Ron and his board anticipated, Petro-Canada again called on Mike Norris at RBC Capital Markets to review its options and answer its questions. Should Petro-Canada sell off some of its businesses and shrink to focus more directly on its core activity as a strictly national integrated marketer? Should it stay with its status quo business plan and find ways to execute it more effectively? Or should it sell or merge the company with a competitor?

When it became apparent that the recommendation would be either a sale or a merger, the board and management agreed to obtain reviews from both Canadian and U.S. sources, given the possibility that an international search for a buyer or partner might be justified. Both reports were submitted to the board for evaluation, and both reached the same general conclusion: The market would not give Petro-Canada the five years needed to establish and grow the various businesses it had acquired in its quest to become the country's flag-bearing petroleum company. The stock would continue to underperform, shareholders would grow more impatient and demanding, and the corporation's objectives would remain unreachable. The best option, the report observed, was a merger with another Canadian oil company, and the best oil company for the role was Suncor. Upon receiving these reports, a group of Petro-Canada directors requested and received an audit confirming that all areas of creating value had been considered.

Ron Brenneman had done a great job shaping Petro-Canada's P&L statements, including a record $904 million profit in the fiscal year 2002, but for all of his good management skills these successes failed to show up in the share price. I had a sense that Ron was growing weary of doing his best without seeing the market recognize his various achievements. Now he was approaching retirement, and as time passed he and I began discussing the idea of bringing both firms under one management group.

By now we were nearing the end of 2008, and the credit crisis of that year had dropped market prices through the floor. Crude oil prices fell as far and as fast as any other, and we began shutting down projects to protect the balance sheet because no one knew where the bottom would be found. Petro-Canada's value dropped at least as far as our own, measured according to cash flow multiples or earnings multiples, making them worth considerably less than Suncor's. This made it even more attractive, from our point of view, to resurrect the idea of a merger, so in December I called Mike Norris at RBC Capital to talk about his firm working on our behalf for a possible merger with Petro-Canada, unaware of his current work on its behalf. Mike's response was to say no, of course, because of the obvious conflict of interest.

In a fifteen-minute conversation with John Ferguson, he and I added up the points in favour of reopening the merger idea. Among the items to tip the scale was the matter of Petro-Canada's healthy cash flow. We were about to embark on Voyageur, a project representing a major expansion of our oil sands operation, and Petro-Canada's cash was an ideal way to finance it.

Before we agreed to reopen the discussion, John asked me to assure him that I would remain as CEO for at least five years. I understood his point. Combining the two firms was going to create problems we hadn't anticipated, and it made sense to have the transition managed by the same person who had initiated it.

But I couldn't commit myself to five years, although my hesitation had nothing to do with my age, health or energy level. Instead, it was linked to my desire to achieve other goals and my sense of what might be best for Suncor. My approach had proved successful in the past, but there was no guarantee it would do so in the future. New leaders bring fresh ways of looking at problems and opportunities, and after twenty years the company was ready for a new viewpoint and a new style.

When I told John I couldn't promise five years, he said, "Okay, how about three?"

Three I could do. And I almost did.

In an informal chat a few days later, John Ferguson and Brian MacNeill agreed that a move between the two companies made sense, and that the major stumbling blocks were the premium price and perhaps the majority ownership rule of the Petro-Canada Act. John and I had discussed this earlier and agreed that it would pose no problem once the complete picture of the deal was revealed.

Brian MacNeill sought and received permission from the Petro-Canada board to begin informal talks with John Ferguson and me. In almost any similar instance a board's response would be to approve the request unanimously. The board, after all, would be privy to all the reasons for proposing the idea, and its unanimous approval would provide the CEO and chair with full support during the preliminary negotiations. Yet some of the same Petro-Canada directors who had found it difficult to ponder the former Crown corporation's end ten years earlier balked once again, and the motion to give Brian and Ron negotiating powers passed with less than full approval.

I've never imagined being a spy in a John LeCarré novel, but

I felt like one during the sessions involving Brian, Ron, John and me. The discussions had to be held in total secrecy, of course. We booked a meeting room at the Palliser Hotel in Calgary, and the four of us scheduled our arrivals alone and at different times. We could not be seen together. No one, we agreed, should even suspect the basis of our talks until a deal was reached.

Brian and Ron quickly made their point that Petro-Canada needed to be paid a premium on its current share value for the deal to work. One way to achieve this was to avoid the term *merger* and label the move a *takeover*. A merger suggests carefully negotiated terms, with each side finding a middle ground. A takeover indicates that the buyer will pay a sufficient premium to acquire the shares, overriding objections from the targeted firm and deflecting price and competition from prospective buyers. The premium would translate into an immediate boost to the Petro-Canada share price, winning over shareholders.

I wasn't surprised at the insistence on a premium, so neither John nor I saw it as a deal breaker. The biggest challenge, we agreed, was setting the price. Everyone could agree on the market price for the Petro-Canada shares. But how much would the premium be? The meeting ended with an understanding that each side, still in deepest secrecy, would set its CFOs to work crunching numbers.

One means of measuring the synergies derived from folding two companies into one is to calculate the savings realized, most of it from reduced overhead, if the two continue to provide the same services under one corporate roof. Our financial people estimated that about $300 million could be saved annually. On that basis alone, the deal could be justified.

By the end of January 2009 we were far enough along in discussions to present the idea to the Suncor board. Things had changed since the first clandestine meeting at the Palliser Hotel. The stock market remained in free fall, taking oil prices with it. Meanwhile, we had made substantial capital commitments toward expanding our oil sands operations and needed cash to finance them.

That made our proposal to purchase Petro-Canada and its healthy cash flow even more attractive. We hadn't launched the idea with this as the sole target, but the appeal of the acquired cash flow and the ideal fit between the two companies encouraged the Suncor board to hand John and me essentially carte blanche to negotiate without involving the directors in step-by-step reports. This gratifying vote of confidence gave us the flexibility to assemble a deal quickly and efficiently.

The first item to tackle was the premium price Petro-Canada was demanding for its shares. We needed a figure that could be justified by a reasonable assessment of each company's values but that would leave negotiating room for a counter-offer, expressed as an exchange ratio for Petro-Canada shares. Suncor stock was trading around $28 while Petro-Canada hovered near $33. When it came to measuring one company's value against the other, the individual share price difference didn't matter, of course. Only the ratio counted. We settled on an exchange ratio of 1.2, meaning that Petro-Canada shareholders would receive 1.2 shares in the new company for every Petro-Canada share they owned at the close of the deal. Brian MacNeill agreed to take it to his board for discussion.

Brian came back with Petro-Canada's counteroffer, and it was a shock. Their board suggested a 45 percent premium, more than double our offer and clearly unacceptable to our board and our shareholders. John Ferguson, who was handling the one-on-one negotiations with his counterpart, Brian MacNeill, began suspecting the deal wouldn't happen if we were that far apart. He and I agreed to let things rest for a while.

A few days later I was reviewing our February 2009 production figures and realized we were about to record an outstanding month. Our production volumes were up, the plant was running more smoothly than ever and we would be posting improved earnings. I expected our share price to soar when the news hit the street. John and I were still eager to see the Petro-Canada deal happen, but I thought we should sit tight. "Let's wait and see what the reaction is when the production figures come out in early March," I suggested to John, and he agreed.

Timing really is everything. By the end of the first week in March, after our production and profit figures had hit the street, Suncor shares were sitting a full 10 percent higher than Petro-Canada's price. At that level the tables had turned, and we quickly set a date for another secret meeting at the Palliser for just us four: Brian, Ron, John and me.

The Petro-Canada board reduced its exchange ratio proposal from 45 to 30 percent, close to the target we had set, and the wheels began turning again. Brian and Ron brought more good news: Petro-Canada would agree to my remaining as CEO, with the freedom to choose my own management team. Suncor could also name both the new board and its chair, and Ron Brenneman would remain in an executive position for some time to assist in the transition before taking retirement.

John and I excused ourselves and went to another room to discuss the offer in private. We wanted the new company to be owned 60 percent by Suncor shareholders and 40 percent by Petro-Canada shareholders. Working from there to the share price gave us a ratio of 1.275, somewhat lower than the Petro-Canada offer but close enough to do a deal. It was going to happen. We were about to create the largest energy company in Canada via the largest business merger in Canadian history. But I was not totally euphoric about the prospect because my mind had been elsewhere for the past few weeks.

My father had been diagnosed with brain cancer, and we didn't know how much time he had left. Surgery might manage to remove the tumour and prevent a recurrence, but the odds of success were not good. More to the point, at eighty-four he might not survive the operation. Still, I favoured the surgery, believing that bad odds are better than no odds at all. My mother opposed the idea, and a family meeting had been called at the hospital in Denver so we could gather to discuss the alternatives and give our directions to the doctors.

I was scheduled to leave on a commercial flight from Calgary to Denver, and making the flight meant I would have to leave the business meeting before everything was concluded. John and I emerged from the room. Both Brian and Ron were aware of my father's condition and in fact had advised their board of the need to finish that afternoon's meeting on time to accommodate my schedule. I didn't raise the issue myself because it would have injected a personal and emotional element into what must be strictly a business deal. I simply apologized for my absence and left John to carry on the negotiations.

Brian and Ron expressed their sympathy and understanding, and when the discussion resumed, John was on his own to find a way past the difference in the two proposed exchange ratios. Brian and Ron soon explained that they had been authorized by their board to settle for nothing less than 1.28 to one. Agreeing to our price of 1.275 would mean returning to their board for approval and, aware how the Petro-Canada board had scuppered the deal ten years earlier, we wanted to avoid this. John thought it over for a moment, then accepted the 1.28 ratio subject to discussing it with me.

Just as I was about to board my flight to Denver, John reached me on my cellphone to announce that he had agreed to the 1.28 ratio and explain why. I assured him it was a good decision. (It was also somewhat more expensive than the 0.005 difference may sound, translating into an extra $70 million.) Then I boarded the plane.

In the end my mother's point of view won out; my father would be permitted to die in as much comfort as could be provided him without surgery, and in retrospect I realize that her decision was the right one. My mentor and first fishing partner passed away four months later.

OTHER steps in the acquisition had to be taken, but things were essentially wrapped up in that meeting in the Palliser hotel room, an event I still find remarkable. We four had quietly negotiated all the key elements of the largest corporate deal of its kind in Canadian history, and we did it without lawyers or advisers hovering at our elbows, prepared to voice concerns and objections.

This remains a remarkable and unique achievement. I honestly don't believe an agreement of this magnitude could have proceeded as it did in any other industry or in any other city. Both the oil industry and the city of Calgary have a tradition of openness and trust, placing as much value on a handshake as on any multi-page contract. After the four of us agreed to the basic terms, no further hitches presented themselves. As I expected, the Petro-Canada Act proved not to be a big factor. It was as if everyone involved recognized that our move benefited both companies and perhaps Canada generally. No one wanted to see the merger derailed.

We went through legal hoops over the next few days before closing the deal, subject to approval by the federal Competition Bureau. Nothing was certain, but at least we didn't have to worry about another last-second rejection from the Petro-Canada board this time. Both boards approved the deal overwhelmingly. Shareholder approval was almost unanimous, as 98 percent of Suncor shareholders and 96 percent of Petro-Canada's gave their blessing. The biggest barrier we had to navigate was an order from the Competition Bureau to sell 104 service stations in Ontario before the deal would be approved. I had expected the process to take as much as a year to complete, but barely four months after the public announcement of our intentions, we had everything sewn up. It was one of the largest Canada-targeted transactions in history, which makes the timeline even more impressive. Yet in its low-key manner it was very Canadian, with no fireworks, no brass bands and little hoopla beyond the standard media announcement and press conference.

Following the last meeting at the Palliser with Brian and Ron, John Ferguson and I left the hotel having changed the face of the country's oil industry. No one we passed knew us or had any idea of what we had accomplished. We were just two guys on a Calgary street.

At the corner, I paused before returning to my office. John was headed in the other direction, and before we went our separate ways he said, "We haven't had any celebrations, have we?" I agreed that we hadn't and that the hard work was really about to begin.

"I think we just made a hell of a deal," John said.

"You're right, John," I agreed. "We made a hell of a deal."

Then we shook hands and both of us went back to work.

8. Blending Cultures and Values
   at the New Suncor

It was true: the hard work began as soon as the documents were signed. How were we going to integrate such different corporate cultures? And what could we do to enhance shareholder value?

I began by tossing out any reference to the word *merger* when describing Petro-Canada moving under the Suncor umbrella. Merger suggests blending two cultures to create a third. I didn't want a third culture. I wanted to retain the Suncor culture we had been building over the years. From a legal viewpoint, we might have concluded a merger, but from a social, cultural or business viewpoint it was still a takeover. With all due respect to my friends Ron and Brian, as well as the shareholders and employees of Petro-Canada, it had to be handled that way.

Leadership in the early days of a merger is crucial. Employees and shareholders alike are often caught off guard, as they were in this case. I wanted to avoid uncertainty by being totally clear about the expectations, strategy, values and beliefs of the new company. I also wanted to maintain the momentum that we had built up over years at Suncor, and nothing would kill that faster than a lack of clarity in delivering the organization's goals and objectives.

◆

MERGERS, takeovers, acquisitions—call them what you will, the biggest immediate impact they make is on employees. For several months, staff at both firms speculated about the personal consequences. Would they have a job in the new company? How would their roles change? Was their future secure? Worry does not create the kind of atmosphere you want to see in a company, and it's not the kind of insecurity that employees deserve. We needed to integrate the Petro-Canada workers into Suncor as quickly and smoothly as possible.

This would be an even more difficult challenge than usual, I sensed, because of the contrasting history and management style of Petro-Canada and Suncor. The same Crown corporation character that had led to the derailment of the earlier proposed merger and the resistance of some Petro-Canada board members would be shared by the company's employees. But now they would be part of a firm that had shaken off its reputation for underperformance and reemerged in the light of success. Suncor had confidence in itself, and we needed the former Petro-Canada employees to quickly grasp that attitude and begin sharing it.

We made a number of essential decisions. One was to announce that the Suncor culture would dominate, especially when it came to defining corporate strategy. That would remain unchanged at its core, except to accommodate improvements as the result of the addition of Petro-Canada people and assets.

Suncor processes and systems would reign, including our ERP (enterprise resource planning) procedure, which was based on the SAP (system analysis and program development) business management system we had deployed. Insisting that only one management system be used and that new employees learn its operation were important steps toward making things work smoothly from the beginning. This decision was driven not by an inflexible attitude but by an emphasis on efficiency. I didn't want people debating the pros and cons of one system over another. In addition to wasting time, leaving the question open would risk creating ill feelings between employees defending one system over the other. Making these kinds of choices without permitting room for opinion was essential if we were to move toward a unified corporation.

We also announced that we would be downsizing, especially in the corporate offices, and that staff reductions would move ahead as quickly as possible. Nothing holds people back in a merger more than doubt about their employment, and I wanted it out of the picture. You either kept your job or you lost your job; if it was the latter I was sincerely sorry, but you knew where you stood and our people would help you deal with it. Every employee from Suncor and Petro-Canada understood this from the beginning.

Telling people they no longer have a job is surely among the most difficult chores any executive faces. It certainly was for me. You can call it downsizing or redundancy or anything you wish, but it's still a matter of delivering bad news. We provided what I considered very good packages to those who lost their jobs, but no offer completely soothes the emotional impact on those who find themselves unemployed.

As soon as the deal closed, I began discussing Suncor culture and values with the management team and the employees, explaining why they were to be implemented throughout the new company. Culture and values are abstract ideas, and they can be a challenge for newcomers to grasp. Compared with adjusting to a different corporate culture, changing day-to-day functions is easy. Your new IT system or other program appears on your screen; you use it every day and soon it becomes second nature. Applying values and reflecting a culture are more difficult because you don't use them— you *live* them.

Before dealing with the cultural issue, I appointed Mark Little from Suncor and Harry Roberts from Petro-Canada to jointly lead the integration teams and coordinate our efforts. (We needed a representative from each side to make the integration process more palatable for everyone.) Beginning immediately after the formal announcement of the deal was made, the integration program lasted almost a year before being handed back to the executive group, which consisted of senior management, for completion. The teamwork between Mark and Harry was exemplary, and they made a massive difference in speeding up the process.

The employees, for the most part, did not resent the fixed directives. In fact, their reaction was overwhelmingly positive, supporting my belief that people value honesty and clarity from leaders. Their performance also confirmed my position that Suncor's most strategic asset wasn't bitumen or the equipment that converted it to petroleum, or the leases we held around the world. It was our people.

This recognition of the importance of people led me to hand the assignment for integrating human resources to Sue Lee, our senior vice-president of human resources and communications. Educated in South Africa, Sue volunteered on behalf of several local and national organizations and had served as chair of the Suncor Energy Foundation, coordinating and approving a range of social and charitable activities for the company.

The number and extent of things to grapple with was mind-boggling. Salary levels, organizational charts, pensions, benefits and collective agreements with unions were just the beginning. Normally it would take at least two years to resolve all the issues affecting more than 12,000 employees, 8,000 retirees and 10,000 contractors. Sue and her staff managed to achieve it in sixteen months. She also worked very closely with members of the management team to impress on former Petro-Canada people why and how they were to think in an entrepreneurial manner when making decisions in their work.

◆

WITH the human resources task in good hands, we were free to focus on hard decisions regarding the Petro-Canada assets we had acquired. Prior to the merger, Suncor had been predominantly an oil sands company. Petro-Canada's activities and assets changed the situation substantially. We went from two refineries to four, and from limited oil field operations to extensive international production facilities. What were we to do with not only these hard assets but the technical and operational knowledge that came with them via the former Petro-Canada employees?

I quickly discovered that while Petro-Canada might have been unloved by industry people and the investment community, the firm had built impressive teams of specialists in areas where Suncor was absent. We had been operating two refineries, as Petro-Canada had, but they were doing a better job. The company also brought a wealth of experience operating in risky environments offshore. I was impressed by the operational expertise of the Petro-Canada people and welcomed their abilities to expand the overall competence of Suncor. This made an even better fit than I had expected: we were outstanding at growing a company, and Petro-Canada was better at operating some assets than we were.

We added Petro-Canada's Fort Hills property and its estimated 3.4 billion barrels of bitumen to our own oil sands holdings. The cash flow from Petro-Canada retail operations helped pay down the Suncor debt much faster than before the merger, and the newly acquired E&P activity strengthened us in that area. Overall we had almost an embarrassment of riches.

We considered selling some assets, including global oil rights in Libya, Syria, the North Sea, the Caribbean and other locations with potential total production of around 200,000 barrels daily. Evaluating them one by one, we sold leases and operations in Trinidad and some properties with declining production levels in the North Sea and the Netherlands. Along with these, we cleaned up our portfolio by selling various North American E&P properties.

The two most vexing properties we gained from Petro-Canada were in Libya and Syria. Libya has the eighth-largest oil deposits in the world, and Petro-Canada had invested about a billion dollars in this play, located onshore in the large Sirte Basin of eastern Libya. In 2009 the site was producing a net 35,000 barrels a day. Linked to these rights was a long-term exploration deal requiring Petro-Canada, and now Suncor Energy, to drill forty-six producing wells. Under the terms of the agreement, we were not permitted to dispose of the rights until we had drilled those wells.

Looking at the geological side of things, I liked what I saw. We could easily bump up our production in Libya to more than 100,000 barrels a day. This wouldn't make it a huge part of our total operation, but it promised a general boost to our production levels at an attractive potential profit. Still, there was that unpleasant reputation of Gaddafi's and hints of unrest among the Libyans. I liked nothing about Gaddafi. Given the violent revolution that swept through the country in the summer of 2011, the fact that we retained the rights to their oil reserves has become an issue among some people.

So why didn't we dispose of those rights immediately? First, it wouldn't have helped the Libyan people. Nor, of course, would it have helped to shut down the entire operation and walk away, leaving it to whoever was interested in taking it over. And it wouldn't have helped us as a corporation. Had we tried selling the property under the terms of the original deal with Petro-Canada, Libya would have seized a significant portion of the money we might have negotiated from a buyer, assuming we could find one prepared to offer a reasonable price.

There was a precedent. While we were closing the deal with Petro-Canada, Verenex, a small oil exploration company based in

Calgary, ran afoul of Libyan process. The Canadian company had negotiated its sale to China National Petroleum Corporation for $499 million, based on rights to the Libyan oil reserves that Verenex owned. Libya blocked the sale for months, claiming it had the option to purchase Verenex itself if it chose. In the end Libya bought Verenex for $370 million, causing Verenex to lose more than 25 percent of its expected earnings. Assuming that the sale of our rights would trigger a loss of similar proportions, I decided we would remain in Libya and watch things carefully.

Petro-Canada had been halfway through the development of a natural gas production facility in Syria in 2009 when we acquired it. Once again, purely from an investment viewpoint, selling this asset did not look like a good move. You can never claim top price on a development that's only partially completed, so I chose to finish the construction and begin drilling on the perimeter of the gas field. The gas plant and the wells proved productive. In fact, the gas field turned out to be much larger than we believed at the time of the merger.

The governments of Libya and Syria have not been admired in recent years, but governments are not the same as citizens. We employed and trained many Libyan and Syrian citizens at facilities in those countries, and I am proud of both our support for them and their commitment to us. Many of them proved to be very productive people who contributed to the company's success despite the upheavals erupting around them. Without doubt, our continued investment in local communities improved the quality of life for people caught up in political turmoil and showed the importance of direct foreign investment on the development of numerous countries in Africa and the Middle East.

Other factors played a role in our decisions. The less-than-commendable human rights records of Libya and Syria raised a dilemma. After international sanctions against dealing with Libya were lifted in 2005, companies such as Shell and ExxonMobil returned to resume petroleum production, but Gaddafi's regime and its reputation for ruthlessness remained a problem. On a practical basis, no one likes working in an environment of political instability, and the 2011 upheaval against Gaddafi was no surprise to people familiar with Libyan politics; it was a long time coming. On a moral basis, you have to ask yourself as a businessperson where your limits are in dealing with regimes with which you disagree. It's not the disagreement itself that tilts the balance, but the degree of disagreement. Most businesspeople are not strongly supportive of the Communist Party's rule in China, but this does not prevent them from maintaining operations there to the benefit of both the country and the investors. When does your distaste for a foreign government override your concern for employees and shareholders? Everyone draws his or her own line in the sand.

The oil industry adds another dimension to the issue. Manufacturers can and do move their activities from country A to country B for any reason they choose. But oil and gas producers have to go where the oil is, which can involve a basket of problems both political and technological.

With the death of Gaddafi, we joined other companies around the world in supporting the new regime by ramping up production levels in that country, expecting that our investment would benefit the Libyan people.

Syria was another matter. Near the end of 2011, it became clear to me that the situation in that country could no longer be tolerated. As much as we believed that our continued presence served the best interests of the Syrian people by providing employment and fuel, the continued actions of the Syrian government and the imposition of sanctions on the country by the European Union prompted me to take action two weeks before Christmas. Applying the principle of *force majeure,* we closed our operations there and I directed that the company explore whatever actions were available to support Syrian employees during the suspension.

I hope that the leadership change in Libya and the unrest in Syria lead to more open regimes that respect basic human rights. If this occurs, and the citizens of both countries witness their standard of living improving as a result of income generated by Suncor and other oil companies, I will be as pleased as anyone about our participation. If both countries slip back to their previous status, I expect that Suncor and others will have to seriously reconsider their future there.

Closer to home, the acquisition of Petro-Canada and its strong retail presence somewhat contradicted my decision to focus on exploration and production assets. It also went against my intention to minimize involvement in the downstream end of the business. The move meant that we were now supplying and managing more than 1,500 retail and wholesale outlets in Canada. Like it or not, we were heavily into marketing, advertising and promotion programs, along with customer loyalty incentives, credit card tie-ins and all the other activities associated with service stations.

In its own way combining the two systems was as complex as Sue Lee's task of blending of human resources. The move succeeded because, once again, I found someone smarter than I was to make it happen. Boris Jackman had been a retail and marketing executive with Petro-Canada and he remained with us through the merger, finding ways to blend the two systems into a single operating unit. By many measures, our downstream operations under the Petro-Canada brand made it one of the best-performing refining and marketing (R&M) groups in North America.

I suspect that future CEOs of Suncor will not get paid to run the retail operations successfully. You cannot drive shareholder

value in a petroleum producer through retail. It's true that retail
success helps move the product from the refineries, which in turn
absorbs flow from the production side. But the service stations represent the tail, not the dog, and the dog still wags the tail. It's one
indication of the way things have changed in the industry. The line
from oil well through refinery to service station pump is no longer
a single, unbroken track. The petroleum industry has grown dis-
jointed, and even integrated oil companies now source and market their products through a variety of means and locations. The
industry of my parents' day—when a company like Texaco located,
produced, transported, refined and sold petroleum products to
consumers along an uninterrupted path—is long gone.

A lot of things began to happen after we absorbed Petro-
Canada, and almost all of them were good. History suggests that
80 percent of mergers fail to benefit shareholders. If the failure
figure is that high, we sure beat the odds. My role in the process
was varied, but the energy I brought to the job was powered by my
determination to succeed and my love for the industry. Most of all,
I was able to rely on a great management team and about 12,000
other people, some familiar with the Suncor culture and some new
to it, who helped make it happen. When it all came together, it generated benefits for employees, shareholders and Canada generally.

This was particularly gratifying because the initial announcement of the 2009 deal shocked the market in several ways. Shareholders of both companies felt a little misled. I understood those
feelings, but given the factors involved, the negotiations had to be
conducted in absolute secrecy. Suncor shareholders had their own
concerns. With Petro-Canada's extensive R&M operations under
the Suncor umbrella, Suncor no longer represented a "pure oil"
play, and the game changed somewhat.

During the early months following the deal's completion, when
we were busy integrating all the activities of the company and estab-

lishing the Suncor culture and values at every level, some people questioned if our team had the skills to blend the two companies without adversely affecting our day-to-day operations. And what about those synergies we claimed? Could we really save as much as we said or were we exaggerating? I understood their skepticism. Measured by size, complexity and almost any other dimension, this was a unique deal. But it worked—to the surprise of some and the immense satisfaction of many.

The biggest error we made was predicting the deal would reduce our total annual costs by $300 million. The savings in overhead, efficiency and other measures have totalled more than $800 million per year!

AMONG the joys of managing a large company, especially one that's resource based, is the chance to shape and participate in partnerships that benefit both sides to a degree that wouldn't be possible if each acted alone. I'm 100 percent sold on the benefits of competition, so I'm a little skeptical about so-called win–win situations, but there's no doubt that our deal with the French oil company Total rewarded both sides. Everybody benefited, including the shareholders and employees of both firms.

The deal began in mid-2010. The Petro-Canada merger was rolling out smoothly, and our production volumes were generally on target. Our debt levels were high due in part to our stalled Voyageur expansion program. Construction of a new upgrader, a key element of Voyageur, had been placed on hold. Meanwhile, cash flow from Petro-Canada's operations was helping us pay down the debt, but I wanted to see it fall faster.

Total was planning to construct an upgrader to process bitumen from its Joslyn Mine area in northern Alberta, which would represent a substantial capital investment. While the French firm was involved in heavy oil recovery and upgrading in Venezuela, it had no experience in the Alberta oil sands, a very different environment. Despite its lack of familiarity with the region, the company was committed to making a major investment in order to buy its way into oil sands production, including constructing and operating its own upgrading facility. Total management recognized, however, that operating year round so close to the Arctic Circle was going to be very different from doing business where the equator was somewhere just beyond the horizon.

Jay Thornton, our executive vice-president of energy supply, trading and development, had begun exploring options for the Libyan and Syrian properties acquired through the Petro-Canada merger. Total already had a substantial presence in both countries, so it was a logical potential partner or buyer. Instead of Libya and Syria, however, the talk turned to Total's plans for the oil sands, which opened up a golden opportunity for both firms. Soon Libya and Syria were set aside, and we were joining forces in the Alberta oil sands.

We managed to negotiate an agreement that left us with a 41-percent share of the Fort Hills area, originally a Petro-Canada site, granting 39 percent to Total with the remaining 20 percent held by Teck Resources. In return we acquired 36.7 percent of Total's interest in the undeveloped Joslyn project, which it would operate in conjunction with Occidental Petroleum and Inpex. Total also picked up 49 percent of our Voyageur upgrader, cancelling its plans to build a similar unit near Edmonton. Fort Hills and the Voyageur upgrader were scheduled to come on stream in 2016–2017, a year or two ahead of the Joslyn project.

The partnership agreement meant Suncor pocketed $1.75 billion to put against our debt load, added about 160 million barrels of oil to our reserves, and reduced our risk level with the Voyageur upgrader, which we would operate. Total found itself partnered with an experienced operator in the oil sands and half the production capacity of an upgrader that would come on stream faster than one it might have constructed on its own from scratch. It all came together in about six months, a short time for such a complex, multi-layered deal.

It's always gratifying to make a play and watch it return dividends of various kinds to a corporation—better cash flow, fatter margins, increased employment, richer dividends and improved security. When you can make it happen with a partner and watch both sides benefit equally from the same deal, you actually smile and say, "That was fun!"

Fun, most often measured on a smaller scale than the Total deal, was a part of all my years at Suncor. And part of Suncor's corporate success as well.

9. Fun and Profit: The Secrets behind Suncor Success

I couldn't be more proud of the manner in which Suncor grew as a company, as a business investment and as a good corporate citizen during my tenure, and I insist that everyone who contributed to the company's success share in that pride. It truly is, I believe, a Canadian success story: a company that occupies a unique position not only in Canada but in the petroleum industry generally.

So I'm a little saddened to note that one aspect of the Suncor culture has already started to change, not because of my presence or absence but because of a natural evolution that all corporations—especially those in the energy sector—undergo. For want of a better term, I call this quality "corporate soul."

Start-up firms tend to be extremely entrepreneurial, driven to succeed and powered by the enthusiasm and individual talents of their employees. Suncor wasn't exactly a start-up firm when I arrived, but once we hit the turnaround point in the oil sands operations, when everyone involved could see the dark cloud of failure lifting, it began acting like one and I encouraged the culture. I wanted every employee to make decisions based on what they knew about the situation and what had to be done to help the company move forward. In smaller companies things get done by people, not by procedures. With the right people, the right environment and the right leadership, the right things get done, and companies at this stage in their development tend to be fun places to work. That was Suncor, and the era extended up to the acquisition of Petro-Canada.

At the other end of the spectrum are companies such as ExxonMobil. It is a superbly run company but not one driven by individual initiative. It works through fixed, rigid procedures. When decisions are made, they're made according to an established process. ExxonMobil is the best operator in the petroleum industry, the safest, the most productive and the most cost-effective, and it achieves this with proven procedures that everyone in the company is expected to follow.

Suncor Energy is on a journey leading toward potentially immense growth in size and influence. Its future role will involve delivering energy that we can only dream of at this point. In the months following the successful acquisition of Petro-Canada, it became clear to me that the company was already moving from an organization driven by the spirit and talents of its people to one powered by the application of procedures. I have no doubt that the growth will continue to be successful, and that Suncor employees will find the experience gratifying. I just hope that the company manages to retain its soul.

The strict process-driven nature at ExxonMobil is no reflection of a dictatorial management style. It is a practical necessity that I understand and appreciate. When the capital expenditures, global scope and international influence are as enormous as ExxonMobil's, you can no longer rely on individuals to make decisions where safety, the environment and corporate assets are concerned. That's when you start relying on processes. Most ExxonMobil employees will agree that working there can be very rewarding, but I doubt many would say it's fun.

To some people, the idea of having fun at your work sounds like an oxymoron because they view work and fun as mutually exclusive. I've always believed they should be connected, and in successful companies they are. I don't mean the kind of fun you have on a carnival ride (although that was certainly part of the Suncor experience); I mean the fun of competition and the enjoyment of being part of a team with a common goal. You work your collective butts off, putting in more hours and more energy than you knew you had, and when you achieve success as a result of your initiative and determination, you think to yourself and maybe say to others around you, "That was fun!"

I like having fun. Who doesn't? But sometimes you have to work at it in more ways than one. It's difficult to have fun and feel good about yourself and life generally if you're not physically fit. I work out at least four or five times weekly and find that keeping in shape grows more important with every year I age. Staying fit has become such an integral part of my life that I don't think about it very much. We didn't introduce an extensive physical fitness program for Suncor employees but I believe in setting standards by example.

Is it fun working out? Sometimes, sometimes not. But it's no fun finding yourself short of the energy you need to enjoy skiing, playing tennis, biking or hiking.

Sometimes there's room for another kind of fun, when you step outside your office or work cubicle and maybe even break down the lines of authority. In my experience, people who can do silly things for laughs alone and still maintain their workload and responsibilities are among the most valuable and productive employees in an organization. The freedom to do this must come from the top, and I admit to adding my support from time to time, sometimes even my participation.

When we moved Suncor from Toronto to Calgary, someone reminded me of a legend: when Calgary fans arrived in Toronto for the 1948 Grey Cup game, a few of them rode horses into the lobby of the Royal York Hotel. Why not ride a horse into the lobby of our new Sun Life Plaza offices in Calgary? someone suggested. The kid from Colorado inside me was game, but when we proposed the idea to the building owners they were less than enthusiastic, and that's putting it mildly. So instead of sitting astride a palomino I was photographed, complete with chaps and ten-gallon hat, riding a plastic horse in front of our new headquarters. And to mark the day in 1996 when Julie and I and our children became Canadian citizens, after the formal ceremony I put on a beaver costume. Fortunately, no photographs of me in that get-up exist—I hope.

I've also turned the tables on employees. Once, a day before leaving on a vacation, I told Sue Lee that Julie and I were attending a charity function that evening. "I understand they're auctioning life-sized wooden sculptures of large animals," I said, "and I thought I might pick one up for the company, maybe display it in the reception area."

Sue served as president of the Suncor Foundation, which manages the corporation's charitable contributions, and she reacted as I expected she would. "Absolutely not!" she said. "We don't need it, we already support that institution and I don't want to spend time looking for a place to put it!" (It's a mark of both Sue's personality and the working relationship we have that she felt comfortable reacting in such a direct manner.)

I mumbled something about trying not to get caught up in the excitement of the auction, and we went on to other things. Later Roger Smith, a member of our executive team who planned to attend the charity event, helped me work out a game plan.

The next day I called Sue from the airport, where we were waiting to board our flight. "Darn it, Sue," I said, "they had this great-looking bear at the charity event last night and . . . well, I couldn't resist. I bought it for the company and it only cost $25,000. It'll be coming to you while we're gone."

I could almost smell the smoke coming out of Sue's ears, so I quickly added, "Tell you what. Julie and I will personally cover the cost, but please try finding a place for it somewhere, will you?"

Sue gave an exasperated reply, wished me a happy vacation and hung up.

A couple of days later, she received a telephone call from someone in shipping and receiving. They had a large wooden crate personally addressed to her, she was informed. Could she come down to reception to open and inspect it? No doubt muttering something unflattering about me under her breath, Sue arrived to confront a massive wooden shipping crate and stood frowning while one of the men began prying it open with a crowbar. When he finally succeeded, a stuffed bear fell out—a teddy bear just big enough to fit on Sue's bookshelf, where it still rests today.

The great value of having fun at your work is the way it helps you deal with stress. I was often asked how I handled the stress of making decisions involving billions of dollars in a famously volatile industry. My response was that I rarely found the job stressful. As I see it, if you work on the right set of skills, especially things like being open and transparent with everyone around you, it becomes easier to deal with any problems that arise.

One of the skills I managed to develop was public speaking. You don't pick up much training as a public speaker in engineering school, and when I moved into the CEO role at Suncor I realized I needed to present the company's story to a wide range of groups, from shareholders and politicians to environmental advocates and the public at large. It took me a year of study, squeezed in among other duties, to understand and apply good public speaking skills by paying attention to tone, inflection and pace and knowing where and how to use humour and pauses. In my last years at Suncor I was delivering forty or fifty speeches a year, and these became not only a means of communicating our position on a wide range of topics to the industry and the general public but also a genuine management tool. I suspect that CEOs or other senior executives who view public speaking as a painful interruption of their work are doing themselves and their company a disservice.

CEOs who are good public speakers can do more than communicate the business side of their firm's work. They can, by the subjects they choose and the way they present them, define the heart and soul of an organization. This aspect of management is rarely discussed because it's difficult to define and measure. As I would often tell Suncor employees, the heart and soul of the company don't show up on the balance sheet, but they were more important than anything else I could name. Job satisfaction, productivity, public approval and, yes, profits all depended on identifying and maintaining just what the company stood for and how well it embodied those qualities in the way it did business. As much as any other quality, the company's values were responsible for Suncor's repeated ratings as one of the country's top-flight employers. I know our integrity was the secret behind much of our success through the 1990s, when some skeptics wondered if we would ever escape the moniker "Canada's unluckiest oil company."

You can learn about management styles and strategies from books, seminars and academic studies, but I believe that many management skills derive from an individual's own background and value system.

One of the things I enjoy doing, and which is at least partly responsible for my success as a leader, is talking to people one on one. Casual conversations with individuals and small groups come to me easily, and it may have something to do with watching and listening to my father.

He was the guy in Brush, Colorado, who you went to when your radio or television needed repair. Dad was a good repairman, but I suspect he was an even better conversationalist. He knew almost everyone in town and could always find something to discuss with them. It was a social talent that, to him, was at least as valuable as his ability to clear up the picture on a TV screen or drop a fly precisely where he wanted it in a trout stream. Some of the warmest memories of my childhood involve heading into the mountains with my dad for a few days of camping and fly fishing. We would find a good spot on the bank of a stream and I would stand near him, breathing the clean air and trying to tempt the biggest fish to strike the fly. Sometimes Dad and I would backpack and ride into the mountains on horseback. The memories remain vivid and valuable to me, and I mention them now because I understand what environmentalists want to protect and why. I share their love and concern for the land, the water, the trees. The only real difference between most environmentalists I encounter and me is that many of them believe we need to ban petroleum production from regions to preserve them. I believe that where the oil sands are concerned, we can have both in the long run.

Whether I acquired a similar conversational skill to my father's through genetics or just from hanging out while he shot the breeze with a neighbour, I've always valued the ability to communicate with others, to listen and to understand their points of view.

Among my memories of growing up in the town of Brush are visions of being busy, even as a kid. If you weren't playing sports, you worked at whatever needed doing. I don't consider myself a workaholic (although Julie may differ)—I gave as much of my time to Suncor as I thought it needed, but I also love fly-fishing and playing golf and riding through the foothills of the Rockies on my Harley-Davidson. It's just that keeping busy doing something productive was expected when I was a kid. I grew up in a time and place where a strong work ethic was a kind of religion. I helped my dad in his repair shop, I helped out on my uncle's farm and I loved the work in the oil patch through my college years.

I acquired other life lessons from growing up in a small town. One of them was to avoid creating a long trail of people whom you have offended or treated unfairly. You can get away with that more easily in New York or Toronto or Chicago because in big cities you're among several million people who have no idea who you are or what you stand for. If you seriously annoy someone or behave less than admirably toward others in a big city, there are always new people to meet and impress. But in a town like Brush, with a population of maybe five thousand, you can't escape a bad reputation, so you find ways to get along with people. I've always made an effort to be friendly with those I meet, and to treat them the way I want them to treat me. Sure it's corny, but it's ingrained in me, and I believe it also made me a better leader and manager.

Too many people try to make the management process complicated. Books, seminars, college courses and luncheon speakers trumpet the various skills and techniques needed to become a successful manager. Somewhere among charts and case studies the two most fundamental management skills—openness and trust—become lost. Maintaining an open dialogue enables you to have a deeper level of communication. Talking with others and encouraging them to share their thoughts is essential to building trust. Without that, all the management window dressing promoted by books and consultants won't amount to much.

Some companies, as I understand it, believe they can bolster corporate qualities through phrases, slogans and mission statements. We engaged in some of that at Suncor when we introduced a core purpose statement, declaring that it would be "a unique and sustainable energy company, dedicated to vigorous growth in worldwide markets by meeting the changing expectations of our current and future stakeholders." We added a list of values and beliefs as a guide to becoming the company we envisioned.

I'm sure the statement filled some purpose in explaining what we stood for as an organization, but where our individual employees were concerned there were other qualities to consider, and if they lacked them no slogan or mission statement would fill the void. One of these is a something I call a *north compass,* an inner device that gives people an innate sense of the right thing to do in any situation. When employees share a similar north compass, they instinctively apply the essence of the mission statement or the core purpose statement or whatever you wish to call it. Most employees at Suncor demonstrated the power of their own north compass. They knew management would not tolerate anything illegal. We weren't cowboys acting as though there were no restraints on us as a corporation. We had shared principles and values, and once they were defined and established everyone knew just what to do and how to act whatever the situation.

Establishing corporate values can be achieved only when the people who work for you fully understand the importance of these values and trust you to explain them. It was especially important at Suncor for employees to understand how these values would help meet clearly defined goals because many of our strategies extended beyond the next quarter or even the next several years, and everyone needed to grasp the long-term objectives.

Being clear about goals and strategies is vital to the success of any organization. Among other things, it makes management's role much easier, effectively preventing cliques and political systems from taking root. When your employees know where the company is headed and why, they don't have the freedom to politicize issues in pursuit of their own agenda; if their actions are not on track to reach the goal supported by the majority of employees, the majority will ignore them.

In my experience, 98 percent of people in any large corporation want to do a good job, leaving 2 percent with other things on their mind. So where should good managers focus their attention—on the 98 percent who are contributing or on the 2 percent who are building barriers and cliques? They concentrate on the 98 percent, the people who show up every day honestly intending to contribute to goals they understand and support.

One more time: a company's most valuable assets aren't the oil that lies in the ground or the factory that grinds out widgets but the quality, skill and dedication of its employees. If that sounds like a cliché, well, a cliché is a cliché because it is true.

The best way to make use of the company's most valuable asset is to treat employees as part owners. That was the approach I took, and encouraged the senior management team to take, whenever human resources issues arose. The guy down the hall handling invoices, the woman in the field driving the Caterpillar truck, the crew maintaining the plant equipment in a January blizzard all had every bit as much of an investment in Suncor as any shareholder in Vancouver, Winnipeg, Montreal or Halifax. We also introduced a long-term incentive plan that would result in compensation for all Suncor employees, provided we met certain targets. This represented another means of encouraging employees to help the company succeed.

Managers succeed in direct proportion to the attributes of the team they assemble around them, and I was fortunate in recognizing the qualities of the people who filled crucial positions at Suncor. Maybe it goes back to that work ethic from growing up in a small town, but I've always believed that honest ambition can make up for all sorts of limitations. Not everyone on the top management team at Suncor had a university degree, but they all brought more important qualities to the job, such as practical knowledge, common sense and determination.

Management is about leadership, and you've got to lead from the front. In my case, especially in the early years when we were constantly grappling with problems in the oil sands, this meant leaving my office in Calgary at least twice a month, changing from my suit and tie into overalls, boots and a hard hat, and heading for Fort McMurray or some other field location. This is a wise move for any CEO, but I considered it particularly important because I had spent so much time in the field myself. I knew some of the difficulties that would arise and how to handle them, and I knew the frustrations that people in the field faced when others back in the office couldn't understand and appreciate their problems. I could also tell when concerns were real and, on the rare occasions it happened, when somebody was blowing smoke.

Whenever I spoke to young engineers at our Calgary office, I emphasized the importance of getting out from behind a desk and heading into the field. "If you sit around here looking only at charts," I would say, "you can't really know what's going on in the oil sands or at the refineries or in the service stations." I knew that an engineer fresh out of university, with a shiny new diploma on the wall, would be tested by people in the oil sands who had grease under their fingernails, and that every encounter in the field was an opportunity to learn. The greetings wouldn't always be warm, but it was the only way to acquire much of the knowledge that universities are unable to provide.

10. The Importance of a Second Market for Canada's Oil

When people speak of management skills, they refer to the ability to create long-term strategies and handle day-to-day decisions on the way to reaching goals—the usual definition found in MBA programs and CEO profiles in business magazines. The other side of that particular coin is the ability to respond to not just routine problems but unforeseen and catastrophic challenges, like the one we experienced early in January 2005.

The news came through a telephone call from Steve Williams, our executive vice-president of oil sands at the time and now the president and CEO. Steve hadn't spoken more than three or four words before the tone in his voice told me this was not going to be good news. He informed me that a fire at our #2 Millennium upgrader had taken it out of production, knocking more than 100,000 barrels off our daily production, just when the oil price was surging past $50 per barrel. This was our newest upgrader, essential to removing impurities from the bitumen and lowering its viscosity so it could be transported through pipelines to refineries.

The cause of the fire was eventually traced to an error made by the contractor during construction, the kind of mistake that is often not discovered until a problem erupts, in this case with disastrous results. In the tallest tower of the upgrader, lighter constituents of the bitumen are taken off at the top of the unit and heavier portions flow down through a pipe to an area referred to as the skirt. From there, other pipes carry the heavy material back through the process as a means of squeezing every drop of oil out of the bitumen. Due to the nature of the material and the process it undergoes, every portion of the pipe network in the skirt has to be either constructed of or lined with stainless steel to resist corrosion, and they were—with one exception. An elbow in a system of stainless steel piping had been made of simple carbon steel. The faulty elbow should have been located and corrected during construction, but it revealed its presence by failing only after two years of otherwise routine operation.

The fire itself was devastating, but we took consolation in the fact that things could have been worse; no one was injured, and the fire had been restricted to a section of the upgrader without spreading to adjacent equipment.

The loss of production and the months it took to rebuild and restore the upgrader knocked our production, our profits and our share price off their pedestals. Some observers wondered if Suncor was falling back into its old ways—being the site of devastating fires rather than the country's most efficient oil sands producer—and they discounted the share price accordingly.

Everyone at Suncor knew the implications of the upgrader fire on their jobs and on the company generally. The people who worked in and alongside the upgrader were pretty shaken up over the destruction of a massive piece of equipment that it was their job to operate and maintain. In times of stress, employees tend to delegate upward. Ultimately, this meant everyone looks toward management to see how they're reacting.

There are many things you can and perhaps should do when faced with a crisis like this. One thing you can't do is show panic or indecision. My first thought when I grasped the scope of the event was the image of a duck in dangerous waters, looking calm and collected on top while pedalling like hell under the surface.

I knew I had to go to the site and see things for myself, but I delayed my visit until the fire had been extinguished completely. Otherwise, too many people would spend their time informing and protecting me instead of dealing with more urgent responsibilities. The weeks and months following the fire were sad times. We were into a long period of teardown, construction and start-up, and I spent a lot of time talking to the people who worked with the upgrader, explaining the situation and informing them of our plans to work around the problem and get everything back on track.

For six months we kept things going without the production levels that the upgrader should have been generating. One gratifying event to come out of this disaster was a demonstration of all the skills needed to get the job done. Led by John Gallagher, the employees got down to their jobs with enthusiasm. This reaffirmed my confidence that the people and programs at Suncor could deal with any crisis, including those relating to protecting the environment.

The upgrader fire represented a serious setback to Suncor. Beyond its effect on our employees and investors, however, it did not have the kind of wide media impact generated by oil spills. The sight of thick, gooey crude oil spilling into rivers, lakes or, in the case of the BP Macando well blowout in 2010, the beautiful blue Gulf of Mexico, is painful and upsetting to watch for everyone, including me. Disasters such as the BP blowout and the 1989 *Exxon Valdez* spill in Alaska are thankfully rare. But it doesn't take a million litres of oil to contaminate water and land. Just a few barrels can cause problems and also produce extensive media coverage that depicts the oil industry as either incompetent or uncaring, sometimes both.

Each time an oil spill occurs anywhere I shudder, because no matter how well it is cleaned up and how much the impact on the environment is minimized, those who are opposed to the use of petroleum generally, and the oil sands specifically, have another reason to claim that their demands are legitimate. It also upsets me because I know that most spills are preventable, especially those stemming from pipelines.

North America is criss-crossed by pipelines carrying oil and natural gas from sources to consumers. The pipelines are part of a complex system to supply energy and material, a system we take for granted when everything operates smoothly. It includes high-tension electrical lines above ground and fresh water and sewer lines beneath the ground. The power, water and sewer lines represent vital chains in the infrastructure of modern society, and most people accept their role. Oil and gas lines are not as widely accepted.

Their length is enormous. Oil produced from our facility north of Fort McMurray may travel via pipeline 2,600 kilometres or more to its destination. Today, a barrel of oil entering the pipeline at Fort McMurray, Alberta, takes about thirty-five days to reach a refinery in Houston, Texas. Along the way the oil passes through hundreds of valves, junctions, pieces of pumping equipment and other necessary devices to keep it flowing.

New pipelines are plotted, engineered and constructed under tight restrictions and with new materials that are highly resistant to corrosion and easy to monitor. Unfortunately, many oil and gas lines snaking across North America are fifty or more years old, beyond the performance life they were expected to deliver, and we are going to need more investment to inspect, repair and replace them. The energy industry is not alone in this predicament. Transportation in North America depends on thousands of highway bridges. As we have seen recently in Minnesota, Quebec and elsewhere, many are aging to the point where they are failing catastrophically.

Fortunately, the inspection, maintenance and repair of existing pipelines is being assisted by advances in technology. Operators inspect the interior of pipelines with "smart pigs," which have nothing to do with bacon and everything to do with spotting troubles before they begin. The "pigs" are electronic inspection units that travel inside the pipeline, measuring the thickness and detailing the condition of its walls. Weaknesses and potential trouble spots are identified before they fail, permitting pipeline operators to excavate the area and correct the problem.

Generally, the pipeline sector is as vigilant about avoiding spills and accepting responsibility for minimizing their impact as any in the industry. Whenever a weld on a pipeline fails, for example, the company routinely examines every similar weld in the system to ensure that the failure was not a symptom of a wider problem. Every oil spill is a disaster of one size or another, however, and every one is preventable. The industry is generally doing a good job of minimizing their impact when they occur, and despite the headlines, it is becoming proficient at avoiding spills entirely.

This doesn't prevent people from raising objections to the construction of new pipelines such as the Keystone XL line from Alberta to Texas, which would double the capacity of crude sent from the oil sands to U.S. markets. In 2012 the Keystone line became more famous for controversy than for its function of providing a long-term source of oil to the United States. The debate appeared evenly decided between two groups: those who viewed the pipeline as the work of the devil, and those who considered it a salvation and a job creator. While some demonstrators opposed so-called dirty oil from Canada, others valued the promise of a long-term supply of crude oil from a friendly, reliable neighbour. They also realized the side benefits of the pipeline to U.S. companies that were struggling in an economic downturn. Oil sands operators buy goods and services from almost a thousand American firms, ranging from Caterpillar trucks to computer software. The impact of these purchases is felt nationwide. The trucks, for example, are assembled in Illinois. They roll on tires made in South Carolina, are powered by engines manufactured in Indiana and include hundreds of other American-made components. The more the oil sands succeed, the more the U.S. economy will prosper.*

In opposing the pipeline, some U.S. critics employed questionable logic. The website of the Natural Resources Defense Council (NRDC), whose trustees include actors Robert Redford and Leonardo DiCaprio, declared that oil flowing south through the Keystone XL pipeline "will be exported, because America doesn't need it. Our nation is already a net exporter of finished petroleum products. That's why a good deal of Keystone's capacity will end up in the international market."[1] The NRDC ignored the fact that the United States imports about half of all the oil it consumes. At a time when the national unemployment rate is hovering around 8 percent, opposition to this job-creating industry could prove a difficult sell to many Americans. The NRDC and others are upset about excess volume from the oil sands flowing into their nation and being processed for export, but are they prepared to shut off the entire flow of oil south from Canada?

The Keystone pipeline is actually a double-edged sword for Canada. While it will boost this country's crude oil sales to the United States, it also will bind Canada more tightly to the U.S. market. This prospect brings some inherent dangers with it, yet I rarely heard that discussed in the exchanges between the two sides of the issue. Tying almost all of Canada's oil exports to a single mar-

---

* As I write this, approval for Keystone has been set aside by President Barack Obama, effectively kicking the can down the road past the 2012 presidential election.

ket, especially when we are dealing with a commodity that is vital to our country's well-being, is a very risky proposition. We need to balance the market share somewhat with a second pipeline to carry oil sands petroleum to Canada's west coast for access to other markets, specifically those on the Pacific Rim.

Two companies are planning pipelines to carry crude from the oil sands to the BC coast. The Gateway pipeline, proposed by the Canadian firm Enbridge, has generated the most publicity, but the U.S. firm Kinder Morgan has a similar plan. Following a route from just north of Edmonton west to Kitimat, British Columbia, the proposed Gateway pipeline would carry 525,000 barrels of Alberta-sourced crude each day to a deepwater port, where it could be transferred to tankers for shipment to Japan, China and other Pacific markets. The distance to the coast is substantial—1,177 kilometres—but not enormous in comparison with similar pipelines. The Kinder Morgan proposal promises a similar route with comparable capacity.

Reaction to the Gateway pipeline by environmental groups has been predictably negative. While I agree that projects of this kind demand extensive review and discussion, I have found some of the arguments against the idea a little misleading. An August 2011 article in *National Geographic,* a publication normally respected for its editorial integrity, severely criticized the pipeline for its impact on a section of BC woodlands called the Great Bear Rain Forest, located along the northern BC coast.[2] The area is more than thirty kilometres away from Kitimat, where the pipeline ends, yet serious concern was expressed for its protection. *National Geographic* was also distressed about possible oil spills at Kitimat, where the oil would be transferred to tankers. That's a reasonable fear, except that the oil transfer equipment and procedures at Kitimat would be identical to those used at similar terminals in Norway, Sweden and Scotland, where pipeline-to-tanker transfers have been conducted for thirty years without incident.

Other concerns are more complex and challenging, although they relate as much to politics as to the environment. The pipeline will traverse land occupied by more than two dozen different bands of First Nations people. Each band will insist on its own agreement and its own set of guidelines before permitting the pipeline to be installed.

Some people, hearing of the proposed Gateway pipeline, might respond, "Why take the risk and go to all the trouble? Can't we keep selling all the excess oil we produce to the United States?" Yes, we probably can. But should we?

Let's begin with a hard economic fact: Energy is one of the largest industries in Canada and is certain to grow even more in future years. The energy sector makes more money, employs more people (almost 300,000 directly and almost as many indirectly through contractors and suppliers) and generates a wider impact on Canada's trade balance than any other business. We grow a lot of wheat, we do a lot of banking, we attract a lot of tourists and we manufacture a lot of things, but when it comes to pure economic power, few things compare with energy.

The energy industry comprises much more than major oil producers like Suncor and the service station operator where you buy gas. It includes a network of thousands of smaller companies that enable the larger sectors to operate efficiently, and their impact on communities everywhere in the country is huge. These companies service and supply oil derricks, pumps, vehicles, computers and untold other aspects of the business, often with specialized equipment and highly skilled employees. If Suncor, Syncrude, Exxon, Shell or any other high-profile petroleum company operating in Canada takes an economic hit, the shock waves extend far beyond their walls to seriously affect smaller companies all across the country.

The Canadian petroleum industry depends on oil exports to employ people and enrich the country generally. Yet almost 100 percent of all the oil Canada exports goes to the United States. Not only is it our biggest customer but we are its largest foreign supplier. About two million barrels of oil flow south every day of the year. The United States is and always will be Canada's largest customer for a wide range of products, resources and services, but of all our large domestic industries only oil relies on that country for pretty much 100 percent of export sales.

An evaluation of the oil demand and supply in the United States by the global information company IHS CERA draws a clear picture of that country's future reliance on Canadian oil.[3] The study noted that U.S. domestic oil production measured 7.5 million barrels per day in 2010, or about 45 percent of total oil supply. This is likely to remain roughly unchanged through to 2030, assuming that technologies now being developed to improve production are successful.

This leaves the United States dependent on imports for about half of the petroleum it requires, based on current and projected usage levels. Where will it come from? CERA makes the following assessments.

Saudi Arabia provided about 1.1 million barrels per day in 2010, 6 percent of the U.S. supply, and the country has expanded its production capacity. Much of this new volume is slated for the country's own growing domestic demand, however, and for export to Asia. In fact, in 2010 the Saudis shipped almost as much oil each day to China as they did to the United States.

Iraq represented just 2 percent of U.S. imports in 2010 and, according to CERA, has the greatest potential for increasing its production. Like Saudi Arabia, the bulk of its oil is probably destined for Asia.

Brazil accounted for 2 percent of U.S. imports and is increasing its production volume significantly. While it will continue to export oil to the United States, Brazil's own burgeoning economy is likely to use a larger portion of its production capacity within the country's borders, affecting its export volume.

Nigeria exported about 1 million barrels per day to the United States in 2010. Ongoing security challenges within the country, often resulting in shutdowns of its oil production, make any growth of exports to the United States questionable.

Venezuela has reduced both its production capacity and its exports to the United States, a move that is not expected to be reversed due to growing domestic demand and the country's response to Asian markets.

Mexico's oil production is declining, and CERA notes that it could become a net importer of oil in the next decade.

Which leaves Canada. At more than 2 million barrels per day in 2010, Canada was the largest single source of imported oil for the United States, representing 12 percent of total crude oil supply. CERA suspects that figure will double by 2030, noting, "Canada is a low-risk source of oil supply. Oil is a key element of deep economic links between the United States and Canada. Increasing supply from Canada offers the United States greater oil supply security."[4]

What about comparing the environmental impact of oil sands production with that of other sources of imported oil? CERA notes the importance of obtaining accurate and reliable information: "In terms of environmental comparisons—such as GHG emissions, water use and land use—environmental data, availability and government needs differ across jurisdictions, making comparisons challenging. Comparing major sources of U.S. oil supply, Canadian oil sands are at the forefront of readily available data. . . . Policies that seek to reduce the environmental footprint could instead shift emissions to countries or sectors with mischaracterized environmental footprints."[5]

CERA's assessment alone is not likely to silence oil sands critics in the United States and vault Canadian exports to that country overnight. But such credible voices will be heard and acknowledged by decision makers, paving the way for Canadian oil sands production to fill the anticipated gaps in import sources between now and 2030.

Is this a good thing? Yes and perhaps no.

Most trade relationships, and all successful ones, are interdependent, with each side benefiting to a similar degree. Where our oil exports are concerned, however, Canada depends almost wholly on the United States for sales, but the United States does not depend on Canada for its supply. It has several sources for the oil it imports; we currently have one customer for the oil we sell. This is not a balanced situation, nor a healthy one for Canada. Either directly or subtly, Canada is vulnerable to U.S. pressure where pricing and other aspects of selling our oil are concerned, and it is naïve to suggest that the pressure would never be applied. The only solution is to create access to other markets besides the United States, and the most promising of these are in Asia. We need to move our oil from its landlocked location to the Pacific coast, and we need a pipeline to do it.

To those who say, "So what? If the United States won't buy our oil, we'll keep it for ourselves," I suggest they examine the entire picture. Without an export market for our oil, we'll suffer a dramatic blow to our economy and lifestyle. The less oil pumped from the ground or retrieved from bitumen, the lower the royalties and taxes paid to various levels of government. Those royalties are measured in tens of billions of dollars pouring into provincial and federal coffers year after year. The Canadian Energy Research Institute (CERI) estimates that the oil sands industry alone will pay the federal government and the province of Alberta more than $775 billion in taxes and royalties between 2010 and 2035.[6] If this source of income vanishes, federal and provincial governments will have to either cut services or raise taxes substantially. Over the same period, the oil sands are expected to foster 905,000 jobs, 126,000 of them outside Alberta, generating employment income of about $25 billion annually.[7]

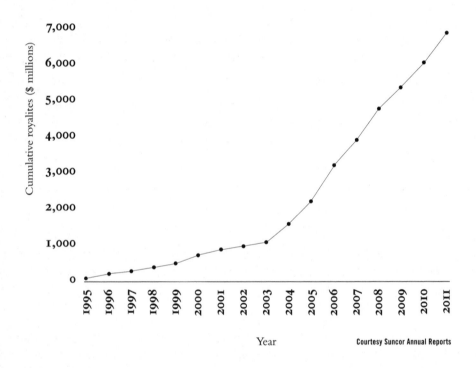

Courtesy Suncor Annual Reports

Year

Fig. 1. Cumulative royalties paid to the government by Suncor

Suncor's contribution to Canada in royalties alone has been impressive. In addition to enriching the public purse, Suncor directly employs about 13,500 people and provides work for more than 13,000 suppliers, contractors and other personnel in all 10 Canadian provinces and more than 40 countries worldwide.

My concern about relying on the United States as our sole customer for oil extends beyond the economic impact, as important as it may be, and reflects my identity as a Canadian nationalist. When we are totally dependent on one market for our largest exported product, it's not just our economic well-being that is at risk. It's our basic sovereignty. It's not inconceivable to imagine the United States insisting that Canada alter various standards to match its own. Why would we let another country dictate environmental policy and commercial terms to us? That's what happens where energy is concerned, and it's a breach of Canada's sovereignty when it occurs.

It's also unnecessary. Alberta's environmental policy and enforcement of the rules where petroleum producers are concerned are far more stringent than those in Texas, for example. Do we really need a member of the U.S. Congress telling Canadians how to run our energy business? We are already overly sensitive about American criticism of Canada on almost any subject. Each time someone in Washington utters a word of disapproval about this country, especially its environmental policies and energy industry, Canadian media scream about it in headlines. The vast majority of people in the United States are unaware that anything has been said, but on the north side of the border it becomes disturbing news. The media play up "news" such as this because they understand Canada's sensitivity to U.S. opinion, and Canadians understand that U.S. interests on almost any topic, from security to water supply, tend to override our own.

Forget for a moment the national sovereignty aspect and think of Canada Inc. and USA Inc. as two private companies. They do business with each other, but the larger of the two, USA Inc., does business with a dozen other firms. Canada Inc. does business only with U.S. Inc. You don't need an MBA to recognize the danger of this "reverse monopoly" arrangement. If you have only one buyer for the product or service you're selling, sooner or later that customer is likely to take advantage of that one-sided relationship. It's just the nature of the market. If you have two customers, you diminish the power of the single customer and raise your bargaining position significantly. Large customers may still abuse you, but now you have an alternative.

If the Gateway pipeline is completed and the port at Kitimat becomes operational, it will influence many aspects of Canadian–American relations in Canada's favour. We won't have to be nearly as concerned about American criticism of our policies. The Canadian prime minister and every Canadian official visiting Washington will be treated with new respect, and the country's voice will be heard more loudly and more clearly.

I appreciate the concerns that environmentalists express about pipelines. I also know the standards that have been set for the proposed new pipelines, the transporting and loading techniques that have been proven safe and the ability of oil tankers to move in and out of port without incident. For this reason, I believe the pipeline to Kitimat can be built and operated safely with minimum disturbance to the environment and minimum risk of a devastating leak.

The pipeline to the west coast is not just an economic issue. It's also a sovereignty issue, a point that becomes clouded amid all the sound bites from protestors. It is not impossible to protect both the environment and the sovereignty of nations, and I suggest that in the grand scheme of things one is just as important as the other.

11. Meeting First Nations Obligations

In the mid-1990s I made what some thought was a strange sugges-tion to the Suncor board of directors. I reminded them that we were committed to managing the company as a quality employer that produced reasonable returns for its shareholders and performed as a proper corporate citizen. We were on our way to achieving those goals, I said, but the board was missing an important element: a First Nations member who could articulate their concerns and remind us that we must all consider ourselves responsible stew-ards of the land, including those of us—*especially* those of us—who develop its resources.

Northern Alberta is a harsh and unforgiving environment, with or without the oil sands. The First Nations people who have called it home for centuries endure hardships that most North American urban dwellers cannot begin to imagine. I believe the development of the oil sands by Suncor should not add to those challenges but reduce them. In as many ways as possible, and with minimal dis-turbance to their way of life, First Nations people should enjoy as many benefits from oil sands development as they choose.

My suggestion wasn't entirely altruistic. Since 1991 Suncor has had a policy of employing First Nations people in as many positions as possible. Frankly, we needed reliable workers and we couldn't think of a better source than the First Nations communities in our operations area.

The petroleum industry has always paid its employees well, and it takes top-level wages and salaries to attract workers to northern Alberta for year-round employment. Even then, the harsh winters in the Athabasca region drive away many. They often depart without notice, creating labour shortages that interrupt or reduce productivity.

Didn't it make sense, I argued, to hire as many First Nations people as we could? We were, after all, working on land adjacent to their communities. We promised to respect the land and restore it to its original condition, and we would, but we could do much more than that. We could offer an open door to First Nations people who chose to become Suncor employees. It seemed like a great fit to me. Suncor would enjoy a core group of employees familiar with both the terrain and the climate, and First Nations people who wanted a career with us would earn wages higher than probably in any other part of North America, participating in and profiting from the development of natural resources in their own region.

On the whole, the idea proved successful. Between 1992 and 2009 Suncor spent more than $1 billion on goods and services provided by First Nations–owned companies in the Wood Buffalo region. Some residents of Fort McMurray and Fort McKay are honest-to-goodness millionaires, many of them First Nations or Métis who have seized the opportunity to improve their economic security and well-being. A lot of these entrepreneurs have expanded their services beyond the oil sands to win contracts with forestry and pipeline firms and the public sector far afield. And there will be more. In 2008 Suncor Energy partnered with the Fort McKay First Nation to launch a business incubator, providing small businesses with guidance in marketing, human resources and finance.

The businesses launched by First Nations entrepreneurs cover a vast range of opportunities. Some are based on the kinds of commercial activity you would expect in an industrialized community, such as catering, maintenance, building contracting and general retailing. Other businesses demonstrate an entrepreneurial spirit that would impress a Wall Street investor.

A group of Athabasca Chipewyan investors recognized an opportunity to profit from tires that had outlived their performance on the Suncor fleet of trucks. Forming a company called Cutting Edge Recycling, they developed equipment to shred the tires and used the material to construct another oil sand operator's landfill site. Another Athabasca Chipewyan partnership launched Chip Manufacturing to produce wristolets from Kevlar, the same material used to make bulletproof vests. The wristolets are important safety equipment for workers exposed to cuts, abrasion and high-heat hazards in oil and gas, automotive, glass-handling, metal-stamping and other industries. Mikisew Slings and Safety, a Mikisew Cree company, manufactures web- and round-style slings capable of lifting up to 45,000 kilograms. A Métis company installs chromium carbide overlay on large-bore piping, and Tech Sonic, another First Nations firm, operates one of the largest ultrasonic cleaning tanks for heavy equipment in North America.

New firms appear almost weekly, contributing valuable products and services to the oil sands producers. I suspect that while I write this, somewhere in the Wood Buffalo region another First Nations group is at work planning a new enterprise that it will own, manage and profit from.

Within an eighty-kilometre radius of Fort McMurray, you will not find one unemployed person who is able to work and wants to work. Admittedly, there were a few bumps along the road to working with First Nations people, most the result of differences in traditions and social values. One of these involved the perception and value of time. First Nations people build their life schedules not on twenty-four-hour days but by other measures of time relating to their environment. This is both understandable and logical. They live off the land, and so the land, not the clock, sets the timetable. Their day usually begins at dawn, and dawn arrives any time between four and nine o'clock, depending on the season. Adjusting to a workday that began at seven regardless of the sun's location in the sky was a challenge for some First Nations employees.

Not all First Nations people are able to take advantage of the employment and economic opportunities available at the oil sands. The most obvious barrier is their distance from the work site. And in some cases, social and economic conditions or problems with leadership have arisen.

Many anti-oil sands protestors are or claim to be from First Nations bands, but few of them are from the Fort McMurray area. Whatever their origins, Native protestors often express concerns that I fully understand and appreciate. At the heart of their objections, I believe, is a distinctive value system. Most North Americans favour progress (especially when it is tied to prospects for greater income and job security) tempered with deep and sincere concern for environmental protection. The impetus remains economic: will this development or project help me earn a living—enough to feed, house and clothe me and my family?

First Nations people have the same concerns, but they are overridden by others, including their relationship with Mother Earth and, perhaps most important, respect for their heritage and way of life. The opening of the oil sands development was just the latest indication of how difficult it would be for them to return to the kind of life practised by their ancestors—although that would be true even if the oil sands had never been explored. In this light, it's easy to understand why Native people view the prospect of long-term, well-paid jobs differently than most residents of Edmonton or, for that matter, almost anywhere else in North America.

Instead of viewing work in the oil sands from an economic standpoint, a lot of First Nations people see it as a means of correcting historical wrongs and perhaps solving the social problems that plague many of their communities in the North. The First Nations people whose land will be traversed by the proposed pipelines through British Columbia to the Pacific coast hold similar views, I'm sure. Petroleum industry assurances of protection from oil spills carry little weight under those circumstances.

One lesson I learned was that no-one can claim to speak on behalf of all First Nations groups. It simply isn't true, except perhaps in the broadest of terms. In the oil sands region alone we deal with five different First Nations, representing more than five thousand Cree and Dene people: the Athabasca Chipewyan, the Chipewyan Prairie, the Fort McKay, the Fort McMurray No. 468, and the Mikisew Cree. Each nation sees itself as an independent body prepared and obligated to deal with issues concerning its own members before falling in line with First Nations society as a whole. Why should this be a surprise? For a millennium or so, the First Nations represented a society of independent tribes, concerned about issues that affected their own unique languages, traditions and values. It's foolish to assume that the point of view of one nation on any issue would represent the points of view of all.

These facts became important over time, because Suncor Energy deals with more First Nations than just those whose homes are adjacent to the oil sands. Activities throughout Canada often require us to be aware of local First Nations concerns and to find ways to address them. The Suncor Energy refinery in Sarnia, Ontario, for example, is located next to a First Nations burial ground and a thriving Aamjiwnaang First Nations community. Any decision regarding the site must take that into account.

Knowing that First Nations issues were so important to our success inspired my proposal that we find someone from the First

Nations to sit on our board of directors. This was unusual because, at that point, no publicly traded company I knew of in Canada had sought to recruit a First Nations representative. In our case, it made a great deal of sense. We were counting more and more on First Nations people as employees, and we were operating in their backyards. A representative on our board could alert us to possible problems arising from policies that affected First Nations and act as a touchstone on those issues. It seemed like a logical move, but it took me two years to convince the directors to agree.

The arguments against bringing a First Nations person onto the board were the same as those that had been tossed around twenty years earlier when it was proposed that women should sit on a corporate board. "It has to be the right kind of person," I heard back then, and "They have to be really qualified," along with "If they don't work out, how are you going to get rid of them?" I wasn't interested in getting rid of anyone. I was interested only in finding someone who brought a unique point of view and a special sensitivity to all the board's decisions.

My persistence paid off when Mel Benson was elected to the Suncor Energy board in April 2000. I couldn't think of anyone better qualified for the job. Born into Alberta's Beaver Lake Cree Nation at Lac La Biche, he had risen from poverty to become senior operations adviser for Exxon in Houston, a job that took him around the world to work in various oil-producing countries. When Exxon was seeking to install a pipeline from Niger to the west coast of Africa, Mel was chosen as the point man to deal with concerns involving indigenous people. His success there demonstrated the universality of First Nations issues; it's not a Canadian phenomenon but a concern of companies everywhere in the world.

The year Mel retired from ExxonMobil was the year the Suncor board elected him. Bringing him on board was not an easy task. Mel had already launched his international consulting firm and joined a number of community organizations both within and beyond the First Nations community. We were fortunate to recruit him, and he served both as chair of the Suncor Energy Environment, Health and Safety Committee and as a member of the Human Resources and Compensation Committee.

Mel bridges both cultures and societies. He has maintained his roots and knows most of the First Nations chiefs in Canada. He also knows the petroleum industry and is totally familiar with its goals and challenges. Interestingly, Mel Benson does most of his work as a director outside the boardroom. For example, many of the issues that arise with First Nations groups concern language— not a simple translation of Cree or some other Native language to English, but the true meaning behind the words being spoken. You can make a literal translation between English and any other language you can name and still fail to understand the meaning of the other side's words. Where the First Nations are concerned, this is even more challenging, and when Suncor people dealing with First Nations representatives feel unsure about their understanding of a situation they often call on Mel to explain things to both sides.

Mel Benson's presence on the Suncor Energy board may not have made everyone happy as far as the company's relations with First Nations society is concerned, but that was neither a sensible goal nor the reason he was chosen to serve as a director. Suncor is, in my opinion, the most sensitive and responsive publicly traded company in Canada when it comes to serious issues affecting First Nations people, and I take as much pride in that as in almost anything else I accomplished with the firm.

♦

Oil sands activity centres on Fort McMurray,* which has become something of a boom town with almost 80,000 residents. It may be a boom town, but it's no rough-and-tumble frontier hamlet. Not with three golf courses, a world-class multi-use community centre, several ice rinks and pools, a full-time college and scheduled airline services. And while Fort McMurray gets most of the media coverage about oil sands communities, Fort McKay is more indicative of First Nations experience in the area.

Fort McKay lies about sixty-five kilometres north of Fort McMurray. Its seven hundred or so residents are almost exclusively members of the Fort McKay band, one of the five First Nations of northeastern Alberta.

As Suncor CEO I made a point of visiting Fort McKay periodically to meet with the chief, Jim Boucher, as well as various elders and leaders, sharing a meal and discussing their concerns. Fort McKay has modern, comfortable housing with good schools and a strong sense of community, free of constraints from outside. The residents have installed their own air-quality measuring facility, which they monitor. They have also created and now manage a sustainability department to build greater efficiency and access to information and services while working with industry to benefit the community. A visit to Fort McKay is an eye opener to anyone who doubts the abilities of First Nations people or the quality of the relationship between them and the oil sands industry.

It is not easy to balance respecting First Nations culture and values while benefiting from their work through industrial development, but I am convinced that by speaking frankly and listening closely, the two sides can find common ground and equal benefits.

---

* The "fort" designation for communities in the area arose from the growth of the fur industry in the nineteenth century. First Nations people settled near the forts where the fur traders gathered, establishing towns and eventually cities.

I'm not sure statistics are available, but I know that directly or indirectly Suncor Energy has provided more employment for more First Nations people than any other company in Canada. And both sides have benefited. I fully expect this process to continue. The First Nations population in Canada continues to grow, and with that growth come rising expectations to share in the country's wealth. Neither I nor the First Nations people nor, I suggest, any other Canadian should have to hear another word about terrible living conditions in First Nations communities and the doomed hopes and aspirations of the people who live there.

With good leadership this country can achieve a balance between providing every opportunity for First Nations people to find steady and fulfilling employment and enabling them to retain their identity and culture. I look forward to the day when that policy becomes universal and unexceptional.

12. How to Steady a Three-Legged Stool

Operations at the oil sands are not as clean and tidy as I would like, whether run by Suncor or by others. They can't be, because the oil sands are sites for both mining and heavy manufacturing, and neither process can be conducted as neatly as running an insurance office or a landscape nursery. Mining, by definition, means disturbing the earth to a degree, and heavy manufacturing requires space, energy and complex support facilities. I wish we could escape the aspects of oil sands production that people find alarming and carry out all the stages in a neatly enclosed environment. It's simply not possible. But neither is the process as cataclysmic as the photographs and descriptions posted by opponents imply.

Images of the oil sands that appear in the media usually depict the mining operations and upgrader equipment, with photos of the upgrader dominated by white plumes pouring into the sky. The plumes are water vapour, the same material that flows from your laundry dryer vent or, for that matter, from your kettle when the water is boiling, and are no more damaging to either you or the environment. Most people understand this, but a few, including some industry detractors and even the odd newspaper photo editor, change the clean white columns to black, suggesting that the stacks are spewing lethal material into the atmosphere.

The mining operation involves trucks and shovels, it's true, but the shovels are powered by electricity, a source of energy that many people who advocate shutting down the oil sands prefer over gasoline or diesel fuel. The trucks use state-of-the-art diesel-electric hybrid engines and need to be maintained to ensure reliability as well as optimal fuel efficiency and the lowest emissions levels.

Which brings up an interesting point. About 20 percent of the drivers at the Suncor Millennium mine are women, and the people who monitor these things tell me that the vehicle maintenance staff actually prefer women drivers. It seems that women are both more detail conscious and more likely to report a potential problem with their trucks than male drivers, who tend to dismiss small glitches as no big deal. On the whole, I'm told, heavy equipment operated by women is in better hands than the same equipment operated by men, especially when it comes to economical and reliable operation. Another lesson in life from the oil sands. . . .

It's worth pointing out that one of the reasons so many unflattering photos of and commentaries about the oil sands are posted by people who may not have visited the site is their location. Canada is a democracy, where environmental standards are regulated and evidence of the success or failure of a company to meet them is available to anyone who wishes to examine it. The public does not have access to either this information or to the fields themselves in Saudi Arabia, Nigeria, Venezuela or many other oil-producing nations. Oil companies in Canada, by contrast, share a sense of social responsibility—an attitude that applies to every business decision they make—and a willingness to reveal and discuss problems.

SHORTLY after it became clear that Suncor's oil sands operation would survive as a successful corporate entity, I insisted that when it came to measuring our performance, we would adhere to the concept of a triple bottom line: our success would be determined by social, economic and environmental standards, and our long-term goal would be to support sustainability for our industry. We couldn't post big earnings for our investors but have substandard performance in social responsibility and environmental protection and still call ourselves a success. Ignoring the economic factor because we focused on the other two wouldn't work either. We would soon be out of business and our employees out of work. Our success depended on steadying the three-legged stool.

One of the best examples of this approach concerned the people in the Wood Buffalo regional municipality, which encompasses much of the oil sands area. Our operations and those of all the other oil production companies could succeed only by attracting workers from both the First Nations people already living in the municipality and from other areas of the country. This was a basic economic need: attract qualified people to achieve a productive, long-term core of workers. No matter how much the workers earned, however, they were not likely to commit themselves to employment in the area if the environment was unsafe, unhealthy and unattractive. Ignoring the social side of things by failing to provide recreational opportunities, entertainment and educational facilities, and a general sense of community would neither attract nor retain the kind of people we needed.

When Suncor and our peers in the oil sands moved into an aggressive growth period around 2008, we lost our balance in the three bottom lines, especially the social and the economic. Housing prices skyrocketed and various stresses appeared throughout the community, making it difficult for workers to seriously consider settling and raising their families there. The long-term consequences of failing to address social and economic matters would not be good.

The challenges were too great and far-reaching for the industry to deal with on its own, so through the Oil Sands Developers Group (OSDG) we teamed up with community groups as well as municipal and provincial governments. The degree of cooperation among the partners was impressive, demonstrating what can happen when different players find common goals and work together to reach them. The fact that we established and met so many of the goals in the midst of a major economic slowdown makes our achievements that much greater.

In an effort to balance our triple bottom line, we accomplished many things. The OSDG and the Regional Municipality of Wood Buffalo reviewed pressing infrastructure needs, including the need for more housing, and asked the Alberta provincial government to release new land for the purpose. The OSDG transportation committee began to work with the provincial government to solve major transportation problems—its projects include the improvement of highways and the installation of bridges across the Athabasca River. And the health care committee started developing and implementing new programs and services, many of them designed to reduce the burden on existing community health care resources.

Some initiatives sound relatively minor in nature yet can make a major positive change over the long haul. For example, OSDG members now coordinate maintenance and construction schedules in a way that limits the sudden influx of contract workers who assume temporary residence in the area, thus placing less strain on the community

In each case, Suncor and its partners focused on generating positive long-term effects that would last throughout the company's projected operating life. Our time horizon stretched far beyond that of other companies in the industry and well beyond most businesses generally. Typical upstream E&P petroleum companies work on a ten- to twenty-year projected lifespan. That's the length of time that the crude will be available through normal drilling and production techniques. When the original oil reserves are in serious decline, E&P companies sell their assets to smaller companies that specialize in scavenging the residue.

Once we solved our major production problems from the oil sands, however, the production schedule for Suncor and other producers would be measured *in centuries*. When your horizon is that far away it's important to take your legacy seriously. Suncor's existence and continued success had to benefit all stakeholders, in both the short and the long haul.

The idea of the oil sands continuing to produce petroleum for the next hundred years or more may disturb some people, but reality dictates that the only practical way to eliminate our reliance on fossil fuels effectively is through research to discover and harness a new energy source and new ways to conserve energy. The investment needed to achieve this on a grand scale is substantial, to say the least, and most of the necessary R&D is being conducted by companies such as Suncor Energy. Shutting down companies operating in the oil sands would eliminate one of the richest sources of funding to find a replacement for petroleum. That may sound ironic, but it's true. Oil companies have both the funds and the impetus to develop alternative energies—and they are doing it now.

The world may be moving away from petroleum as a primary source of energy, but if so it's moving at a crawl, not a sprint. One way or another, we'll be depending on reliable sources of oil for at least the next hundred years, and it's that time frame that prompted my advocacy of a triple bottom line and dictated many of our plans. If Suncor's operations last well beyond the end of the current century, so will its impact on local communities. With this in mind, conventional planning and operating principles become inadequate and irrational.

The concept of the triple bottom line grew into an intuitive means of tackling many aspects of business. It also raised the bar by demanding that both sides of the environmental issue be cognizant of, and sensitive to, the ways in which their circles overlap. Business leaders cannot ignore the fact that their firms will not attract the workforce they need to operate efficiently if they do not heed at least basic standards of sustainability. Environmentalists have to recognize that excessive demands could very well doom a community, creating major social and economic upheavals.

Honestly seeking opinions from a range of stakeholders, listening to them closely and responding in a manner that satisfies all sides can pay remarkable benefits. It's not easy and it's rarely fun, but Suncor has banked more than just goodwill through this policy. The company involves stakeholders in each of its major decisions. In many cases, this manages to replace confrontation with collaboration. As a CEO, you get a good feeling standing in front of a crowd that hurls compliments at you instead of brickbats. It feels even better to find that your efforts have saved the company money while earning it goodwill.

This happened on several occasions during the most recent periods of heavy growth at Suncor, including the expansion of the Steepbank Mine operation and the launch of the Firebag in situ project. In both cases we conferred with community stakeholders early in the process and addressed almost all their outstanding needs—so much so that regulators decided there was no need for public hearings. In the case of Steepbank, the community consultations actually shaved two years off the original schedule because some of the decisions resulting from open discussions reduced the project's environmental impact and improved its cost efficiency.

It all comes down to dialogue—listening, understanding and appreciating the other side's point of view, trusting that the various goals do not conflict as much as it may first appear.

✦

THE optics of the oil sands may not be all that attractive, but the technology to deal with various environmental concerns continues to evolve at a rapid pace. What's more, the steps we take to protect the environment and their success at reducing air and water emissions are not immediately apparent. Technology evolves constantly but sporadically, making it impossible to use the state of the art as the basis for future operations. By the time anyone, including those within the industry itself, has fully evaluated a process or standard, it is likely to have been improved or replaced. We've seen a similar evolution with automobiles. When I was a teenager, twenty miles to the gallon (or about 8.5 kilometres to the litre) was considered good mileage for a family car. Today the same vehicle would be considered a gas guzzler; cars burning half as much gasoline are producing twice as much horsepower, and cars manufactured and marketed in 2012 are far ahead in terms of safety, efficiency and longevity of those made by the same manufacturer just five years earlier. Compared with the auto industry, oil sands technology is moving at lightning speed.

Over the years, the technology employed to recover bitumen from the oil sands and prepare it for refining has yielded far greater efficiency and sharply reduced the environmental impact. The advances race ahead of the mass media's ability to understand them and communicate their significance. Much has been made, for example, of the amount of water needed to capture the bitumen and produce a barrel of crude oil from it. Many oil sands opponents claim that it takes five or more barrels of water drawn from the Athabasca River to produce one barrel of oil. Wherever and whenever that figure originated, it's no longer true. We have made enormous progress in this area, reducing our water consumption by 40 percent between 2003 and 2011. In 2012 it requires about 2.08 barrels of water per barrel of oil, and with in situ production more than 90 percent of that water is recycled. It's also cleaner. All the water released into the Athabasca must pass the province of Alberta's standards.

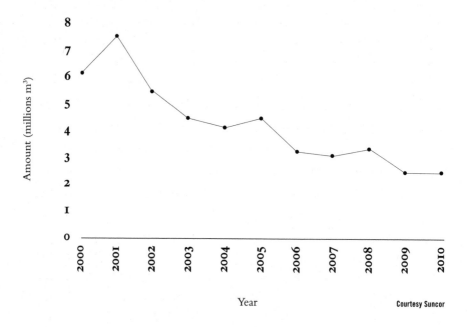

Fig. 2. Water withdrawal for oil sands operations

A major concern for stakeholders is the quantity of water that the oil sands use. Over the years we have managed to reduce dramatically the volume of water drawn from the Athabasca River, and that amount is dropping still. The water is treated and purified before being returned to the river.

Is that still a lot of water? Not when compared with the amount needed to produce some consumer products. I was fascinated to read that scientists had calculated the amount of water required to produce various foods and products at every stage of development.[1] They used the term *virtual water* to describe the amount required to produce any given item. For example, it takes a thousand litres of water to yield one kilogram of wheat, and fifteen times that much to land a kilogram of beef on your table. That's 15,000 litres of water needed to serve roast beef to your family. Some measurements were even more startling; producing a pair of jeans weighing just one kilogram requires 10,850 litres of water to grow and process the cotton, weave and dye the jeans, and go through all the other necessary steps before you carry them home from the store and step into them. Against these figures, the use of water in the oil sands becomes reasonable.

It's the scale of the oil sands that stuns people initially. The Millennium Mine is an open pit as much as a hundred metres deep and covering about fifteen square kilometres. It's not the prettiest thing you've ever laid eyes on, but the mine will not remain as it is forever.

One of the most visible aspects of a mine operation are tailings ponds. All mining processes create tailings, the material remaining after the mined resource has been removed. Oil sands tailings consist of water, clay, sand and residual bitumen. Before the mineral content of tailings can be returned and the land restored to close to its original condition, the water must be removed. This sounds like a simple process, but it's more difficult than you might think.

Traditionally, the tailings mix has been deposited in ponds where, over time, the heavier material sinks to the bottom and the water evaporates or is removed. That's what happens in the oil sands; the heaviest material, primarily sand, settles on the bottom and water rises to the top, where it can be removed and recycled. It's the middle layer that creates the challenge. Made up of about 70 percent water and 30 percent fine clay particles, this layer, the mature fine tailings (MFT), has the consistency of yogurt and resists drying for literally decades. It can take thirty years or more for MFT to solidify sufficiently for the land to be restored. Meanwhile the tailings ponds have been the Achilles heel of oil sands PR.

When I arrived at Suncor, the problem was not new to the company. Over time, we could control smokestack effluents with scrubbers, we could dramatically reduce our water usage and we could cut the amount of energy it took to produce a barrel of crude oil, but the tailings ponds sat year after year like massive black eyes on the entire oil sands production activity. They were unsightly and potentially risky to wildlife, and nothing could be done to restore the sites to their original condition until the material solidified.

Suncor had been tackling various means of settling the tailings faster since the late 1970s with little success. In the early 1990s, we pioneered a technology to speed up the drying process by adding gypsum and coarse sand to the ponds. This helped settle the material and improve our water recycling, but it was still taking far too long to eliminate the ponds.

We developed a program we titled TRO (tailings reduction operation), which cut the drying time to a matter of weeks. It was also unique, and effective enough to be granted a patent. We introduced TRO in 2010. By about 2018 tailings from our entire oil sands operation, including those that have sat in ponds for several years, will have been processed with TRO technology. Once this occurs, most of the tailings ponds created prior to 2010 will be gone, and the majority of the mines in operation will function with just one tailings pond at any given time. We invested about $250 million developing TRO and will have spent another $1 billion by 2013 to install it throughout the operation. That's a lot of money by anyone's standard but we saw it as a good investment.

Suncor employees are generally proud of their work and of the company they work for. They are especially pleased when the firm makes a dramatic breakthrough that addresses criticisms of the oil sands. The success of TRO, marked by the launch of Wapisiw Lookout, was a great source of pride for everyone associated with Suncor.

Wapisiw Lookout sits on the site of the first Suncor tailings pond, which opened with the launch of the operation in 1967. It remained in use until 1980, when it was closed. In 2011 the land that the pond occupied was restored and will be almost identical, botanically and geographically, to the surrounding boreal forest. Wapisiw represents a model for the future restoration of Suncor mine sites. Mine sites that look like a moonscape today will be indistinguishable from any corner of the surrounding boreal forest when our operations are completed.

As time passes and the industry moves toward greater in situ recovery of bitumen, the question of mining and tailings will grow less pressing. As I described earlier, in situ replaces trucks, shovels and open pits with precision drilling that inserts heat through one well bore and recovers warmed and liquid bitumen from another. In addition to causing much less disturbance to the earth than pit mining, in situ technology enables operators to recycle water even more efficiently than before.

Everything is a trade-off, of course. As it exists today, in situ processing requires substantial amounts of heat energy, and the heat is generated from burning natural gas, a concern for all of us. Some critics question the wisdom of using natural gas to produce heavy oil, suggesting it's a matter of trading one source of energy for another with no real net gain. But natural gas is readily available in North America; petroleum isn't, which explains why the United States needs to import about eight million barrels of crude oil each and every day. Oil is also far more flexible as a source of energy, not to mention safer in most applications; no one has yet developed an aircraft that uses natural gas. In other applications, natural gas may replace oil to a degree. Some cars and commercial transport systems have been converted to natural gas, and millions of North American homes rely on it for heating. Converting other services to natural gas, however, would represent an extensive (and expensive) long-term project. The capital investment and the impetus to make such a conversion are currently nowhere in sight.

The use of natural gas as a way of yielding oil from bitumen produces a net gain in energy. The gas-versus-oil equation for in situ production from the oil sands indicates that, with current technology, the energy equivalent of a barrel of oil is about five to six times greater than the gas needed to produce it. As with other oil sands technology, this process will improve considerably in the coming years. We have already recorded major steps forward in reducing the energy needed to recover oil in situ through the use of organic-based surfactants and solvents that help the oil flow more freely and more efficient pumps to bring it to the surface.

My confidence in both the continued global demand for petroleum and the advent of technology to improve production efficiency at the oil sands was behind my decision in 2008 to launch a second major production expansion. We had just negotiated a new royalty agreement with the province of Alberta under which we were to begin paying the government between 25 and 30 percent of net profits from our mining operations from January 1, 2010, running through to January 1, 2016. The deal guaranteed Alberta substantial income from its petroleum resource and gave us the assurance that we could substantially increase our production capacity within a fixed royalty format.

The day following the royalty agreement announcement, we christened Voyageur, our plan to boost oil sands production by 200,000 barrels per day. Planning for Voyageur had begun five years earlier. Its implementation had been delayed while we waited for oil prices to stabilize at a level that would make the investment worthwhile. It was another Big Bet, committing Suncor Energy to $11.6 billion for a new upgrader facility plus $9 billion for expansion of the Firebag in situ operation.

When I arrived in 1991 Suncor's oil sands operations were best known for rarely making money. Today, besides generating returns for investors, the oil sands employ tens of thousands of people, most of them earning wages that they could never hope to make in other occupations.

More important is the manner in which the environmental footprint of the industry is being reduced well beyond the oil sands themselves. For example, we're looking at dramatically cutting the energy intensity needed to upgrade and transfer product to our customers. Individual advances in technology may not appear impressive on their own, but the incremental improvements are dramatic and continuous. These advances are being explored and introduced by a critical mass of companies, each watching, competing with and being inspired by the others. Improvements in reducing carbon emissions and environmental impact are generally not treated as proprietary. Suncor shares many of the advances we've made with our competitors, which accelerates the wide implementation of new ideas.

In the petroleum industry, once something is successfully implemented it becomes the new floor. There is no ceiling, no point at which we say, "Well, that's the ultimate. Nobody is going to do it faster, better, with less energy and more precision." As soon as a company becomes aware of a new device or technique that promises greater productivity or cleaner operation or less fuel consumption, the immediate reaction is, "Let's see if we can find a way to improve it."

And someone always does.

13. The Always Present (and Frequently Frustrating) Politics of Petroleum

The petroleum industry is complicated partly because oil is more than a source of energy. It's also a political issue locally, domestically and internationally. Nothing that involves oil, from exploration and production to refining and pricing, is free from political intervention. All commodities are subject to one kind of political involvement or another if they represent a major element of the economy, but the significance paid to petroleum often exceeds that paid to food, water and other energy sources such as coal and natural gas.

This is a tribute to the role that oil plays in our modern life, and no one in a democratic society can legitimately argue with the need for countries and regions to be involved in the issue. My concern, and the concern of every other oil company executive I have encountered, is the degree to which oil and the companies producing it become a political football.

When it comes to power for transportation, heating homes and businesses, and a wide range of other global applications, oil provides 25 percent more than coal and 60 percent more than natural gas.[1] Wind, solar, nuclear and hydroelectrical power all represent smaller parts of the overall energy supply picture. In Europe and North America, and increasingly throughout the world, the presence of

175

oil in a region signifies a strategic asset as a source of not merely energy but of vital income through royalties and taxes. The province of Alberta earned about $3.7 billion from oil royalties in 2010, most of it from oil sands production. Some $18 billion in industry taxes and royalties went to all the provincial and federal governments in total. Here's another way to measure it: from every dollar earned by the petroleum industry in Canada, fifty-four cents flows to various levels of government.

I don't have a problem with paying either royalties or taxes. Royalties are the means of valuing a resource that belongs to the residents of a province, state or nation. The way governments use the royalties earned from oil production ranges from brilliant to outrageous, in my opinion. In many oil-rich nations in the Middle East, billions of dollars in oil revenue flow into the pockets of despots and their friends and family year after year. That a small group in power makes extravagant use of this money while other citizens in the same country are living in abject poverty taints the industry's image in the eyes of many people.

Other countries, such as Norway, have treated their income from petroleum royalties as a widely held resource whose profits should be shared by current and future generations. Since 1995 the Norwegian government has deposited oil revenues into a sovereign investment fund, adding billions to its value year after year through returns on its investments and new oil royalty earnings.* With the country's petroleum reserves now past their peak production, this has become a crucial way to ensure financial and social stability for the country and its citizens. Elsewhere, Kuwait has also done a good job of sharing its wealth among its citizens.

My major concern with respect to Canada, and to a degree the United States, is not how petroleum royalties are shared but the

---

* Disclosure: As I write this, the Norwegian sovereign fund is a shareholder in Suncor Energy.

lack of a national dialogue on energy policy that takes into account the needs of both the industry and the country. Canada, like the rest of the world, is facing long-term energy challenges that need successful management. These range from ensuring security of supply to supporting sustainability while determining the ideal mix of resources to meet the country's energy requirements.

A well-constructed energy policy would define the role of Canada in a world that is expected to consume 50 percent more energy by 2035 than it did in 2011.[2] One of the biggest difficulties in creating an effective policy is doing so within a political time frame. Steady and reliable energy production on a global scale demands vision spread over a century or more; in politics, time is measured primarily as the space between elections. It's a challenge to persuade politicians to look beyond the next campaign, let alone the next decade.

When speaking of energy policies, I'm not referring to federally mandated national energy programs (a term that still sends chills up the spine of Albertans who recall the National Energy Program of the Trudeau years). This is something quite different. Canada and every major energy-producing and energy-consuming country should have a comprehensive and coherent strategy that addresses a range of issues. In Canada's case the policy needs to consider our regionally diverse natural resources and the various ways the country's energy production and consumption levels affect the economy. We are a resource-rich country, and we need to choose how to make the most of this legacy in ways that will benefit not only our children's generation but our grandchildren's and their descendants.

I understood the lack of a defined national energy policy during the years of a federal minority government, when the Conservatives were focused on retaining power. With the advent of a majority in 2011 they should have the opportunity and the impetus to begin dealing with the subject. It may even encourage the United States to follow suit by persuading its leaders that their nation requires a national energy strategy as much as Canada.

The need for an energy strategy in Canada has become so vital that in 2010 several of the largest companies in the country, including major energy producers and consumers, formed the Energy Policy Institute of Canada (EPIC) to address the problem. The goals of EPIC were simply to start the discussion rolling. Since the federal government appeared reluctant to deal with the issue, the primary industries involved in energy production and consumption attempted to shine a spotlight on the topic. EPIC's actions were not entirely self-serving, since it was composed of producers and consumers, both of which shared the need for stability and security of energy supply. Without these factors, neither side could set long-term goals or make plans to reach them.

Unfortunately, EPIC's mandate ended in 2012, and while it made some important points during its life I'm afraid it accomplished less than might have been expected. The inherent barrier was a familiar one in Canada: the management of natural resources is considered a provincial responsibility, and attempts by other jurisdictions to get involved tend to create immediate suspicion and opposition. This view extends to setting energy policies, and the strongest opposition to a national strategy originated in Quebec.

With its extensive and profitable hydroelectric facilities, Quebec sees itself as a green province with neither the need nor the incentive to participate in a collective dialogue under a national energy policy. Quebec's position is this: we are already the largest producer of pollution-free renewable energy in all of North America; why should we permit others to set goals and standards relating to environmental protection and long-term energy supply that will affect us? Quebec is not alone in its suspicion of establishing national objectives where energy is concerned; Alberta and much of the Prairies share the same concerns.

Despite what I consider a limited success, EPIC managed to establish several broad principles that are worth reviewing:

- Ensure that energy and environmental imperatives go hand in hand in ways that will result in the most innovative and positive outcomes.
- Advance the primacy of the Canada–United States energy relationship and ensure that mutual clean energy goals focus on cooperation in the development and implementation of ground-breaking technologies.
- Contribute ideas and solutions that enhance the openness of world energy markets and strengthen global rules relating to investment, carbon management and energy security.
- Help design regulatory processes that aid, rather than impede, responsible energy development.
- Promote certainty and predictability in energy policy, which are vitally needed to support investment decisions.[3]

Several countries have established energy policies with success, and their experience could serve as a model for Canada and the United States. France, for example, with no oil or gas reserves, made a decision in the early 1970s to minimize its reliance on oil and gas and construct an effective electricity grid powered almost exclusively by nuclear fuel. As a result France is in a better position to determine and provide its basic energy needs than many other countries.

Japan made a similar decision that worked equally well—with the exception of approving the installation of nuclear reactors on the shoreline. The government did not anticipate the devastating tsunami following the earthquake of March 2011, and many critics of nuclear power use that incident to decry nuclear energy. The fact remains, however, that no meltdown or widespread dispersion of lethal radiation occurred as a direct result of the event.* The tsunami, of course, horrified the world not only with the extent of the damage but the loss of life. I found it interesting and even reassuring, however, that the structures of the multiple nuclear reactors remained intact. Radiation problems that stemmed from the tsunami were a direct result not of failures in the system but of the fact that a seawall to protect the Fukushima Dai-Ichi nuclear facilities had been built too low. Designed to divert a rise in water levels of 6.3 metres, the wall proved inadequate for the 7-metre-high wave that overwhelmed the Japanese coastline, and the resulting flooding knocked out the reactor back-up systems.[4] Should this unique event serve to turn the world away from nuclear energy everywhere? I don't believe it should.

Along with various other nations, China is also preparing an energy strategy that will play a vital role in the country's development.

Contrast these approaches with that of Canada and especially the United States, where the view is strictly short term. When oil prices go up, Congress votes to tax the oil industry. Then, when Congress notes that investment in the United States by the same industry drops off a cliff, Washington can't figure out why.

I'll go out on a limb and suggest that some long-term policy decisions are too important to leave to the federal government if it appears reluctant or too distracted to deal with them. There may

---

* It's worth noting that, according to the United States Department of Labor, Mine Safety and Health Administration (*Comparison of Year-to-Date and Total Fatalities for M/NM & Coal*), forty-eight lives were lost in the U.S. coal mining industry in 2010. In China, an average of seven coal mine workers were killed on the job each day during 2009, a decline from almost eighteen deaths per day five years earlier (Tania Branigan, "China Claims Big Drop in Mine Deaths," *The Guardian,* January 20, 2010).

be a role for business to take the lead, along with other concerned parties such as non-governmental organizations (NGOs) and various sectors of society. I'm not necessarily advocating hard-nosed decision making by these groups, but I suspect if enough of them got together and debated an energy policy, political leaders would begin to take notice.

This in no way suggests usurping the role of government in the energy industry. Government's primary task is regulation, and I favour tough and fair regulation for the petroleum industry, including the oil sands. We are all judged by the lowest common denominator. The deaths of those 1,600 ducks in a Syncrude tailings pond brought all kinds of nasty comments raining down upon Suncor and other operators. Sensible regulation, uniformly enforced, is essential not just in the petroleum industry but wherever consensus exists that it is needed. I also have no problem with government providing incentives in one area and disincentives in another. Helping the developers of wind power and solar energy with inducements, for example, is a good thing for governments to do, just as imposing heavy taxes on cigarettes is an effective way to cut down on smoking. Such measures encourage companies to seriously investigate the potential returns of investing in new ideas and alternatives to either satisfy market demands or create entirely new market sectors.

In too many instances, however, governments are behind the curve when it comes to dealing with subjects of broad relevance such as environmental protection. Carbon emissions have been of concern to many people for years, with little effective government response. Imagine if governments in Canada and the United States had introduced a reasonable carbon tax of perhaps $5 per ton when the issue came alive around 2005, and then dedicated all the money collected to the support of urban rapid-transit systems. The plan would have been so logical, and its impact on urban North Americans so positive, that it would have been relatively easy to implement.

True, the fringes would complain as they always do; right-wingers would object to any new tax, and more radical environmentalists on the left would demand a $50 tax instead.

The majority of taxpayers would have understood that modern, efficient rapid transit in metropolitan areas is the best way to encourage people to leave their cars at home. (I'll admit that I am not an exclusive rapid-transit rider, but I choose transit to get back and forth to work at least periodically.) People either ignore or forget that at least 80 percent of carbon emissions associated with cars and trucks is not the result of extracting and producing the oil and gasoline pumped into the vehicles but of burning the fuel in their internal combustion engines. Want to cut carbon emissions in urban areas? Reduce the number of vehicles—especially those belonging to commuters—on the road. The best way to cut down on vehicle traffic is to create extensive and comfortable rapid-transit systems.

Which raises another point that addresses both the need for a national energy policy and the benefits of widespread rapid-transit. All across North America immense reserves of natural gas are becoming accessible and economically viable through advanced technology such as *fracking*. Fracking (the term is derived from *fracturing*) is an advanced technology that has proven effective in releasing natural gas from shale deposits. As its name suggests, the technique involves separating layers of shale to release trapped gas, then feeding it through pipelines and into storage vessels. It remains to be seen how effective the process can be in light of concern that it may pollute aquifers that act as vital sources of fresh water, but I believe it can be proven safe. Numerous people are enthusiastic about the export potential of natural gas, which involves liquefying the gas before loading it aboard tankers to be shipped across the world.

So here's my question. Why would people in North America export natural gas at $5 to $7 per million cubic feet while importing about nine million barrels of oil a day at $100 a barrel? How can this possibly make sense? Instead of exporting natural gas, why not convert coal-fired electricity-generating plants to natural gas? In addition, why not introduce mass-transit vehicles that run on natural gas instead of buses that consume gasoline and diesel fuel, much of it derived from imported crude oil? I expect the average North American would agree that it makes more sense to employ the energy in our own backyard before negotiating a price to import energy from someone else's. What would it take to make this a reality? Although the market will largely determine what energy source is preferred, a little government impetus wouldn't hurt.

Unfortunately, governments not only lag behind the people they appear intent on leading, but they try to make up for lost time with exaggerated responses designed to generate the most press coverage. When the issue finally grows too big to ignore, the reaction of political leaders often is to create headlines by swinging for the fences, scoring a home run with every new idea. Good baseball teams never try to win a game by hitting only home runs, and governments shouldn't try to change an industry or a society with a single swing that too often produces only major disappointments.

We saw the home run philosophy in Canada in 2008 when Liberal party leader Stéphane Dion based his election campaign on a "big picture" move to cut emissions with a carbon tax. People who understood his objective agreed that the goal was worthwhile, but the leap was too wide for the public to grasp. Those who understood, and perhaps even supported the concept, disliked the idea that the money collected would flow into general revenue instead of toward environmental issues, and Dion, his leadership and his party all crumbled as a result.

We saw the philosophy again in 2009, this time in the United States, when Speaker Nancy Pelosi attempted to ram the Waxman-Markey Bill through Congress. Waxman-Markey was a massive bill designed to control greenhouse gases and affecting a range of energy sources and industries, and it proved so complex that it alienated even those who supported its objectives. The bill was badly flawed, giving a large exemption to the coal industry while penalizing petroleum. This was undoubtedly a bone thrown to congressional representatives from coal-producing and major coal-consuming states, but it undermined the supposed objective of cutting carbon emissions.

The use of coal as a source of energy to produce electric power generates quantities of carbon and other greenhouse gases on a scale that dwarfs the impact of oil sands production. Putting it bluntly, coal is the most carbon dioxide–intensive energy source available for industrial-scale applications. Its only attractive qualities are that it is cheap, accessible and abundant. The impact of burning coal extends well beyond any association with global warming. Coal is also responsible for a general deterioration in air quality; it contributes to smog and, according to some sources, is responsible for thousands of deaths each year in addition to those of coal miners. The province of Ontario, which generates just 8 percent of its electricity from coal compared with almost 74 percent by Alberta, estimates that the health-related damages of coal costs it $3 billion annually.[5]

Why does Alberta continue to burn coal in its generating plants? Because it's cheap. The province lacks appropriate waterways to generate hydroelectricity, which would normally be an economical alternative to coal, and generating a kilowatt hour of electricity in the province's existing coal-fired plants costs only one-third as much as it would to build nuclear facilities and produce power in that fashion. Here's the downside of coal: it is also very dirty. One source estimates that air conditioning an Alberta home for a single day emits a ton of carbon from a coal-fired power plant in the province.[6]

If burning coal produces far higher carbon emissions that burning oil-based products, why claim to be cutting carbon by restricting petroleum when the largest fuel source of carbon receives a free ride?

The Waxman-Markey Bill would have encouraged even more use of coal because it proposed wider applications of electrical energy, such as electric-powered cars. With no provision for building nuclear power plants, and apparently no recognition that coal-powered plants produce more than half of all electric power in the United States,[7] Congress bowed to pressure from the coal industry lobby when drafting Waxman-Markey. This may be the reality of practical politics in the twenty-first century, but any U.S. government bill that tries to reduce carbon emissions and ignores the role of coal in firing its generators lacks perspective.

I met Congresswoman Pelosi during a trip she made to Ottawa in 2010 with Congressman Edward Markey, co-sponsor of the Waxman-Markey bill. During her visit Pelosi demanded that Canada halt future oil sands development. "Why did you try to make such a massive change with one bill?" I asked her, referring to the Waxman-Markey legislation. "Society doesn't change that way overnight. Instead of trying for a grand-slam home run, why not lay down a few bunts and singles, and let people get used to the idea?" All I got was a blank stare. I hadn't expected a detailed response because if such a route had been considered at the outset it might have succeeded, and I suspect Congresswoman Pelosi realized it in hindsight. It was clear that she and the rest of her committee were looking primarily for a grand gesture that would score points with voters who were demanding legislation to deal with carbon emissions. Everything else was ignored.

I was more concerned about another aspect of Pelosi's visit to Canada. The committee members had ventured north from Washington, a place that even the most rabidly patriotic American will admit has become a symbol of ineptitude, to scold Canadians about their own energy policy. Their message was that Americans should get off oil as a primary source of energy and Canadians should slow down or cease development of the oil sands because the plants were emitting too much carbon. Besides, if the United States no longer needed oil, they wouldn't need the oil sands production—the source of about 25 percent of that country's supply.

Congresswoman Pelosi arrived in Ottawa fired up to scold Canadians on the worldwide need to use less oil, but she had no game plan that would move her own country off the fuel. She also showed no compunction about lecturing a foreign country on how to conduct its own business. I tried to make the point with her that the entire carbon footprint of all the operations at the oil sands is less than the amount of carbon dioxide emitted by coal-fired electricity-generating plants in the state of Wisconsin alone. Would she advocate shutting down Wisconsin's power stations to eliminate the release of as much carbon into the air as the oil sands?

It was a rhetorical question but a valid argument. If the United States does not effectively eliminate coal to drive its electric power plants, what difference does it make to the overall picture if every oil sands operation shuts down tomorrow? Unless and until the United States addresses its long-term reliance on coal, Canadians could walk, ride bicycles, pull wagons and never drive a gasoline-powered vehicle ever again, and it would make almost no impact on carbon levels worldwide compared with emissions from south of the border. Back in Brush, Colorado, my dad might have said, "Pull out your own dandelions before you complain about the ones growing in your neighbour's yard."

We invited Congresswoman Pelosi and her entourage to visit the oil sands and learn some facts about its operation. As of mid-2012, she had yet to accept the invitation.

It wasn't just the Pelosi crew's message that got under my skin. It was the negative manner in which it was delivered. I question the wisdom of one country criticizing another for its internal policies, but if it must be done I'm sure there are diplomatic ways of going about it. In the meeting I attended the tone sounded instead dictatorial and demeaning. It was also symptomatic of the trend that has developed in American politics to demonize any individual or group that disagrees with the other side's political or moral point of view.

I love Canada for many reasons. One is that we appear to have avoided the polarized approach to problems that seems to dominate the United States these days. I am disturbed, however, at the way Canadians in general, and much of the media in particular, overreact to every criticism of their country from anyone associated with the U.S. government. The more we allow American views to influence our domestic policies, the more our sovereignty is threatened. The threat does not come from Washington alone. U.S.-based corporations and organizations pour millions of dollars into Canada to support groups whose goals they favour. Many of these goals concern Canada's production and distribution of petroleum, an activity that makes an impact on every Suncor employee and, to one degree or another, on every Canadian.

When I questioned Canadian NGOs about accepting funding from American interests to influence Canadian policy, they quickly responded by drawing a parallel with Canadian corporations raising money from various locations around the world. Suncor and other oil sands operators, including foreign-owned ones, accepted funds from outside the country, so why shouldn't the NGOs?

I understood their point, but the big difference concerns transparency and accountability. Yes, Suncor raises capital from foreign sources. When it does, the source of those funds, the manner in which they will be used and the terms to settle the debt all become public knowledge. Foreign-owned oil companies also invest money in Canada, hire Canadian employees, reveal their operations and pay enormous amounts of money in royalties and taxes. Foreign pressure groups do none of these things. When Canadian NGOs use substantial sums to support their position, people assume the funding comes from within the country's borders as an expression of groups and individuals representing Canada. If NGOs want to use money from the United States or any other country to influence Canadian policy they should be obligated to demonstrate total transparency regarding the source of those funds and how they are spent.

Between 2003 and 2010, U.S. environmental lobbies spent about $15 million to campaign specifically against Alberta oil sands and the prospect of tankers carrying oil to China and other Pacific nations. An organization known as the Tides Foundation alone funnelled almost $6 million to more than two dozen Canadian organizations or Canadian subsidiaries of U.S. organizations to support American aims. Well over $4 million of that figure was directed toward actions to shut down oil sands production.[8]

We need policies in Canada to affect energy production and consumption while providing environmental protection and controlling emissions into the air and water. These policies should be developed by Canadians and for Canadians, however, and they should not be influenced by groups with deep pockets located outside the country whose primary interest is their own agenda, not that of Canadians. I'm aware that 80 percent of Canada's trade is with the United States, an imbalance that even the most diehard U.S. patriot would agree is not in the best interests of Canada. But we cannot permit the United States or any other country to dictate national policy.

This activity by U.S. sectors is especially galling because, if I may be permitted to say so, the United States has fouled up many issues that Canada has managed to put right. If we can control our national debt levels, provide imperfect but still effective universal health care, ensure a solid banking system, avoid the most devastating effects of crime and drug trafficking and manage to score high in every international rating system on the health and happiness of our citizens, we should be able to manage and regulate our petroleum industry on our own. And we can.

14. The Challenge of Global Warming

A s Suncor CEO, I met with every major environmental advocacy group in North America regularly. I have debated with and listened to members of Greenpeace, the Sierra Club, the David Suzuki Foundation and at least a dozen others. I enjoyed meeting most of them; the sessions were enlightening, entertaining and, as long as we exercised mutual respect, often productive.

From time to time I surprised them with my presence. When our daughter Emily was sixteen years old, she expressed an interest in the ideas that Greenpeace was promoting. The World Petroleum Congress was being held in Calgary at the time, and it included a "village" of booths set up by various NGOs representing environmental concerns. I took Emily along and we asked to meet Steven Guilbeault, a member of the Canadian delegation and the Quebec spokesperson for Greenpeace.

When I identified myself and introduced Emily to Guilbeault and other Greenpeace representatives, I couldn't help noticing their shock at my presence. What was the CEO of a company that Greenpeace considered an enemy doing in the middle of so many zealous environmentalists? Well, he was introducing his daughter to the environmental movement and letting her absorb their message first-hand. We both lived on the same planet, after all, and while we saw the problem from different angles we were equally concerned about preserving clean air and water.

A breakthrough of sorts occurred sometime later when we agreed to provide space for a Greenpeace booth at our annual general meeting. This took place in the midst of our involvement with the Stuart shale oil project in Australia, an activity that Greenpeace opposed. I arranged a session between the Greenpeace reps and the Suncor board and management group at which we tossed positions back and forth in a constructive manner. My motive was to demonstrate that it's better to listen and respond than declare and defend. The oil industry and the environmental movement had applied the second tactic too often and been too inflexible over the years, and it was time to change. And one of the things we needed to change was the use of labels and stereotypes.

Whenever we discard labels and stereotypes, it's easier to relate to the person on the other side of the table, and easier to agree to disagree. If we dispense with titles, protocol and posturing and exchange points of view respectfully, it will surely lead to progress. Government representatives, industry leaders, environmental advocates, social activists and others should not segregate themselves and hide behind labels or positions but instead find ways to appreciate opposing opinions on complex and significant matters and search for areas of agreement at the core. I'm not being idealistic. I believe I'm being practical. Shouting at each other across the table doesn't work, and shouting at the general public through press releases, advertisements and commercials hasn't proved very successful either. During my years at Suncor, I think both sides achieved real progress when we dealt with environmental groups on a warm and sincere basis, demonstrating respect for their opinions and expecting it in return. To me, this represented a badly needed "adult conversation."

Formal meetings tended to begin either coolly or heatedly, with table thumping and name calling on their side. After about an hour of back and forth, things would change and we would find ourselves agreeing on at least 90 percent of the subjects at hand.

Most of the 10 percent difference related to global warming. I always refused to discuss this issue in detail because the discussion too often became an all-or-nothing discourse with no room for an honest exchange of viewpoints and ideas. It was a two-way street. Some of the environmental groups I met chose not to talk about issues that I considered significant. Like global poverty. "Think of the hundreds of millions of people in this world who are constantly on the edge of starvation," I challenged a Greenpeace delegation at one session. "If your proposals result in crude oil prices of $200 a barrel, how does that help people in poverty, either here or in Africa or anywhere else?" I received no answer. They didn't want to talk about it.

I am concerned about climate change, and I appreciate the risks involved. But what I cannot accept is simplistic solutions to what is clearly a complex and challenging issue.

More to the point, I cannot find anyone who proposes a permanent and practical solution to the current state of global warming. And I cannot understand how environmental activists believe that shutting down the oil sands and generally eliminating fossil fuels will reverse the trend and avoid a future cataclysm without causing short-term crises that almost nobody is willing to endure. The only response I receive when I raise the matter is a demand that the world cut back on the release of carbon into the atmosphere. Okay. How much? At what cost? And with what impact on society?

You cannot correct what you cannot measure, and measuring the release of carbon components from energy sources is a real challenge, especially when the source is petroleum based. One way to measure carbon dioxide emissions from petroleum products burned in internal-combustion engines is the "wells-to-wheels" method. This technique calculates the GHG (greenhouse gases) produced through every stage of the fuel's life, beginning with the energy needed to pull the crude oil from the ground, followed by the energy required to pump it to the refineries, transport it to the end user and burn it within an engine.

Studies have indicated that, based on a "wells-to-wheels measure," refined products made from oil sands–derived crude oil range from 5 to 15 percent higher in GHG than those from conventional oil sources.[1] But "conventional" oil means the light "sweet" crude oil that represents the very best quality produced, and this is becoming a rare commodity. More of the crude refined around the world is heavy oil, similar to that from the oil sands. And much of this same oil is being produced in Venezuela, the Middle East and other regions that cannot be compared, on the basis of long-term security and things like human rights, with Canada.

On that basis, Athabasca–derived oil from Suncor and other producers is "on par with other sources of U.S. crude imports, including crudes from Nigeria, Venezuela and some domestically produced oil."[2]

Or here's another way of putting things in perspective. Canada is currently responsible for 2 percent of GHG emissions, and oil sands production, in turn, is responsible for 5 percent of Canada's total emissions. Put those numbers together and you get about one-tenth of 1 percent of global emissions, which represents a small fraction of GHG produced by the transportation sector and by coal-generating plants around the world.

I don't deny the reality of global warming or question its predicted effects. But my response to those who think we should immediately ban fossil fuels is two-fold. First I ask what alternatives to petroleum products they propose to use in various applications, from powering our modes of transportation to providing industrial and domestic heat. Second, I explain that demanding the oil sands be shut down would only complicate things, not solve the problem.

This has nothing to do with my long-held interest in maintaining the oil sands and everything to do with future realities.

Those future realities, as I see them, can be explained by picturing our society choosing to walk through one of three doors it is facing. Enter door number one and be prepared to encounter catastrophic consequences of climate change caused by excessive production of greenhouse gases. This is the door that many high-profile environmental groups fear we will choose, meaning we continue to use fossil fuels as our primary source of energy for heating, electricity generation, transportation and a host of other purposes.

Door number two leads to economic ruin as a result of limited growth and development by industrialized nations trying to meet unrealistic emission-reduction targets. We can walk through that door and down a path toward immediate closure of the oil sands and other petroleum-producing facilities, along with severe limitations on all fossil fuels. The industrialized world, it's worth recalling, has been built upon a reliable source of relatively inexpensive energy, and there isn't any that I know of behind this door.

Through these contrasting and unattractive doors, we either commit ourselves and our descendants to a world grown warm enough to destroy glaciers, raise the ocean levels to disastrous heights and turn vast areas into desert . . . or we cripple our economic base.

Or maybe not. Nothing in life can or should be so distinctly separated. Door number three is located between the other two, and it avoids both stark visions of the future. Instead it opens onto a path of significant reductions in GHG that do not destroy our economy. Instead of responding to a complex challenge by proposing a single, one-dimensional solution—*Shut down the oil sands and ban fossil fuels!*—this third route recognizes all the elements that contribute to GHG production, both primary and secondary. Fossil fuels are a fundamental element in the economic strength of the developed world and will continue to play this role through the foreseeable future. Advocates for reducing carbon dioxide emissions drastically and for doing it *now* may have a problem with this fact, but they cannot deny it.

No matter how you slice it, the majority of GHG from petroleum-based sources is emitted from vehicle tailpipes. We can begin lowering GHG levels substantially by reducing both the volume of emissions from vehicles and the need to use them at all.

More than any alternative currently available, improving our energy efficiency and exploring methods of conserving the energy we consume will positively address questions of rising carbon dioxide levels and their effects. These steps can be taken by every sector of society. People who drive their gasoline-powered cars two city blocks to purchase a quart of milk rather than walking the short distance may think it makes little impact. A million or more people who make the choice to walk instead once a week over a year can make a noticeable impact on consumption and GHG levels (and, by the way, improve their physical fitness). Driving an oversized car with a similarly oversized engine to transport one person back and forth to work each day is another example of unnecessary energy consumption. So many opportunities to cut emissions exist in transportation alone that we could all measurably reduce our carbon footprint starting right this moment. Expanded public transit facilities and services would make it easier to leave the family car at home five days of the week at least, and if North Americans made use of bicycles to the same extent as residents of many European countries, more volumes of carbon would be avoided.

Imagine the amount of carbon dioxide and other gases that would be cut by more limited urban sprawl, more bike paths, better rapid transit (especially for commuters) and national energy policies that addressed GHG levels. And imagine how much further emission levels would drop if all energy production and energy consumption sectors were as successful at lowering emissions and cutting water use as Suncor Energy and other oil sands producers were from 1990 to 2009, when we lowered emission intensity by 53 percent.

The opportunity to reduce energy consumption in these and other ways is available to every one of us. And that presents an opportunity for businesses to explore, develop, market and profit from new products and services geared toward saving energy.

I'm not proposing that modern society revert to a pioneer life-style. I still support my freedom to ride my motorcycle for relaxation on weekends and for others to make moderate use of energy derived from fossil fuels. When my schedule permits, I would take public transit more frequently. It's the unthinking consumption of energy that we can reduce by being aware of our own day-to-day activities. Much of that sort of reduction will incrementally make the impact that environmentalists demand, but in a far more practical and less disruptive manner than more dramatic solutions.

MY approach to life and business is to focus on the things I can control and to draw on my essential optimism. If global warming is a cyclical phenomenon and repeats temperature fluctuations that have occurred since long before the advent of fossil fuels, reversing the trend is beyond our control. If a cause-and-effect connection exists between the use of petroleum as an energy source and rising global temperatures, that is also beyond the control of North Americans for at least a generation. Why? Because about two billion people in China, India, Brazil and other emerging nations are determined to share the lifestyle we have enjoyed for a hundred years. That lifestyle has been built on petroleum, and nothing exists in the foreseeable future to replace it.

We could plead with the Chinese, the Indians, the Brazilians, the Indonesians and the citizens of all the other emerging nations to eliminate their carbon emissions to the same degree we do. We can ask them to forego owning automobiles, using low-cost electricity and various other benefits of a comfortable middle-class life based on petroleum—the same kind of life tens of millions of North Americans have experienced for the last few generations. How likely are they to heed us?

Of the 20 million cars China built in 2011, only 500,000 were electric or hybrid. Projecting a production run of 25 million cars from China in 2015 and assuming that the number of electric and hybrid cars is doubled by that year, something more than 20 million new petroleum-powered cars will be on China's roads, and they will all operate on gasoline or diesel fuel.

To its credit, China has also set impressively low targets for fuel consumption and emissions on the cars to be built for domestic use, but it's inescapable that the Chinese middle class will want to own and drive internal-combustion vehicles. So will Indians, Brazilians and tens of millions of others.

We have to deal with the fact that climate change of any kind and any cause is a global issue. Whether carbon dioxide is released from a manufacturing plant in Canada or a fleet of trucks in China makes little difference; they have the same impact on the atmosphere. This does not mean that all of us—corporate citizens or private citizens—should throw our hands in the air, but that the problem cannot be dumped on the shoulders of one sector or one industry. If climate change has a substantial enough impact, let's all play a hand in dealing with it.

As Suncor CEO I recognized that large sectors of society and the scientific community support the need to cut carbon dioxide emissions. While riding that horse, however, I was also aboard another as CEO of a major energy producer that played a vital role in contributing to the economic and social well-being of people across Canada and the United States. I needed to find a way of riding both horses in comfort and safety, so I proposed that we follow a strategy that became known as Parallel Paths.

Parallel Paths was based on Suncor acting not just as a supplier of petroleum but also as a source of alternative energies. It would prevent a polarization within the company, a sense that we were committed solely to the production of petroleum from the oil sands. The wealth created by the production of non-renewable carbon-based fuels would enable us to explore, develop, produce and potentially profit from renewable energy sources such as wind and solar power. No conflict exists between these multiple goals. They represent diversification, and we discovered an unexpected synergy among them, an insight into long-term developments in energy production in general.

Could Suncor be equally successful as an energy supplier and as a corporation making a positive impact on the carbon dioxide emissions/global warming debate? Yes, but we couldn't be perfect. "Perfect," in the eyes of some, would mean shutting down not just our oil sands operations but our entire petroleum production facility, a move I assume would have to be taken by every other petroleum supplier around the world. In the early 1990s I decided that Suncor would take a middle ground between doors one and two, focused on reducing our emissions of greenhouse gases without sacrificing the economy, and working on developments designed to meet the energy needs of today as well as the anticipated needs of tomorrow.

IN essence, I think that the environmental movement itself is stumbling, and has been since it became evident that the Kyoto Protocol of 1997 is basically dead. I keep seeing evidence that some corners of the movement have engaged in at least hyperbole and sometimes outright falsehoods. I understand the importance of dramatizing situations to attract attention to your cause, but some of the more outrageous claims and the manipulation of facts to support them have weakened the position of a few environmental advocates.

The weakness has been felt at the highest levels of government, including in the United States. At one time, Washington was seriously discussing a "cap and trade" approach to tackling environmental issues without restraining economic growth. No one discusses the idea in Washington any more, just as no one in the United States seriously believes that the country will implement a carbon tax in the foreseeable future.

Practical concerns always win out over philosophy. Since late 2008 the biggest practical concerns for many people have been related to global economic crisis. It's difficult to deal with issues promising rewards in 2050 or later if your current problem is ensuring you'll have a job, a home and a way to feed your family today. Global warming continues to be a point of discussion, but it no longer dominates the agenda among governments.

At Suncor we never pretended to have all the answers to legitimate questions about the issue. Our specific goal was to assume the lead in our industry when it came to environmental action. I believed we could succeed over the long term by drawing upon the skills of several enthusiastic and creative problem solvers in the company. The same people who had skyrocketed Suncor's production capacity from the oil sands could, over time, make a similar positive impact by reducing the volume of greenhouse gases our activities produced and improve our overall environmental protection record accordingly. My job was to provide the resources, establish the policy and encourage the teams.

We began by investing an average of 16 percent of each year's capital budget in environmental programs. That's one out of every six dollars the company spent, and we maintained a similar policy of searching for the means to sharply reduce greenhouse gases in our operations. I have great faith in the ability of technology to address the problem of GHG, whether it involves an economical means of capturing and storing carbon or some yet-to-be-discovered method that will effectively remove carbon from the production side.

My belief in the potential of technology to deal with greenhouse gases is at least as valid as broad-based regulations that mandate performance standards on specific sources of emissions, or programs like the state of California's Low-Carbon Fuel Standard (LCFS).

LCFS, introduced by former California governor Arnold Schwarzenegger, attempted to measure and regulate the carbon footprint of fuels from their production in oil fields, oil sands or corn fields through to their combustion in automobile engines and other applications. Announced with great hoopla, the California regulation was initially lauded as an example for other states and countries to follow. But it is unlikely to be implemented in anything close to its original scope and design.

One problem was its sheer complexity. How do you assign, with openness and fairness, an equitable measurement of GHG impact and the penalties to be imposed on a hundred different sources? The calculations required to measure carbon dioxide emissions under the LCFS are based on life-cycle analysis (LCA), which involves carbon dioxide from first recovery of the raw material to consumption by end users. This might work if the carbon intensity of gasoline and diesel fuel were a fixed chemical property subject to accurate measurement, but it's not. Finding the LCA of fuel involves semi-quantitative subjective analysis with a margin of error as large or larger than the reductions required under the regulation. As I noted earlier, the difference between the volume of GHG involved in producing gasoline from the oil sands and the volume from producing it from "conventional" sources is calculated at 5 to 15 percent. Split the difference and call it 10 percent. If the margin of potential error in the LCA is 15 percent, what have we learned about the impact of oil sands petroleum in this context? What will the environment gain?

The LCFS definition of "conventional" was also questionable. The regulation listed three different methods of recovery under that term, but fuels from the oil sands were labelled non-conventional and grouped with oil from shale and liquid fuels derived from coal and gas. These last two methods are still in the early stages of development. The oil sands process is already mainstream, with a record of sharp reduction in carbon emissions during production, and the emissions level per barrel produced continues to drop year by year. Grouping oil sands production with coal-to-liquid experiments is simply not realistic.

The LCFS was unbalanced in other ways as well. Within days of the proposal being announced, the biofuels lobby in the United States objected to the methods of measuring their product's impact and convinced California to modify its rules and favour the use of ethanol.

An even bigger problem with LCFS was the overall feasibility of the concept. If the goal was truly to reduce GHG in internal-combustion vehicles, the focus should not have been exclusively on the source of the fuel because 70 to 80 percent of all GHG is produced in the combustion chambers of engines, not in the sourcing and refining of the fuel. The best way to lower carbon emissions from road traffic would be to improve fuel efficiency and dramatically lower the number of kilometres driven by each car and truck every year, perhaps by providing better public transit. Yet nothing in the LCFS would put more electric cars on the road (assuming this would produce a net benefit) or encourage more people to ride rapid transit.

But the most cynical and distressing aspect of the whole exercise was California's decision to exempt heavy crude oil produced within the state from the same penalties and restrictions imposed on oil sands petroleum. This exemption was awarded despite the fact that the production of California heavy crude generates more GHG than the production of an equal volume of oil from the oil sands.[3] When this was pointed out to the California regulators, their response was basically, "So what?" All politics are local, and in the case of California's environmental regulations local means state-wide. But this action raises a legitimate question. Is California more interested in reducing GHGs or in bolstering its own state-based petroleum producers?

California's less-than-objective approach failed to prevent other jurisdictions from emulating its actions. A group of northeastern American states—Connecticut, Maine, Massachusetts, New Hampshire, New Jersey, New York, Rhode Island and Vermont—employed LCFS as a standard for imposing similar restrictions in their region and urged the federal government to pass national legislation supporting the same effort. They were followed by several Midwestern states suggesting similar legislation, and all of them singled out the oil sands as a source of carbon-intensive fuel.

No one, it appears, gave much credence to the increasing proportion of heavier grades of crude oil from "conventional" fuel sources, which require processing almost as energy intensive (and carbon dioxide–producing) as oil sands–derived fuel. Nor was it sufficiently emphasized that most GHG production derives not from producing the fuel but from burning it within internal-combustion engines. Reduce the GHG level in the production phase of petroleum to zero and the resulting fuel will still produce exactly the amount of GHG per litre as any fuel from any location and any production process. The product of the combustion process will account, on average, for 80 percent of the wells-to-wheels GHG volume no matter what the source of the crude oil.

I don't know if the LCFS is dead or merely on life support at this point. I know that many states that initially applauded the move are rethinking their plans, waiting for California to shape LCFS into something that will achieve its overall objective instead of just creating impressive headlines for politicians.

IN Canada, I don't believe we need a low-carbon fuel standard or any version of such a program as badly as we need a national energy strategy. With a well-devised and widely supported strategy to assess the country's energy requirements ten, twenty and fifty years down the road, we could determine the mix of proven and potential energy sources needed. Targets and goals for lower GHG levels would form an integral part of the mix, enabling everyone to review how energy is both produced and used. With this broad picture in place, an array of key concerns could be defined and addressed—things such as improved vehicle efficiency, better building construction techniques and wider use of mass transit. We should allocate financial and human resources to these goals instead of playing political football with GHG production levels.

The oil sands industry could play much more than a cheerleading role because it is able to mobilize capital and apply technical expertise to drive the transition. Its participation would become even more crucial within a cooling economy, when the substantial capital needed to stimulate innovation begins to dry up. The industry could also act in persuading the public to make whatever changes are required, and in getting consumers to evaluate and ultimately embrace new ideas that are likely to develop.

If individuals and leaders in industry or politics are serious about reducing GHG, we can take actions that appear small on their own but that collectively make a far bigger impact than banishing the oil sands or limiting the petroleum production. We can all drive smaller cars and choose energy-efficient appliances. I also support a fair and reasonable tax on carbon consumption, providing that the revenues collected do not flow into the general revenue stream but are directly applied to related activities such as supporting energy-reduction programs, expanding rapid transit systems and developing additional ways to move society away from fossil fuels in the long term. Industries can keep making use of resources more efficient, as Suncor Energy did when it invested millions of dollars to raise its recycled water use in oil sands production employing in situ technology from 94 to 96 percent, with the continuing goal of getting as close to 100 percent as technologically possible.

Most of all, the petroleum industry must begin assuming a more positive stance. Reality-based optimism always trumps gloom. Demands from governments, NGOs, the media and private citizens may interrupt our focus on business, but they cannot be disregarded or met with knee-jerk dismissal. Over my years in this business I witnessed many instances when the industry rejected a challenge only to find that the new standards could be met with much less cost and effort than originally claimed.

This occurred when governments banned lead from gasoline and insisted on much lower levels of sulphur in various fuels. The four words heard too often from people within the industry were "It can't be done," but it was done eventually, and usually at less cost than originally projected. It's reminiscent of the naysaying response from American auto manufacturers ordered in the 1970s to increase the efficiency of their vehicles and yield more miles per gallon. When Japanese car makers Honda, Toyota and Nissan announced they had developed technology that achieved the goals without sacrificing reliability or power, the U.S. domestic manufacturers had to quickly backtrack. Of course, you can't cry wolf over and over and still maintain your credibility when the demands are eventually met—and they usually are.

The oil sands are the largest, most conspicuous industrial site in Canada. Most Canadians, I believe, take pride in what is being accomplished there, and benefit at least indirectly from the money the project generates. Along with this pride comes an expectation for oil sands operators to do better, and it's true—we can do better. We are already doing an enormous job reducing our carbon footprint, cutting our overall energy and water needs, and protecting and restoring the environment. But there is no finish line to this race. I have great faith in the engineering expertise and expanding technology associated with oil sands operators. When we are handed a challenge we should meet it not by claiming that it can't be done but by reviewing our methods and searching for ways to better them. Given enough effort, I'm sure improvements will be found more often and more easily than we expect.

It's in the interests of everyone associated with the industry to take this attitude. Because we all know what happened to the boy who cried wolf once too often.

15. The Legendary Two-Jawed Fish

I consider myself a fairly tolerant guy. My theory is that it would be a very dull world if everybody held the same opinions as Rick George on every subject.

Thanks to my training as an engineer, however, I tend to value facts over speculation. I'll listen to every opinion tossed my way, but when it gets down to taking action I prefer to have it backed with reality than with supposition. I share the opinion of environmentalists who want to protect national parks and wilderness areas from encroachment and pollution. We find ourselves on common ground there, particularly after I suggest that I have probably spent more nights in a tent than anyone else in the room. I want my children and their children to sample the same joy of exploring nature that I have all my life. I want them to breathe clean air and drink pure water, and I want them to grow up with access to and respect for all the precious natural resources of this country.

I also like to point out that it needn't be, and rarely is, a matter of Us versus Them. There is no contradiction between being an employee in the oil sands industry and being concerned about the environment, just as environmentalists should not contradict support for an industrialized capitalist society. Some environmentalists and I part company regarding the degree to which industrial development is permitted to disturb open lands, but that's a continuing dialogue

I not only respect but treasure. The meetings I have held with environmentalists offered an opportunity to exchange ideas and viewpoints, and the distance between us was rarely insurmountable on all fronts. Eventually we would join company on the importance of setting and enforcing regulations to limit the impact of industrial development and ensuring that the land is returned as closely as possible to its original state.

In too many instances, though, criticism of the oil sands is so far off base that its premises and conclusions are almost laughable to anyone with the most basic knowledge of the facts. When delivered by a pseudo-celebrity like former U.S. vice-president Al Gore, however, the message is accepted as unquestioned gospel in some quarters.

In 2009 Gore had the audacity to make this bald-faced statement: "Gasoline made from tar sands gives a Toyota Prius the same impact on climate as a Hummer using gasoline made from oil."[1] I'll overlook the suggestion that gasoline from the oil sands is made from something besides oil and deal with the fantasy that gasoline originating in northern Alberta can turn a Prius into a Hummer where carbon levels are concerned.

GM never released gas consumption figures for its original Hummer models, although one credible site suggests that 24 litres per hundred kilometres (10 mpg) is a reasonable expectation for a combination of city and highway driving.[2] Toyota declares that the owner of a Prius can expect more than 3.8 litres per hundred kilometres (50 mpg) under similar conditions.[3] Does producing oil from bitumen generate five times as much carbon as pulling oil out of the ground in Saudi Arabia or anywhere else in the world? No. It produces perhaps 10 percent more, not 500 percent more. That's either a major mistake or a substantial exaggeration by someone who is supposedly equipped to deliver facts, not fairy tales.

Fairy tales arise when some of the fiercer advocates of environmental protection invent an idea that they cannot support with available facts, so they create their own data instead. This approach exists in the murky ground between gross exaggeration and absolute falsehood when it comes to the oil sands. Much has been made of the impact of oil sands operations on the Athabasca River, for example, with some critics claiming that carcinogenic materials were routinely being dumped or were leaching into the water, causing horrific health problems to First Nations people living downstream. But those substances all occur naturally in bitumen, and bitumen had been leaching into the Athabasca for several millennia before anyone even considered drawing crude oil from the region.

A report that generated waves of outrage against the oil sands was issued in the *Proceedings of the National Academy of Sciences of the United States of America (PNAS)*, a publication associated with Stanford University.[4] The study measured the levels of various elements upriver and downriver from the oil sands to discover if there were any differences. It made a point of distinguishing the levels of these materials in winter and summer, noting that they were significantly higher in winter.

The *PNAS* report created a good deal of interest from people such as David Suzuki, who built an hour's worth of coverage around it in an episode of the CBC television show *The Nature of Things*. Much of the attention generated by the report focused on the group's leader, University of Alberta professor David Schindler, a long-term critic of the oil sands. The list of pollutants measured in the report appears disturbing at first glance: mercury, lead, arsenic, nickel, silver, copper, cadmium, chromium and zinc. Nobody wants these materials in their air or water, yet all of them are produced to a certain extent by every motor vehicle on the road. They also exist naturally in soil and water. The critical factor here is not their presence but their concentration. And in many instances the amounts were below the measurement capability of the instruments used by the researchers. The instruments could detect some pollutants but were unable to confirm that they were anywhere near hazardous levels.

Presence alone does not equal risk, and levels too small to be measured by sophisticated scientific instruments are hardly grounds for the kind of overstated comments that appeared in the media. Dr. Schindler himself did not speculate on the health hazards, if any, these levels represented. This did not prevent some news sources from declaring that the substances were present, as they have been for probably millions of years, without noting that similar levels can be found in any urban centre anywhere in the world.

Dr. Schindler himself called the results "kind of boring."[5] I wish some environmentalists and the media had seen it that way. The Sierra Club almost shouted, "New study links tar sands and carcinogens." The CBC claimed, "Oil sands adding carcinogens to Athabasca River." *The Globe and Mail*'s coverage pointed out that "some levels exceeded those recommended by Alberta or Canada for the protection of aquatic life"[6] but failed to note that the report stated no drinking water guidelines had been exceeded by any of the pollutants in the study and that Dr. Schindler had made no reference to specific health hazards represented by any of the contaminants.

My sense is that the researchers were aware not only of the limited impact the materials were having on the health of local residents but also that the materials would continue to enter the river and its tributaries as long as bitumen remained in the drainage area—whether or not oil sands production continued.

Various groups in Canada and the United States that see the oil sands as a huge problem delighted in the PNAS report, although the report itself drew no conclusions regarding the levels of materials in the water and the health risk they may represent. These groups also discounted a report addressing similar issues, which was published almost simultaneously by the Royal Society of Canada (RSC).[7] The RSC expert panel consisted of ten scholars from major Canadian

universities whose fields of study included analytical and environmental toxicology, land reclamation, re-vegetation and restoration
ecology, hydrogeology, environmental and occupational health and
other disciplines pertinent to the subject.

Here are key findings from the RSC report's executive summary, according to the defined objectives:

> Feasibility of reclamation and adequacy of financial secu-
> rity: . . . sustainable uplands reclamation is achievable and
> ultimately should be able to support traditional land uses.

> Impacts of oil sands contaminants on downstream residents:
> There is currently no credible evidence of environmental
> contaminant exposures reaching Fort Chipweyan at levels
> expected to cause elevated human cancer rates.[*]

> Impacts on population health in Wood Buffalo: There is
> population level evidence that residents of the Regional
> Municipality of Wood Buffalo (RMWB) experience a range
> of health indicators, consistent with "boom town" impacts
> and community infrastructure deficits, which are poorer than
> those of a comparable Alberta region and national averages.

> Impacts on regional water supply: Current industrial water
> use demands do not threaten the viability of the Athabasca
> River system if the water management framework developed

---

* In the detailed portion of the executive summary, the report stated, "There is no credible evidence to
support the commonly repeated media accounts of excess cancer in Fort Chipweyan being caused by
contaminants released by oil sands operations, notably polycyclic aromatic hydrocarbons (PAH) and arsenic.
In particular, common references to PAHs in relation to human cancer risk have been loose and inconsistent
with the scientific understanding of human cancer risk from this class of compounds" (12).

to protect in-stream ecosystem flow needs is fully implemented and enforced.

Impacts on regional water quality and ground water quality: Current evidence on water quality impacts on the Athabasca River system suggests that oil sands development activities are not a current threat to aquatic ecosystem viability. . . .

Tailings pond operation and reclamation: Technologies for improved tailings management are emerging but the rate of improvement has not prevented a growing inventory of tailings ponds. . . .

Impacts on ambient air quality: The current ambient air quality monitoring data for the region show minimal impacts from oil sands development on regional air quality except for noxious odour emission problems over the past two years.

Impacts on greenhouse gas emissions (GHG): Progress has been made by the oil sands industry in reducing its GHG emission per barrel of bitumen produced. Nonetheless, increasing GHG emissions from growing bitumen production creates a major challenge for Canada to meet our international commitments for overall GHG emission reduction that current technology options do not resolve.

It's not a perfect report card. The authors felt that land reclamation was not keeping pace with the rate of land disturbance and expressed concern about control of NOx (nitrous oxides) and "regional acidification potential." The industry has and will continue to reduce GHG emissions per barrel of oil produced, and the size and number of tailings ponds will decline in proportion to the increase in production in situ, as will other expressed sources of concern. The reference to boom town impacts included "general price inflation, extreme housing shortages, labour shortages in most sectors, family stress, drug and alcohol abuse, increased crime and other social negative impacts." These are serious matters, and various agencies within and beyond Suncor continue to address them.

I saw much coverage of the PNAS report, some of it bordering on hysteria and some of it based on baloney. The hysteria was strange, because the PNAS report did not link any health risks to the low levels of compounds found downstream from the oil sands operations. I saw almost no coverage of the RSC report because, I assume, it was even more "boring" than Schindler's study.

Earlier, much was made of the discovery of a "malformed" fish pulled from the Athabasca River by a member of the Mikesew Cree First Nation band and presented to various media representatives. The fish appeared to have been born with two sets of jaws, precisely the kind of horrifying deformity that appears to define the risks of industrial pollution. Only when the fish was closely examined by a retired biology professor was it reported that the second mouth was no deformity. The fish had been dead for some time, and the additional "mouth" was the result of decomposition, not genetic abnormality.[8]

It's true that other samples of fish from the Athabasca revealed lesions and tumours, including one displayed by Dr. Schindler, but these were attributed to natural leaching of various elements from the bitumen embedded in the oil sands. Many people remain unaware of this fact. Meanwhile, those who shuddered at the "two-jawed fish" recall it very clearly—proof that fancy often overrides facts.

IT'S not unusual for reports from qualified sources to reach different conclusions in their findings. The PNAS and RSC reports do not fall into this category because their procedures, goals and focus differed. It's important to note, however, that the reports do not contradict each other. The PNAS study set out to find if the levels of various naturally occurring compounds were measurably higher downriver from the oil sands than upriver. They were. No big surprise, although the study made no attempt to connect the findings precisely with the activities of oil sands producers or to determine if the downstream levels represented a threat to health. Approaching the same question from a different direction, the RSC report was designed to determine if activities by the oil sands industry, including the levels of materials measured by David Schindler and his staff, represented a risk to health. It discovered that, for the most part, they did not.

None of this prevented people from continuing to make outrageous claims about the safety of the oil sands and their impact on the environment, even when their only qualification for commenting was a recognizable name and face. Actor Daryl Hannah managed to get herself arrested in front of the White House in the summer of 2011 for protesting against construction of the proposed Keystone XL pipeline. I assume that many people who neither knew nor cared about either the pipeline or the oil sands were drawn to the story of her arrest based on recognition of her name. If that was the case and they read beyond the headlines to absorb some of her reasons for protesting, they were unknowingly being fed a litany of exaggerated claims and questionable "facts."

Here are the statements[*] she delivered to U.S. media sources, followed by accurate responses that no one in the United States, to my knowledge, employed to repudiate her claims:

---

[*] CBC News reviewed Ms. Hannah's criticisms about the oil sands and found serious faults with each of her statements (Mark Gollom, "Analysis: Examining 5 Oil Sands Claims by Daryl Hannah," *CBC News*, September 2, 2011, www.cbc.ca/news/canada/story/2011/09/01/daryl-hannah-oil-sands.html).

"It's well documented that the tar sands itself is one of the world's largest ecological atrocities and disasters."

If she meant the existence of a trillion barrels or so of bitumen within a wilderness setting, she may have had a point—but an empty one. The sands have been there for a few million years, after all. I suspect, however, that she was referring to the development of the oil sands by Suncor and other firms as a means of providing North Americans with petroleum-based energy.

The RSC report compared a number of industries with the oil sands and found that, as an industry, the oil sands ranked fifth for mercury, sixth for cadmium, and eighth for lead and some carcinogenic pollutants. These rankings made no reference to the actual volume of pollutants released, which continues to measure well below the acceptable level set by various government regulators. RSC members also added, "The claim by some critics of the oil sands indicate that it is the most environmentally destructive project on earth is not supported by the evidence."

"The contribution [of the oil sands] to the carbon in the atmosphere is unprecedented."

According to the RSC, the entire oil sands operation contributes perhaps 5 percent of Canada's total carbon emissions. Sounds like a lot, but the report also noted that fossil-fuelled electric power generation in Canada contributes 16 percent of carbon emissions, and transportation services add 27 percent. How does the oil sands contribution possibly qualify as unprecedented?

"I've been hearing about how many people have cancer that live downstream from the tar sands project."

Whoever Ms. Hannah was listening to did not include physicians and researchers from Alberta Health Services. In 2006 a physician claimed he had diagnosed several cases of a rare form of bile cancer in the village of Fort Chipewyan and immediately blamed emissions from oil sands operations. This became rich fodder for every critic, and soon headlines around the world were trumpeting stories about the carcinogenic impact of the oil sands.

The news was personally unsettling to me. If our oil sands production was responsible for elevated cancer rates, I wanted to know about it. The doctor's claims were taken seriously enough to warrant a detailed study of cancer rates in the area, conducted by Alberta Health Services. The findings confirmed a slight rise in the rate of biliary cancers—three confirmed cases over twelve years—compared with the general population. Other cancers were measured at or below expected levels. The physician conducting the tests wrote "I believe the community should be reassured that numbers are not as high as reported. These results were based on a small number of cases—there is no cause for alarm."[9] He recommended continued monitoring of the situation, and I totally agreed.

The study, launched by Alberta Health Services, was reviewed by independent cancer experts in Australia, New Zealand and the United States, as well as two Canadian First Nations researchers, one recommended by a health board in Fort Chipewyan. All agreed on the study's statistical exactness and general validity.

"[The oil sands have] poisoned everyone who's lived downstream."

I find it unacceptable that no one seriously challenged this statement. One more finding from the RSC report: "Environmental contaminants at current levels of exposure are unlikely to cause major health impacts for the general population." The report added that projected emissions levels were not likely to change that prospect.

Hollywood personalities are one thing, but from time to time sources with impressive credentials make claims that reveal a distinct bias against the oil sands—a bias that the scientific evidence fails to support. James Hansen of Columbia University has made many unreasonable claims about the oil sands and other carbon sources. Some have been contentious enough to make his supporters disassociate themselves from him.[10] They have been upset, for example, about his demand that U.S. President Barack Obama and Secretary of State Hillary Clinton be placed under citizen's arrest on charges of violating the Security Act if they give the go-ahead to construction of the Keystone XL pipeline.

Hansen has taken facts and twisted them to support his position. He did this in a paper titled "Silence Is Deadly," submitted to Congress and placed on the Columbia University website in June 2011.[11] In it he claims that the oil sands contain an estimated four hundred gigatonnes of carbon. When released into the atmosphere, this amount of carbon would add about two hundred parts per million of carbon dioxide to the atmosphere, elevating the atmospheric level accordingly. If this occurred, he warns, it would be "essentially game over." His original statement indicated "game over for stabilizing the climate," but most media coverage phrased it as "game over for the climate."

Hansen's projection implies that the elevation of carbon dioxide from the use of oil originating in the oil sands would occur in one sudden emergence of carbon from the soil, an impossibility. At a daily oil sands production rate of five million barrels of oil, it would take more than a millennium to extract, process, burn and release all that carbon into the air. That's an annual release of one-thousandth of the carbon he is referring to. Every grade nine science student knows that carbon dioxide is absorbed by living vegetation, which uses it to sustain itself and, in the process, emits oxygen. Whatever imbalance were to occur over the next thousand years, the impact from the oil sands based on Hansen's premise would be too small to measure, yet his claim no doubt generated at least mild panic among some.

I understand those who find themselves disturbed by photos and headlines about the oil sands, and by the environmental impact of the petroleum industry generally. Before they use a high profile to repeat questionable comments as though they were facts, however, I would like to see some effort to pursue the truth. And while I don't agree with the strategy, I understand that environmental activists appreciate the need to hit people over the head verbally to get their attention. Saying that the earth is getting warmer would not have been enough to sway public opinion sufficiently to inspire protest marches and attention-getting headlines. Identifying a demon such as the oil sands, and claiming, as Hansen did, that life on earth may be doomed if they continue operating, was both over the top and effective.

I have little regard, however, for people of any political stripe or personal agenda whose lifestyles and values are in direct opposition to the lecture they deliver to others with great passion. This is called hypocrisy, and no one has demonstrated that particular trait with greater audacity where the oil sands are concerned than Hollywood movie director James Cameron.

Cameron is a master at creating epic presentations on a massive scale, and I admire him for that. His movies—among them *Aliens, Titanic* and, of course, *Avatar*—were fine entertainment, earning him piles of money and great acclaim. This success appears to have convinced him that he has a duty to influence a major industry in his native country (he was born in Canada, leaving for the United States at age seventeen), tossing potentially tens of thousands of people out of work while flaunting with great display the polar opposite of his sermon.

For those of you unfamiliar with the details, Cameron arrived in Alberta in 2011 at the invitation of a former band chief in

Fort Chipweyan. Before coming to the province, Cameron had declared the oil sands a "Pandora" and "a black eye for Canada," generally condemning their operation and management. He also stated, "I think it's the wrong solution for us to be doing greater and greater environmental damage, pursuing a dead-end paradigm which is fossil fuels instead of spending those billions . . . on building wind turbines. Those same areas are a great wind belt and we could be generating . . . wind energy out of the same place. Why aren't we doing that?"[12] He chose not to speak to me or to any other CEO engaged in oil sands production. Instead, he took a helicopter tour of the oil sands, met with Alberta Premier Ed Stelmach and received the kind of fawning attention from the media, including television networks CTV and CBC, traditionally offered to Hollywood royalty. I will say that he came to the oil sands with a more open view than some of the press reports suggested.

His widest coverage in Canada was an hour-long interview with CBC news anchor Peter Mansbridge, who in my opinion tossed softballs for Cameron to catch. I don't believe in bad manners anywhere or toward anyone, and I'm not suggesting that Mansbridge should have exposed Cameron for his hypocrisy. I wish, however, that he had provided an opportunity for the director to reveal some of the more blatant contradictions in his attitude on his own, by asking questions such as "How many houses do you own?" Cameron owns three homes in Malibu, totalling about 2,200 square metres, or 24,000 square feet, ten times the area of an average U.S. home. None has solar panels, windmills or any other energy-saving device. All appear to rely on electric power for heating, cooling and lighting. About half of all electricity generated in California is produced by either coal or natural gas. California cannot produce enough electricity on its own, however, so it imports enormous amounts from other states, most of them using coal as a fuel on a much bigger scale than California. Cameron also owns a forty-hectare ranch in Santa Barbara.[13] The carbon-offset payments Cameron has made appear to be a means for him to assuage his conscience, but they do not neutralize the hypocrisy of his sermon. Here are some other questions Mansbridge might have asked.

> *"How do you travel between your home, your ranch and other locations?"*

Cameron owns a JetRanger helicopter. He also owns a fleet of cars, motorcycles and submarines, a Humvee fire truck and, of course, a yacht.

> *"How did you get to Alberta from your home in California?"*

He flew there in his private jet.

> *"What have you done to persuade American states that produce electricity from coal-burning turbines to move to a fuel source that releases lower levels of contaminants into the air, including GHG?"*

I don't know of any activity on his part beyond using this as a theme in his movie *Avatar.*

> *"What did you say to the* Los Angeles Times *in 2010 regarding how the world must deal with energy in future years?"*

This one I know. He replied, "We're going to have to live with less."[14]

♦

JAMES Cameron can live in any style he chooses. But I think he should assess his own values and their impact on the world before he proposes that others "live with less" and attacks an industry affecting 33 million Canadians, including the 100,000 or so who rely on the oil sands, directly and indirectly, for their livelihood.

I have the greatest respect for people who give a lot of thought to aspects of life that concern them, and whose actions reflect the values and concerns they express. I find it more difficult to admire someone who lectures the world about living with less while maintaining an extravagant lifestyle. Such hypocrisy weakens not only Cameron's position on the oil sands but also his status as a credible commentator.

16. The Promise of Alternative Fuels

Whenever someone says to me, "We need to shut down the oil sands" I reply, "That's an interesting idea."

I don't reject the demand outright or go into a defensive mode about the need for this resource or the environmental advances the industry has made. Instead, I usually refer to the triple bottom line philosophy of satisfying economic, social and environmental concerns, pointing out that you cannot seriously alter one of the three elements without making a serious impact on the other two. For example, what kind of impact would eliminating 100,000 jobs and the royalties earned from the oil sands have on Canada's ability to support various social programs and keep tax levels at a reasonable rate? Which would be better: to ensure that the oil sands make a minimal impact on the environment and fund the development of alternative sources of energy, or to shut them down entirely?

My reply disarms oil sands critics to some degree because they expect a passionate defence. It also leads to serious discussion about the implications of not only abandoning the oil sands but of ditching the entire concept of petroleum as a source of energy. I also suggest that any consideration of the issue must extend beyond our own borders to include the 1.5 billion people who have no access to electric power. Electricity isn't a matter of convenience or a luxury that enables us to watch television or have a reliable source of light in our homes. It is often a matter of survival itself.

People in areas of Africa, for example, must walk for hours to reach a source of drinkable water instead of being able to draw it through pumps at wells in their village. During an emergency, it is difficult for them to call for help. The lack of electricity means that many of the basic aspects of life that we in the industrialized world take for granted are simply not available. Whenever I met with powerful environmental groups and mentioned the need to assist other regions of the world, I would note how millions of children die each year because they do not have access to clean water. The discussion usually went nowhere. People like Al Gore don't want to discuss how to make life better for these people; they want only to deal with banning the oil sands. Yet there is a link between cheap available power and the solution to that tragic death toll.

The world, and especially North America, runs on relatively cheap energy, and in most places petroleum-based fuels are the least expensive and reliable sources. They also tend to be the focus of environmentalists seeking to move society away from its dependence on fossil fuels and to ban or at least severely restrict their use. Surely this is not the best route to follow, given society's currently enormous dependence on petroleum. We should be widening the sources of energy, not limiting them. Instead of crossing petroleum off the list, we should be finding a way to reduce its carbon footprint while we search for renewable alternatives that will perform with the same efficiency at comparable cost.

Many advocates of shutting down the oil sands and dropping our "addiction" to oil enthusiastically embrace alternative energy as the solution. Well, it's not the solution yet. Not in 2012, or in the next ten years or in the foreseeable future. That is not the voice of skepticism. It's the voice of experience.

In 1997, I suggested to the board of directors that we change the company name to Suncor Energy and rationalize that change by investing in other energy sources, including biofuels and wind power. I also recommended that we commit the company to pursuing new concepts for energy production, distribution and use. The program that became our venture into alternative and renewable energy sources, Parallel Paths, aimed to make Suncor as energy efficient and environmentally impact-free as possible, while actively developing renewable energy sources to replace fossil fuels. It took a powerful sales pitch to convince both the directors and the shareholders that this was a good idea, but I eventually succeeded. I wanted to be able to say that Suncor had made a difference, and that our focus was on producing energy generally, not oil sands–based petroleum exclusively.

I also wanted to move beyond the rhetoric and panic on both sides. Environmentalists were making claims about climate change that I believed to be at least overstated and at times outrageous. Meanwhile, many leaders in the oil industry were growing defensive and inflexible, putting all their energy into deflecting the charges instead of solving the problem. "If we talk more slowly and more loudly, and produce better PowerPoint presentations, we can get our point across" was the attitude.

My anti-herd mentality kicked in. Unprepared to join either side in the battle, I talked to Gord Lambert, our vice-president for sustainable development. "Everybody seems to be panicking over climate change," I said. "Where is the opportunity side of this issue for us?"

After giving the question some thought, Gord proposed that we begin pursuing less carbon-intensive forms of energy on a much wider scale than we had in the past. "We have to change the energy system to reflect a need for renewables," Gord emphasized. From out of that talk we developed a program to invest $100 million over the next five years to enter the renewable energy side of our business. We named Gerry Manwell, who had played a key role in the success of our Millennium project, vice-president for renewable energy business development.

This proved to be one instance when I felt a need to break our policy of not blowing our own horn. We announced the $100 million commitment as a declaration of how serious we were about the venture and, perhaps, to inspire our peers to take similar action. Unfortunately, the move generated little more than skepticism from other oil and gas companies in Canada. The investment community, which I thought would be most likely to question the wisdom of our move, had no comment either way.

Meanwhile, Gord Lambert was instrumental in forming the Clean Air Renewable Energy (CARE) Coalition. Jointly started with the Pembina Institute, CARE grew to include an eclectic mix of stakeholders and openly described itself as "a counter-intuitive group of strange bedfellows" who were asked to "check your biases at the door" whenever they gathered together.

This was no window dressing created more for good PR than for practical progress. The group consisted of a truly mixed bag of organizations, ranging from Suncor, TransAlta and ConocoPhillips Canada to Friends of the Earth, the Federation of Canadian Municipalities, Pollution Probe, World Wildlife Fund Canada and the Toronto Environmental Alliance. To use a sports analogy, it was like the Toronto Maple Leafs, the Chicago Bulls, the Los Angeles Dodgers, the Dallas Cowboys and Manchester United getting together to advance the cause of professional sports. Instead of sports, CARE became focused on promoting the growth of wind power energy in Canada.

It made progress. In 2000 barely 150 megawatts of electricity was being generated by wind power. This leaped to 4,862 megawatts in 2011, thanks in large part to CARE's success in persuading the federal government to launch the Wind Power Production

Incentive (WPPI) program, effective from April 2002 to March 2007, which paid one cent per kilowatt hours of electricity generated by wind power. This was sufficient to build momentum that is predicted to result in almost 10,000 megawatts of wind-generated electricity by 2015.[1]

Our first major step on the Parallel Paths route was a joint development launched in 2002 in partnership with Enbridge. Together we created a new entity, Sunbridge, as the investor and operator of twenty wind turbines in Gull Lake, Saskatchewan, that would feed more than 11 megawatts onto the province's electricity grid. The installation was preceded by an assessment of the impact on rare birds and plant life in the area and included a comprehensive environmental review conducted by Saskatchewan Environment and Resource Management (SERM) and Natural Resources Canada. When Gull Lake showed sufficient promise, we began adding other installations in planned stages until, by 2011, Suncor together with various partners had almost 160 wind turbines in operation at various locations across Canada, generating more than 250 megawatts of electricity. This amount of power offsets about 260,000 tonnes of carbon dioxide that would be produced through conventional coal-fired turbines creating the same amount of energy.

The project made us feel good about reducing the company's environmental impact. More than that, it gave us a seat at the table when alternative energy options were being discussed and, in the wider picture, the right to be in the business of reducing to at least a measurable degree the influence of fossil fuels on the environment.

It's easy to envision business people, especially those in the petroleum industry, as caring little about protecting the environment, but if it's possible to keep two diametrically opposed ideas in your mind and recognize the validity of both, it's also possible to favour both the success of business and the pursuit of environmental protection.

It's more than possible; it's a moral necessity for any company with aspirations to act as a good corporate citizen.

Wind turbines use impressive technology to generate electricity, but even with government subsidies they bring the lowest return on investment of all the projects we have funded. It's difficult to earn a profit in the first few years of operation, although assuming a productive life of twenty-plus years for each unit, Suncor will eventually be able to record acceptable financial returns from the investment. For now, the turbines represent a sincere effort to explore and evaluate an energy source other than petroleum, and I am proud of Suncor's leadership in this area.

The investment in wind power and other sources of renewable energy reminds me of the investment required to locate petroleum in conventional deposits. Long before holes are drilled to tap subterranean oil reserves, a lot of research is carried out at great expense and with great effort. By the time the first drill bit grinds its way into the earth, the discovery of oil is almost considered a sure thing. It isn't, of course; the odds still average nine to one against striking oil. I'm not aware of the odds against finding practical alternatives to petroleum for all its energy applications, but so far the comparison remains; it's a long shot, no matter what energy source is being developed.

Following the Parallel Paths strategy, we built Canada's largest ethanol facility, located near Sarnia, Ontario, where 40 million bushels of corn—about 20 percent of Ontario's annual corn crop—is converted annually into ethanol. The residue of the process becomes premium cattle feed, and the corn yields about 400 million litres of ethanol each year, which is blended with Petro-Canada gasoline produced by the nearby Sarnia refinery.

Both wind power and corn ethanol production are fascinating technologies with some net benefits in lowering GHG levels. Suncor earns a small profit from these operations, but neither technology comes close to matching the energy needs of North America, and I can't see any evidence that they will in the foreseeable future. This hasn't prevented many people who are anxious to ditch oil as a source of energy from presenting these and other technologies as reasonable solutions while ignoring the drawbacks of each.

The plain fact is that every source of energy has both costs and benefits, beginning with the sun, the world's ultimate energy source. Spend too much time in its rays and you risk a case of sunburn and even more serious health hazards. This doesn't mean that we should avoid the sun, only that there is no silver bullet that will generate usable energy without an accompanying by-product.

Go back to wind power. In 2011, wind power delivered about 1 percent of the total electric power consumed in North America.[2] If we worked very hard and invested several billion dollars, we might increase this to 2 or 3 percent in ten years. Most environmental groups love wind power, pointing out that it amounts to a "free" source of energy. I like it as well, especially on a purely ecological basis—the wind is free, after all. But the cost to capture its power isn't, and the price is measured beyond dollars invested. The most visible cost, literally, is aesthetic. The sight of one large wind generator is interesting. The view of a field crowded with thirty or forty or more is obtrusive. Everyone, it seems, supports wind power as long as the generators are located somewhere out of their sight.

Wind-powered generators create more than a visual blemish. Along with high-rise office buildings, they can become killers of migrating birds, limiting turbine locations even further. We have also discovered that wind generators are efficient at killing bats. Anyone who appreciates the value of bats in controlling insects will not be happy with this reality.

Ethanol and other biofuels are safer for birds and bats, but they are not a reasonable replacement for petroleum. Unlike petroleum, ethanol is a renewable source of energy, which is its primary

advantage. Elsewhere, its value remains questionable. Burning ethanol in an internal-combustion engine reduces GHG emissions to
some degree if assessed via a life-cycle analysis. One study suggests
that a 10 percent ethanol blend cuts GHG emissions by 4 to 6
percent, and a 100 percent ethanol blend would reduce GHG levels by 40 to 62 percent.[3] This would require, of course, that every
existing motor vehicle be converted to 100 percent ethanol use,
and that all future vehicles be engineered for this fuel. This is not
going to happen, nor will enough corn-based ethanol be produced
to meet the demand because not enough land is available to grow
the corn.

Yet annual production of corn ethanol in the United States rose
from 190 million litres (50 million gallons) in 1979 to 49 billion litres
(13 billion gallons) in 2010. Why the great push on behalf of ethanol?
In two words: politics and money. Governments in the United States
and Canada decreed that ethanol must represent 10 percent of fuel
sold for passenger car use and backed the order with massive subsidies to farmers and producers. In 2010 alone, the U.S. government
provided subsidies of more than US$5.68 billion to support corn
agriculture specifically for processing into ethanol.[4] These enormous levels of ethanol production could not have occurred in an
open market, where price depends on demand and net production
costs. But that's not the most disturbing part of the story because,
once again, the real cost can be measured by the Law of Unintended Consequences.

It took 13 million hectares of U.S. agricultural soil to grow the
corn as raw material for those 49 billion litres of ethanol in 2010,
which is enough land and feedstock to nourish 149 million people
with edible crops. The corn dedicated to ethanol production represented about 40 percent of the total corn crop of the United States
in 2010. Pulling that much land out of production drove up food
prices because farmers recognized that they would get more money

and a far more secure market growing corn destined for ethanol plants than growing crops to feed people. This has become a powerful incentive in certain markets, especially the United States, where recent free trade agreements have reduced or eliminated export markets for American farmers. The federal government's response, with its subsidy for growing corn as a source of ethanol, begins to make economic and political sense. Why pay farmers for not growing products (or not having a market for their harvests) when you can pay them to grow corn destined for ethanol that will reduce the country's reliance on oil imports? And from the farmer's viewpoint, why risk assuming that a market will exist for your food harvest when buyers of ethanol-directed corn are guaranteed?

There is another unintended consequence of cultivating all that corn to produce ethanol. Those 13 million hectares of U.S. land are located for the most part in the Midwest, where almost all the water runoff drains into the Mississippi River. In their effort to maximize yields, many farmers apply large quantities of fertilizer to their crops, often more than is necessary. The excess fertilizer, not absorbed by the plants, finds its way into the Mississippi and downstream to the Gulf of Mexico, where it creates a massive "dead zone." Algae thrive in the zone, using up available oxygen and preventing fish from surviving in large numbers.[5]

It gets worse. If every cornfield in the United States were dedicated to raising crops for use in the production of ethanol exclusively, it would replace less than 14 percent of the annual gasoline consumption in that country. To replace 100 percent of the gasoline consumed in the United States each year would require three times the total agricultural land under cultivation in the United States—leaving, of course, no room for food production.[6]

This is distressing enough, but it becomes even more upsetting with the realization that despite the government subsidies, the loss of farmland for edible food crops and the impending disaster due to fertilizer runoffs, nothing has been achieved. Ethanol is about 61 percent as efficient as gasoline in powering internal-combustion engines, so one-third more of it needs to be burned to generate the same amount of power as burning unadulterated petroleum-based fuel.[7] Where are the net gains?

Perhaps there is a better source of biofuels than corn. Over the years at Suncor Energy, I watched and encouraged various efforts to produce biofuels from sources such as cellulose and algae. None to date has showed promise of success at an acceptable cost while reducing carbon levels associated with their processing. I would never suggest giving up the effort to find a practical process. After all, from 1967 to 1992 many people believed that the oil sands would never become a productive and profitable venture either. I have great faith in technology and am prepared to be surprised, but when it comes to displacing petroleum with biofuels, I am not optimistic in the short term, and the medium term doesn't look much more promising.

In the summer of 2011, Germany launched a program to move away from both fossil fuels and nuclear power toward renewable energy sources. That's an ambitious goal. In 2010 more than 40 percent of the country's electric power was generated by coal-fired plants, 14 percent was generated by natural gas, and almost 23 percent more was based on nuclear energy. About 17 percent of the country's electric power needs were drawn from renewable energy sources, including hydro, biomass, solar, wind and waste power plants.[8] The balance, less than 5 percent, came from miscellaneous sources such as geothermal. As Europe's industrial leader and a country with a long tradition of engineering skills and developments, Germany should be capable of setting a pace well beyond that of other countries with similar goals. So here is the best they can do: in 2011 Chancellor Angela Merkel promised to shut down all of the nation's nuclear plants by 2022 and projected that her country would be generating 80 percent of all its electric power requirements from renewable energy sources by 2050.

"We want to . . . reach the age of renewable energy as fast as possible," Chancellor Merkel stated. She deserves respect for her foresight and determination, but buried within the details are a couple of significant facts.

The first is the timeline. It will take forty years for Germany to reach the goal of moving four-fifths of its electric power needs to renewable energy sources. Merkel demonstrates confidence and independence in breaking the rule that politicians rarely look beyond the next election date when setting goals. On the assumption that Germany can meet this deadline and other countries can match the schedule, we are not going to reduce our consumption of petroleum significantly for almost two generations. That's the timeline we face. And that's from the country perhaps best positioned to set and achieve such a goal, based on its economic power and technical expertise.

The other fact is Germany's annual investment in renewable energy installations, estimated in 2010 at 26.6 billion, or about C$37 billion.[9] I'm not suggesting the investment is not worth it, or that Canadians wouldn't support equivalent expenditures of public money. The forecast expenditures for the oil sands over the next few decades are also substantial, but they will be generated by the sale of petroleum products produced by the facilities. They will also spin off significant taxes and royalties to feed government coffers. How much of Germany's cost to move to renewable energy will be derived from private investors? It's unclear. It is very clear, however, that the move to renewable energy will be expensive and long term, and we should be prepared for it.

I disagree with the chancellor's decision to eliminate nuclear power, but I congratulate her on framing a vision, a goal and a strategy for long-term energy for her country.

◆

THE ultimate solution to drastically cutting the use of petroleum-based fuel, in many people's minds, is the electric automobile. Charging a battery instead of filling a fuel tank for propulsive energy promises a bright new future free of oil. This may well be the most encouraging form of widespread incremental advance on reducing our dependence on petroleum for transportation.

GM introduced its Volt hybrid electric car in late November 2010 with great fanfare and a price approaching $42,000, expensive for a compact car. If you bought one in the province of Ontario, you received about $8,000 as a government incentive, but even at a reduced price of $34,000 the purchase would be based more on impressing your neighbours than on making a dent in gasoline consumption.

The Volt is not a purely electric-powered vehicle; it requires a 1.4-litre gasoline engine to extend its range beyond about sixty kilometres and ensure heat for winter driving and air conditioning in the summer. Should the world switch to hybrid vehicles like the Volt overnight, it would clearly reduce the level of carbon emissions, but it would not eliminate the need for petroleum-based fuels.*

Other cautions have been raised about the growing enthusiasm for hybrid or fully electric-powered vehicles, most related to the manufacturing and disposal of the batteries to power them. They are heavy, expensive to make, and often contain large amounts of toxic materials. And like the batteries in your cellphone or TV remote control, they have a limited life, ranging from five to ten years.

---

* While the Volt garnered a good deal of press coverage following its introduction, initial sales have not been encouraging. Even with a modest 600 units coming off the assembly line each week, production was halted for five weeks beginning in mid-March 2012 while dealer inventories were reduced.

It may be easy to dispose of and even recycle small batteries like the ones you use around the house, but giving the same treatment to vehicle batteries on a large scale will not be so simple. For one thing, they are much more difficult to handle. In addition to weighing as much as 250 kilograms, even depleted automotive batteries may hold enough stored electricity to represent a serious risk to workers. They cannot, of course, be either incinerated or dumped in landfill sites without generating serious pollution, and recycling presents a problem, especially for lithium-ion batteries, the most popular and efficient formulation. In fact, according to one source, it costs five times more to recycle lithium from existing batteries than to mine and refine it from ore.[10]

Recycling vehicle batteries presents an enormous task in the coming years. One authoritative source estimates that the world will be dealing with over half a million units each year by the early 2020s.[11] I have no doubt that the process of retrieving and disposing of vehicle batteries will spawn a large industry, and that technology will improve both the life and efficiency of the batteries. But let's face it: they will require special treatment and place new demands on the environment to one extent or another.

Like the Toyota Prius and others, the Chevrolet Volt has set a pattern and sustained a trend toward hybrid-powered automobiles using small, highly efficient gasoline engines to supplement pure electric power. It's clear to me, and to people who watch the automobile industry closely, that developing and marketing hybrid vehicles represents a wise and beneficial development. No one can quibble about the wisdom of reducing gasoline consumption and emissions.

But one unassailable fact relating to petroleum-powered vehicles remains: the average life of a car in Canada and the United States is now more than ten years. Cars are much better built than in our parents' day, with effective rust proofing and more precise engineering, and they can be kept running efficiently for several hundreds of thousands of kilometres. Unless we are prepared to support an immediate ban on all petroleum-powered vehicles, it will take years for these cars to be replaced by electric power or hybrids. And hybrids will still require gasoline or diesel fuels. This is not an effort to propose that the move to electric power is doomed—just further proof that globally, transportation will depend on petroleum for many years to come.

Even if unforeseen breakthroughs enable the manufacturers of electric-powered vehicles to dispense with internal-combustion engines in favour of plug-and-go designs, their supporters overlook the source of all that power. In Canada during 2010 about 20 percent of electric power was generated by fossil fuels, primarily coal.[12] In the United States fossil fuels accounted for more than 70 percent of electricity generation, and the vast majority of that was coal.[13] Given the influence of the U.S. coal lobby, coal is likely to serve for several more years as the go-to energy when it comes to producing electricity in that country.

If, in an unrealistically short period—say five to ten years— cars in North America became electric powered, where would this power come from? Current electric power generation would be overloaded to the extreme, with more than 100 million electric-powered cars and trucks draining the grid. New power generation facilities will be desperately needed, and based on current knowledge most will burn fossil fuels, primarily coal, which releases far more carbon into the air than petroleum-based fuels.

Nuclear energy is the ultimate clean source of electric power generation, in my opinion, but concerns remain about the disposal of nuclear waste, and even in the best of times it takes decades to bring new nuclear plants on stream. The anti-nuclear lobby is as loud and influential in many states as the anti-petroleum lobby, even though nuclear energy solves more problems than it creates. Much was made of the 2011 Fukushima tsunami and resulting nuclear shutdown, to the point that Japan announced a total move away from nuclear power as a means of generating electricity. But even in that massive disaster none of the catastrophic events predicted came to pass. The basic lesson from that experience was "Don't build nuclear plants on fault lines or near shorelines." Unfortunately, I suspect the near miss will squelch a lot of efforts to construct nuclear generators in the United States for some time.

Until the development and widespread use of solar panels capable of generating several thousand megawatts per installation year round, and the creation of facilities to store and release massive volumes of electricity in the absence of sunlight, solar generation will remain a local source of electric power on a global basis. In Canada the prospect is even less promising. How much electricity will solar power generate in January in a city like Edmonton, which averages barely three hours of sunshine per day? Or in more southerly Toronto, where residents can count on even fewer hours of sunshine per day, on average, during that month?[14][15]

Hydroelectric power is popular in some quarters, and is a major generator of electricity in Ontario and Quebec. On the surface it appears ideal, being both renewable and non-polluting, assuming that a year-round source of flowing water is available. But an assured source of hydroelectric power involves building dams to create reservoirs, backing up the flow of rivers and flooding vast areas of land. Dams and reservoirs have an enormous impact on wildlife, disrupting spawning patterns for fish and migratory trails for caribou and other animals. If an acceptable location for a hydro generating plant is identified, it will almost certainly be several hundred kilometres from the urban centres that will rely on it, requiring a long chain of massive towers marching across the landscape with suspended cables carrying electricity at very high voltages.

In the short and medium term at least, the most promising means of generating electricity may lie with natural gas. The success of this fuel in North America is a direct result of technological advances that are similar to the kinds of advances being made in oil sands production.

Technical advances have made fracking highly efficient, producing a glut of natural gas and a collapse in market price. In 2005 natural gas prices spiked at US$14 per million BTU. By early 2012 they had slid to less than US$3 per million BTU, and natural gas reserves in the United States waiting to be unlocked through fracking technology remain immense—in excess of 2 trillion cubic feet, according to one estimate.[16] Based on current consumption levels, this translates into a supply of seventy-five years or more. With low prices and high reserves, it makes a good deal of sense to convert electricity-generating plants to run on natural gas, a fuel considered far cleaner than coal. We may also see wider use of natural gas in public transportation and fleet vehicles.

While everyone agrees that natural gas is the fossil fuel with perhaps the lowest overall impact on the environment, the fracking process is not without its critics. Forcing liquids under high pressure into layers of shale brings its own share of risks, proving once again that there is no free lunch.

I'm still very much an optimist. The engineers, environmentalists and almost everyone else at Suncor consistently surprised me with the advances they made in cutting our environmental impact while bumping up our productivity, sometimes simultaneously. It all led to reductions in the quantity of water used in production, deep cuts in emissions from all sources of production, restoration of oil sands mining areas after the removal of bitumen and dramatic improvements in the safe handling and transmission of oil.

Meanwhile, other people as bright and dedicated as the Suncor team keep searching for that mythical silver bullet that will deliver the energy the world needs at a price it can afford while creating minimum disturbance to our environment. I, for one, hope they find it.

17. Emphasizing Deeds over Words

It would be impossible to spend twenty years as the CEO of a company as large and dynamic as Suncor without absorbing a great deal of practical knowledge along the way. One of the most important lessons I acquired is an axiom familiar to the construction industry.

It's based on the idea that managing large projects involves three measures and recognizes that you can focus on only two out of the three. Attempting to succeed equally in all three is almost a guarantee of failure. The formula works as well when you're constructing a house as it does when you're building a billion-dollar bitumen upgrader, and you ignore it at your peril.

Here's how it works. You choose two out of the following three measures: schedule, cost and quality. The ones you choose—or, if you prefer, the one you discard—depends on your overall objective. The important point is to focus on just two.

In the inflationary period of 2005 to 2008, when we were busily expanding our Voyageur project, the industry emphasis was to get the project done on schedule. That was fine, but to do so while striving to reach essential quality standards would send the third factor—cost—through the roof. Similarly, with an inflexible schedule and a cap on costs, you had to be prepared for lapses in quality control. We made a decision to focus exclusively on costs and quality, letting the schedule unfold as it would. We would have been pleased to see some aspects of the project come on stream sooner but this would have meant sacrificing quality, which was simply not on the table, or relinquishing control of costs, which were already skyrocketing.

Good management is many things: clear vision, consistent strategy, open communication and so on. It's also, as this three-point formula illustrates, a matter of identifying standards you must achieve and ones you learn to live with.

The approach served us well because we also followed another guideline when establishing our objectives in the expansionary phase. We decided that we would make news with our accomplishments more than with our promises. We achieved a great deal at Suncor from 1991 to 2011, perhaps more than any other corporation of its kind in Canada. We broke new ground in the technology used to recover and process bitumen, we increased our production and decreased our impact on the environment, we boosted revenue dramatically, and we built the company from assets of less than $1 billion to more than $70 billion in the process.

But I preferred to let our actions speak for themselves, and although we eventually made our objectives known, we avoided patting ourselves on the back before we actually got the job done. That's becoming a rare approach in business generally, and in the petroleum business in particular, but I believe it's the best way to operate. I'll admit there's a drawback. As an industry, we have been so busy getting things done that we haven't spent enough time talking about the positive side of things in the oil sands. Nature abhors a vacuum anywhere, including the arena of public opinion. There has been a vacuum of understanding about the true nature of the oil sands, and this has made it easy for people to accept erroneous or outdated claims about our operations there. I have no doubt that when more people understand how the oil sands fill a need that is simply not going to vanish overnight, they will appreciate the crucial role the project plays in the economy of Canada, the United States and elsewhere.

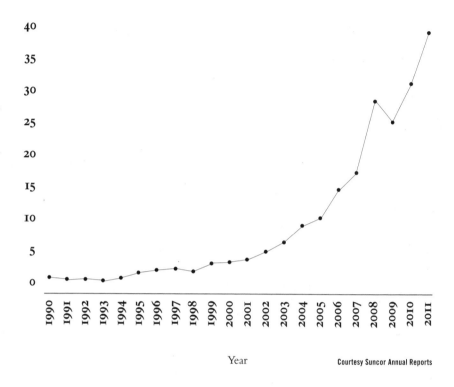

Courtesy Suncor Annual Reports

Fig. 3. Suncor's total revenue

Hard work by the Suncor team let us grow the company's revenue in spectacular fashion, along with its capital value. (By mid-2011, the firm was the second-largest by capitalization in the country and had long surpassed the value of its U.S. parent.)

The progress I witnessed over my twenty years in the oil sands is almost too extensive and complex to explain in detail. It's enough to say that we are doing more with less—more oil from the bitumen and less impact on the environment—than anyone, including me, could have dreamed possible back in 1992. And it's not over. Advances that no one can foresee will be made over the next twenty years, removing most of the concerns that disturb environmentalists.

They will be made in part because the equipment and processes employed at the oil sands have been refined over the years to deliver, among other qualities, far higher standards of reliability. The kinds of breakdowns that plagued Suncor and other operators for so many years have become rare, and the time once spent on keeping the equipment running can now be invested in ensuring that the same equipment runs more efficiently.

Some steps will demand that the culture of our business change first, especially when the reduction of energy use is involved. When you're awash in a substance, it's difficult to remind yourself to conserve it. The oil sands, like the rest of the petroleum industry, produces the world's primary source of energy in daily volumes measured by millions of barrels. So while every oil sands worker may be aware of the need to do more work with less energy, it's difficult to put this idea into practice to the extent that's required. We dramatically reduced the volume of water needed to generate a barrel of oil from the oil sands. The next stage is to make similar reductions to the amount of energy required, and this will arrive with a shift in the culture. We're already making strides in that direction, and more progress will be made as the importance of energy conservation becomes deeply ingrained.

I hope to see another shift among other oil sands firms that do a good job but don't always share the sense of united dedication to quality performance that's needed to offset global criticism. In 2009, we took a step to address this when we proposed the need to establish an operational standard for firms participating in the oil sands, perhaps through an umbrella organization that could encourage and promote the advances being made in production, energy conservation and environmental protection. Steve Williams, now Suncor CEO, and Gord Lambert, VP of Sustainable Development, roughed out an idea for the organization and called it the Oil Sands Leadership Initiative (OSLI). Members of OSLI would lead the way in decisions to protect the environment, pay attention to social needs, post good economic performance and develop major technical advances.

This would be an elite group no matter how you measured it. We didn't want empty gestures or PR. We were looking for companies that were setting the pace in the industry. By assuming responsibility for the highest standards of performance in the oil sands, we would share our knowledge, experience and innovative ideas to accelerate change across the entire industry. When OSLI was launched in 2010 the founding partners included Suncor, ConocoPhillips, Nexen, Statoil Canada and Total E&P Canada.

OSLI represented the kind of enterprise the oil sands industry needed to generate real advances. I was so sold on the premise that I mentioned the organization in an address to the 2010 World Energy Congress in Montreal. Pointing out that OSLI was composed of progressive oil sands producers with a focus on innovations leading to improved overall performance, I said we were actively looking for ways to achieve a zero-carbon footprint and perhaps waterless extraction.

My description of OSLI earned general approval from the audience, but my suggestion that it represented a serious commitment to innovation and bold thinking was unflattering to firms that were not members of the group. Their reaction prompted a reassessment of that concept, and we began taking steps to open OSLI to other companies that support its goals. We also began sharing our TRO technology for effectively handling tailings ponds with all the companies engaged in oil sands production.

If nothing else, the experience demonstrated the importance of deeds over words when it comes to improving both the performance and the optics of the oil sands. OSLI, whose strategy is based on taking positive measures rather than issuing defensive responses to critics, has helped achieve widespread technological advances far faster and more efficiently than could have been imagined a few years ago.

The industry needs to make these kinds of advances, which generate real benefits to all sectors because the oil sands continue to come under attack by organizations and corporations concerned primarily with promoting their own interests and image. This became apparent with announcements from consumer firms such as Chiquita and others that they would boycott petroleum products derived from oil sands crude. The futility of tracking the origins of gasoline and diesel fuel from its retail distributor back to the original source soon became apparent to these firms, and they quietly backtracked. They were dealing, after all, with a commodity whose origins from day to day are as likely to be Saudi Arabia, Nigeria or Venezuela as the oil sands. Their actions qualified for the term *greenwash* as an attempt to curry favour with consumers without necessarily living up to their intent.*

Among the firms reacting to these pressures was Virgin Airlines. Instead of falling into lockstep with NGOs that insisted it boycott jet fuel originating from the oil sands, the company dispatched people to Calgary to investigate the situation for themselves. With the realization that it was impossible to purchase jet fuel anywhere in Canada west of Montreal not derived from oil sands crude, or to ensure that fuels sourced from anywhere in North America did not contain an oil sands product, their attitude shifted dramatically. Virgin began working with OSLI to track developments in oil sands production, marking the first of what may become a network of partnerships between OSLI and consumer-based companies to advance and promote environmental improvements in the industry.

◆

---

* The Chiquita banana brand, which generated the most press coverage from its boycott, issued a statement in December 2011 that earlier press reports "inaccurately stated we have boycotted or banned Canadian oil" and that Chiquita "will continue to source Canadian oil" (*Ottawa Citizen*, December 23, 2011).

ONE of the things I love about the petroleum industry is the amazing scale of opportunity it provides. Earlier I mentioned it's a business of big bets, where the market is actually the entire world and where billions of dollars are invested with a quick nod of the head. Yet there is always room among the giants for somebody to shake things up a little while building a company based on little more than a good idea. Large organizations are concerned about growth, of course, but much of their effort is directed toward creating stability and permanence. Start-up companies just want to get into the game and will look for and work at any advantage they can find to do it.

It's not just the nature of the oil business but the nature of large companies generally. The bigger a corporation grows, the more focused it becomes on avoiding, or at least minimizing, risk. Whenever plans are being made by large corporations, an individual or a group is always at hand to say, "But what if . . . ?"—"But what if prices don't rise?" "But what if the equipment doesn't work?"

Suncor and other major players in the industry have come up with great new ideas, but it would be foolish to believe they are the only source of them. From time to time I read reports or heard stories of two or three people who had launched a small company intent on finding a better way to extract bitumen, or process it into crude, or to do one of a hundred different things more efficiently, and I would secretly envy them. Some were strictly promoters with their eye on the profits and nothing new to contribute, but there were not many of these and they rarely succeeded in fooling anyone. In this business it's close to impossible to deceive others about your knowledge and experience. But to sincerely believe you have a better process and be prepared to work 24/7 to make it a success—because time may be the biggest asset you have—is at the core of every entrepreneur. Statistics suggest that the majority won't succeed, and I suspect they are all aware of this. Knowing the odds just makes them work harder.

I estimate that at any given time, there are about three or four hundred such small companies operating in Calgary alone, and they play an important role because they are the source of so much innovation. They are the people who say, "I've got a better mousetrap," and until you've seen it work, or not work, who can dare say they are wrong?

I'M not sure this qualifies as a lesson learned, but it's at least a bit of wisdom acquired over forty years of married life.

I've been blessed in many ways, but none more so than in my marriage with Julie. Through all the travels that my career has taken me on, she has retained her enthusiasm for exploring the world. Many couples grow apart as they grow older, but I can honestly say that Julie and I have grown closer, perhaps because we've shared the excitement of discovering different cultures. She has also maintained her fierce independence, a trait that has not only helped me navigate my way through life but that I greatly admire and respect.

We moved our family twelve different times over the years, and with each move, Julie refused to dwell on the downside of saying goodbye to friends and relatives. Instead, she looked at the next stage in our lives as a new adventure. I think, because we moved so often, she especially valued her independence and resilience.

Julie has scored enormous achievements on her own, many of them inspired by her upbringing and her experience teaching at an inner city high school when we lived in Houston. She believed that the best way to learn about the schools our children attended was to work within the culture. She volunteered wherever she could and took on leadership roles such as serving as president of the International School Parents Forum, associated with TASIS (The American School in England), while living in London.

She is co-chair of the Canadian Women's Foundation, which raises money to research, fund and share the best approaches to ending violence against women and also works to move women out of poverty and to empower girls. While in Calgary, she helped create the Juno House for adolescent girls and their families, and launched the Juno House Foundation to build capacity and provide support for those in need of its services. She also served as chair of Hull Child and Family Services for five years.

I could easily fill a chapter of this book detailing all that Julie has accomplished beyond being a wife and mother. Julie and I share the belief that to have a lasting and fulfilling relationship, each partner must encourage and support the other in achieving their goals and dreams. Sometimes two people open the doors for each other, enabling both to become the best they can be. That's been my practice in managing people, too.

Julie and I recently celebrated our fortieth wedding anniversary, and while many executives can talk about forty years of marriage, it often involves two or three wives. Julie is my first, second and third wife, so it appears that our philosophy is working.

18. A Green and Pleasant Future

Of all the good times I enjoyed as CEO of Suncor Energy, I don't believe any exceeded the day in September 2010 when we officially opened Wapisiw Lookout. Wapisiw (pronounced *wap-a-sue*) was where Sun Oil's initial oil sands production site had its first tailings pond, in 1967. The tailings ponds have probably stirred more animosity than any other by-product of mining activity at the oil sands. No surprise there. They are unattractive and to the uneducated eye they appear to be evidence of permanent disturbance to the land.

There's probably no way to make tailings ponds attractive, but from my earliest years at Suncor I was determined to reduce their number and abolish the notion that they were permanent. Their number and need would be cut with our move to in situ production, where tailings ponds are unnecessary. And they would not by any means be a lasting legacy of our presence in the oil sands because each pond site would be restored to a state as close to its original condition as soon as possible.

Wapisiw Lookout (wapisiw is Cree for *swan* and is similar to Wapasun, the name of the first person to bring a sample of bitumen-soaked earth to a Hudson's Bay Company outpost in 1719) covers about 220 hectares. No new tailings have been added to the pond after 1980 and it was thought that the older tailings would settle out quickly, but it took many more years than expected. In 2010, when the tailings surface was finally sturdy enough, we covered it with fifty centimetres of soil, added large snags and rock piles to encourage predators, then seeded it with native grasses and oats before adding 630,000 native shrubs and trees. The area was watered and fertilized, and the vegetation growth will be monitored for many years to ensure that it develops into a self-sustaining ecosystem.

The transition cycle from tailings pond to mixed-wood forest and small wetland took more than forty years for Wapisiw, which is obviously much too long. This cycle has been and will continue to be shortened considerably.

The opening of Wapisiw was important because it served as visual evidence that Suncor was serious about respecting and restoring the environment. Our achievements in the reduction of water consumption and various emissions were important, but their proof was borne out in statistics and noted, for the most part, by researchers and technologists. Wapisiw was something you could see, measure and walk around on. It was fresh, green, and quickly grew populated with local wildlife ranging from mice and voles up to the hawks, eagles and other predators that feed on them. Long after I and all the other Suncor employees who played a role in restoring the site are gone, and as much crude oil as the world needs or wants has been produced by the oil sands, Suncor tailings ponds will appear as natural and life supporting as Wapisiw.

Back in 2009 we gave ourselves a list of goals to be achieved at the oil sands location by 2015, using 2007—the latest year for which we had full and reliable statistics—as a baseline. Those goals include reducing fresh water consumption by 12 percent, increasing the reclamation of disturbed lands by 100 percent, improving energy efficiency by 10 percent, and reducing air emissions of nitrogen oxides, sulphur oxides and volatile gases by 10 percent.

We did most things quietly but made a substantial impact nevertheless. We provided $1.5 million for Ducks Unlimited Canada to expand its activities in protecting wetlands in the western boreal region, and offered similar levels of support for groups such as the Pembina Institute, the Alberta Wilderness Association and the Nature Conservancy of Canada, where Mike O'Brien served as chairman of the board of directors.

These and other goals and actions brought flak from both sides. Many environmentalists believed we should be doing more, and the investment crowd accused us of being too ambitious. Besides, the investment community wanted to know, what did this have to do with enhancing shareholder value? My response was to suggest there is no contradiction between strong economic performance and environmental stewardship. They are mutually supportive.

We would have received a more positive response, I suppose, if we had scored some headline-grabbing breakthroughs on emissions and water use, but like many technological advances, the improvements in our oil sands operations are for the most part incremental. The amount of carbon emitted for each barrel of oil we produce was cut by more than 30 percent between 1990 and 2010, with a roughly equal reduction in the amount of water used. It's difficult to predict how much more efficient the production of crude from the oil sands will become in the next decade, but I have no doubt that more advances are waiting somewhere over the horizon. Year by year Suncor and other oil sands producers will require less energy to pull bitumen out of the sands and release fewer emissions per barrel produced in the process.

At least some of my confidence in future technological advances is based on the investments in oil sands operations predicted to be made between 2010 and 2035. According to a report from the Canadian Energy Research Institute (CERI), a not-for-profit independent research firm launched jointly by government and academic institutions, investment and reinvestment in oil sands projects over that twenty-five-year period will range from a low of $2.197 trillion to as much as $4.783 trillion.[1] The lower figure assumes that only existing pipeline facilities will be used for transport primarily to the United States—an unlikely scenario. Even then, however, the amount of money is staggering and needs some kind of analogy to put it in perspective.

So how about this? With $2.2 trillion in 2010 you could purchase every sports franchise in the NBA, the NFL, the NHL and major league baseball . . . thirty times over. Here's another way to measure it: CERI projected that based on such an expenditure Canadian employment in oil sands–related activities would grow from 75,000 jobs in 2010 to more than 900,000 by 2035. The same study found that for every two new jobs created by the oil sands industry in Canada, a new job is created in the United States. With hundreds of thousands of new jobs in both countries, this expenditure will finance volumes of research on greater productivity, slashing energy use and emissions levels during the production process.

It's important to grasp that it's not just a matter of throwing money at research to address industry problems in a simple PR gesture. The advances to be made in future years will represent a steady effort to achieve continuous improvement. Research in these areas by every oil sands producer will be ongoing, and improvements can be expected to flow year after year.

It's also important to be aware that government agencies don't automatically rubber-stamp changes in oil sands production facilities. The province of Alberta, as the primary regulator, created the Energy Resources Conservation Board (ERCB), which demands that operators meet a long list of requirements before approvals are granted. It's hardly an overnight process.

Consider the time and effort needed to obtain approval for a new upgrader at the Suncor Energy oil sands site. The full procedure took six years from our official announcement to receipt of formal approval from the ERCB. The application was first submitted to, discussed with, and approved by twelve First Nations bands, seven community and regional groups, seventeen environmental organizations and almost forty other representatives and alliances. It took four thousand pages of data, filling ten large binders, to contain all aspects of the proposal. There were more than five hundred requests for further information or clarification from the ERCB and Alberta's Ministries of the Environment and Sustainable Resource Development, and each had to be responded to in detail. The terms and conditions established by Alberta covered more than a hundred pages; many of its requirements addressed detailed provisions for wildlife protection.

It's a demanding and time-consuming process, and I mention it here not as criticism—I appreciate the complexity of the issues and the number of interested parties—but to counter any assumptions about the relationship between industry and government over the oil sands. The province is a tough regulator. We not only accept their role but also support it, as long as the regulations are applied fairly and equally. Given the nature of our business and the location in which we conduct it, plus the very vocal environmental organizations that monitor the industry, we need the presence of a strong regulator.

On a broader scale, Canada needs to set higher standards for its competitiveness as a nation. Competitiveness, after all, drives productivity, and Canada's productivity continues to lag behind that of the United States. This is not just the view from a CEO's office, by the way. It's the view from a guy who sees everyone paying more for products and services than they should, and the root cause is almost always a lack of competition.

Consider cellphone charges. Canadians pay far more for cellphone access than Americans, Europeans and people in almost every other country in the world, in part because we lack a highly competitive environment. We should also have more than two railroads competing for freight contracts and more than five banks setting the service standard in that field. Canada may be a relatively small country in terms of population, but if we can overcome that with more competition we could raise our standards right across the board.

I'm not suggesting by any means that Canada model itself after the United States. But the most competitive entrepreneurs, producers and marketers sit right on our doorstep and set a pace that we can't afford to ignore.

We can do more, as Canadians, to drive productivity and competitiveness. I've done business literally all over the world, and I've learned that Canadians are just as smart and just as hard working as anyone else. The one element holding us back when it comes to being both highly competitive and highly productive is that we're very comfortable. We're prosperous, secure and generally content with our lot. Yes, we have problems, just as other nations have. But our problems are for the most part solvable, given sufficient time and effort. With comfort comes complacency, however. If we don't learn to foster a greater entrepreneurial spirit and improve our productivity, we will find ourselves falling behind.

That's a tall order, I'll admit. But sooner or later, falsely assuming that we can maintain our position by continuing to operate in the same easy-going manner will prove faulty. Countries everywhere would love to have the economic comfort that Canadians enjoy, and if they cannot gain it via natural resources or geography, they will gain it some other way—at our expense. It's all a matter of being hungry, ambitious and shrewd enough to overcome the other person's advantages. In a poker game, it's not the player sitting with four aces who wants a new deal. We may have four aces now, but several other players would like to reshuffle the cards.

I believe that fostering a more competitive approach in Canada begins by encouraging young people to enrol in college and university business courses, and not restricting access to these studies. The other steps sound like textbook answers only because they represent the policies of the most productive firms across a range of sectors:

- Invest more in machinery, equipment and technology, particularly in the information and communications sector.
- Invest more in R&D and foster innovation at several levels within organizations.
- Employ more workers with higher education levels, especially for specific functions such as engineering.
- Launch a staged program for competing in foreign markets.

This has been the story of many things, almost all of them big—big bets, big expenditures, big developments and, especially, big challenges. I have faith in the skills and determination of people in and out of the industry to find new ways to meet these challenges with technological breakthroughs. The scope and number of the advances I witnessed over my career are beyond counting. And I'm proud to say that Suncor Energy led the way in many developments and continues to do so. Our leadership in the industry—not just in production techniques but in respecting the concerns of environmentalists, First Nations people and others—is the single most important factor in the company's success.

Leadership is always about boldness and about risk. If you're not bold enough to make decisions that are the direct result of your own perception, vision and instinct, you can never be an effective leader. And if you're not willing to acknowledge the risk involved in every bold decision you make, few of your decisions will be effective.

Of course, what's risky to me may not be nearly as dangerous to you. It depends on how much you know about the situation. The risk involved in climbing a vertical cliff using only your bare hands and strength is far greater to me and most other people than it is to the men and women who know where to step and where not to. In a similar fashion, the decisions I made to boost oil sands production at Suncor by moving from the problem-plagued bucket wheels to shovels and trucks, and the billions invested in the Millennium project, held less risk to me than to outsiders. Neither was a sure thing, but I have long suspected that the risk became amplified in the minds of some people simply because everyone else was so cautious.

While Suncor is and always will be closely associated with the oil industry, its activities stretch around the world and well beyond petroleum itself. I have yet to see the kind of technological advances necessary to make wind power and solar power significant energy sources as commercial ventures, especially in Canada, but I'm not dismissive enough to say that this will never happen. My confidence in the potential of engineers and entrepreneurs to revolutionize that corner of the industry was behind Suncor's investment in these alternative sources. Somewhere right now, I suspect, a future Steve Jobs is busy in the corner of some suburban garage trying this idea and exploring that idea, working toward realizing a dream.

The degree of success we scored at Suncor stirred much of the criticism directed at us. This was no surprise to me. Our profile was the most prominent of all the oil sands operators, and the biggest targets attract the most shots. While not every encounter with critics was fun, I tried to make them all educational for both sides. Discussing my love of outdoor activities such as fishing, hiking and canoeing with someone who enjoyed the same pastimes gave us something to share. How, each of us would think, could this person be so bad if we both believe in the same things? I'm not suggesting every meeting changed minds, but sharing our concerns and interests made it easier to listen carefully to each other's point of view, and to look for ways to accept it.

I have spent more than forty years in an industry based on the concept of thinking big. Now I'm prepared to start thinking small.

I have stepped away from a company that has been as closely identified with big ideas, big investments, big production volumes and big capitalization as any in Canada in recent years. A new team with new ideas and new energy has assumed the reins, and I have no doubt that it will continue to manage one of the great success stories in the petroleum industry.

THE official announcement in December 2011 used the word *retirement* as an explanation for my leaving Suncor, but that's not quite correct. While I plan to squeeze in as much time as ever playing golf, fly-fishing and being with my family, that's not what this new stage in my life will be about. I love the petroleum business, and I intend to remain associated with the oil sands in a totally different capacity.

Few businesses are as involved in constant change as the petroleum industry. Change occurs everywhere, often with little notice and major impact. It involves political changes—think of Iraq, Iran, Libya, Syria and perhaps some other locale that's not even on the radar as I write this, but may be in the headlines as you read it. It must deal with enormous economic changes as well; if the price of some other major commodity moves with more volatility and wider effects than that of crude oil, I'm not aware of it. And it cultivates technological changes that are at once rapid and revolutionary. The industry is using tools and techniques today that would have been considered the fantasies of an over-imaginative science fiction writer through the early years of my career.

Many important developments are changing the way we recover petroleum at the oil sands, and their impact will continue to be felt throughout the industry. Some are entirely new, while others are refinements to existing systems and techniques. The improvements may be incremental, but their total effect will be to make the recovery of oil more energy efficient and environmentally friendly year by year. A large number of these steps forward will be made not by corporations such as Suncor, which will implement them, but by small enterprises with maybe a handful of staff, all free to explore ideas that others consider off the wall.

But that's where some of the best ideas come from, isn't it? The personal computer that has changed our lives in barely a single generation wasn't developed by giant IBM. It was created by two young guys in a garage. I'm not suggesting I'll be part of anything as revolutionary, but I'm looking forward to focusing exclusively on developing ideas with the freedom to fail, and without the myriad responsibilities associated with heading a massive corporation. I had fun playing the role of CEO at Suncor Energy. Like the imaginary new Steve Jobs, though, I plan to keep busy and out of the limelight, perhaps in some small, nondescript building, being bold and taking risks, looking for something that no one else has tried and been successful with in the past.

It would give me enormous pleasure to recognize the groups and individuals who wished me well when I retired from the CEO position at Suncor in May 2012, but I have already expressed my appreciation to them personally. I can't ignore mentioning one event, however, because it touched me in a unique manner.

Over my years with Suncor, I built a relationship with a number of First Nations leaders. Among them were Mel Benson, a member of the Cree nation whom I mentioned earlier in his role as a Suncor director; Michael Lickers, a Mohawk who has done outstanding work with youth in Ghost River and elsewhere; and Casey Eaglespeaker of the Blood tribe, an active educator whose work has been recognized by First Nations groups across North America.

All three men acted as my hosts, if that's the correct word, for a pipe ceremony held at the headquarters for Hull Child and Family Services in Calgary. Julie and I have supported Hull's operations for many years, and we are great admirers of the volunteers who work on behalf of people in need.

The pipe ceremony is perhaps the most sacred ritual of First Nations people. Although tobacco is used in the ceremony, its function has no association with the reason some people smoke cigarettes and cigars. To people of the First Nations, the pipe represents a physical form of their prayers, and the smoke from its bowl becomes their words. The entire ceremony serves to bond earthly and spiritual realms, and these bonds are not to be broken.

I'm not a very religious guy, but the sombre nature of the ceremony and the goodwill I sensed from these leaders affected me deeply, especially when Casey Eaglespeaker gave me my First Nations name: White Wolf. We all shared the pipe together, and I left the ceremony not only with a new name (and the pipe) but with an even deeper respect for First Nations people, their culture and their values. It was a moving and memorable way to mark the beginning of another chapter in my life.

My years at Suncor Energy changed me in more ways than I can describe, and probably more ways than I'm aware of. One of the primary and personal changes was the decision Julie and I made to become Canadian citizens. This led to recognition of my work within and beyond Suncor.

In December 2007 I was named an Officer of the Order of Canada. Rideau Hall in Ottawa, where I was formally presented with the honour by the Governor General, is a very long distance from Brush, Colorado, and I had sure come a long way from the envious teenager who watched oil patch roughnecks drive by in their shiny new pickup trucks.

It's probably unnecessary to mention how much pride I took in receiving that honour or how happy I was to share the moment with Julie and our children. Nobody sets out on a career determined to win that sort of recognition. The others who received similar honours that day were driven by motives similar to mine. We enjoyed what we did, we considered it important and we wanted to do it to the best of our abilities—and perhaps better than anyone else. When I stood to receive the Order of Canada, I thought of the thousands of other people who owned a portion of that honour, all of them employees of Suncor and all of them deserving recognition as well. Nothing important in business gets done by one person alone.

I couldn't help noticing that most other members of the Order were artists, authors, musicians or athletes. In fact, on that day the honour was granted to only two business leaders, including me. I haven't closely examined how many other business people have received this great honour over the years, and I don't intend to look it up. The guidelines say the award is granted to "Canadian citizens for outstanding achievement and service to the country or to humanity at large." It says nothing about how many jobs are created or how big the impact has been on the economy, nor should it.

I have begun to suspect, however, that some aspects of succeeding in business have grown more important in recent years, and I hope that one in particular can be recognized and adapted by politicians. The world faces immense and complex challenges over the next few decades: enormous government debt in Europe and the United States, major demands on social services in developing countries, and practical alternative energy solutions to serve future generations. Instead of exchanging viewpoints in a united effort to deal with these problems, we allow too many polarized debates in which each side is demonized by the other and mutual respect is absent.

No better example can be found than in the ongoing impasse in the U.S. Congress during the early years of this new century. America is hardly the only source of this attitude—just the most visible and dramatic. The United States and every other democratic nation need to deal with the pressing matters of the day in a responsible manner, especially when social issues are at stake. I say this not only as a father and grandfather but as a fan of free enterprise, because businesses cannot succeed in societies that fail. Business leaders must be attuned and responsive to the needs and concerns of everyone who lives and works beyond their office windows, and they and the people we elect to represent us can begin going down that road by practising something I learned from my father.

My dad knew how to do many things well, but he was exceptionally gifted at expressing interest in the lives and concerns of others and listening to the things they had to say. Of all the lessons he taught me, including the pleasure of fishing a free-flowing trout stream, nothing has been more valuable than the importance of listening.

I've made bold bets over my career, and at Suncor I managed to surround myself with a team of people whose talents, dedication, hard work and loyalty were as good or better than those in any comparable organization, anywhere in the world.

But when it comes to naming the single most important talent I managed to develop over my years since leaving Brush, Colorado, my response is immediate and simple: I learned to listen. Carefully. To everyone.

ACKNOWLEDGEMENTS

M y sincerest thanks and gratitude to John Lawrence Reynolds, who brought my words and thoughts to paper. This book would not have been completed without John's hard work and dedication, and I admire his diligence and professional skills.

Deepest thanks to Pat O'Reilly, who was at Suncor when I first joined the company and remains there at the time of publication. Her assistance in reading and correcting many drafts, as well as researching material, was invaluable.

I wish to express my appreciation of Mike O'Brien, Mike Norris and Dick Falconer, who lived through Suncor's initial public offering, the subsequent equity sales by owners, and both the attempted and the successfully completed Petro-Canada takeovers. Mike O'Brien was a key executive who filled a number of roles at Suncor during my first decade as CEO and has been a great friend. He remains on Suncor's board of directors today.

I'm grateful to Sue Lee and Gord Lambert, whose counsel and advice was important for the book and the growth of Suncor, and to Lamya Abougoush, who reviewed several drafts and offered encouragement and her usual critical insights. I would also like to thank Madeleine Oxenham, who has been a great executive assistant and a wonderful support; Jim Gifford and the HarperCollins team, whose help has been amazing; and Camilla Blakeley, who refined the manuscript with her careful and nuanced copy edit. Many thanks to the employees of Suncor for their hard work and their determination to turn a very weak company into one of Canada's strongest.

And thank you, Julie, for sharing the magic carpet ride.

Notes

Ch. 2. A Business of Big Bets

1. International Energy Agency, *The IEA, an Overview*, www.iea.org/about /docs/Overview.pdf.

2. How Stuff Works, How Oil Drilling Works, http://science.howstuffworks .com/oil-drilling.htm.

3. Hewitt D. Crane, Edwin M. Kinderman, Ripudaman Malhotra, *A Cubic Mile of Oil: Realities and Options for Averting the Looming Global Energy Crisis* (New York: Oxford University Press, 2010).

4. N.a., "Motoring Ahead: More Cars Are Now Sold in China Than in America," *The Economist*, October 23, 2009, www.economist.com /node/14732026.

5. Norihiko Shirouzu, "China Uses Green Cars to Bolster Auto Sector," *The Wall Street Journal*, March 23, 2009, http://online.wsj.com/article /SB123773108089706101.html.

6. International Energy Agency, *World Energy Outlook 2010, Executive Summary* (Paris: IEA, 2010), http://www.iea.org/Textbase/npsum /we02010sum.pdf, 5.

7. Crane, Kinderman, and Malhotra, *A Cubic Mile of Oil*, 78.

CH. 4. SUNCOR BECOMES PROFITABLE…AND CANADIAN

1. Alan Bayless, "Suncor's Dismal Prospects," *Financial Times of Canada*, February 10–16, 1992, A1.

2. Jim Doak, First Marathon Securities Ltd., as reported in "Suncor Stock Offering Sharply Cut Back," *The Globe and Mail*, March 5, 1992.

CH. 6. MOVING WEST: RELOCATING CLOSER TO THE ACTION

1. N.a., "The Next Shock?" *The Economist*, March 4, 1999, 37, www.economist.com/node/188181.

CH. 7. THE PETRO-CANADA SAGA

1. Peter McKenzie-Brown, "Melting Away: Like the Wicked Witch of the West, Petro-Canada Has Met Its Demise, and Few Are around to Mourn," *Oilweek*, November 29, 2009, www.oilweek.com/index.php/en/news /government/5044-melting-away.html.

CH. 10. THE IMPORTANCE OF A SECOND MARKET FOR CANADA'S OIL

1. Switchboard, National Resources Defense Council Staff Blog, Peter Lehner, "Keystone Pipeline, Tar Sands Oil, and Climate Change Are Not in Our National Interest," August 31, 2011, http://switchboard.nrdc.org /blogs/plehner/keystone_pipeline_tar_sands_oi.html.

2. Bruce Barcott, "Pipeline through Paradise: Why Oil Sands, a Sunken Ferry, and the Price of Oil in China Have the Great Bear Rainforest in an Uproar," *National Geographic* (August 2011), http://ngm.nationalgeographic.com/2011/08/canada-rainforest/barcott-text.

3. James Burkhard, Jacki Forrest, and Terry Hallmark, *Major Sources of U.S. Oil Supply: The Challenge of Comparisons*, Special report (Cambridge, MA: IHS CERA, October 17, 2011), 6. IHS is Information Handling Services, which in 2004 acquired Cambridge Energy Research Associates (CERA) to become IHS CERA, advising international energy companies, governments, financial institutions and technology providers.

4. Ibid.

5. Ibid., 19.

6. Dawn Walton, "Ontario Urged to Speak up for Oil Sands," *The Globe and Mail*, February 27, 2012, A8. The estimate includes $311 billion in federal taxes, $105 billion in Alberta provincial taxes, and $350 billion in Alberta royalties.

7. Ibid.

CH. 12. How to Steady a Three-Legged Stool

1. A.K. Chapagain, A.Y. Hoekstra, H.H.G. Savenije, and R. Gautam, "The Water Footprint of Cotton Consumption: An Assessment of the Impact of Worldwide Consumption of Cotton Products on the Water Resources in the Cotton Producing Countries," *Ecological Economics* 60, no. 1 (2006): 186–203.

CH. 13. The Always Present (and Frequently Frustrating) Politics of Petroleum

1. Hewitt D. Crane, Edwin M. Kinderman, Ripudaman Malhotra, *A Cubic Mile of Oil: Realities and Options for Averting the Looming Global Energy Crisis* (New York: Oxford University Press, 2010).

2. U.S. Energy Information Administration, International Energy Outlook 2011, (Washington, DC: U.S. EIA, September 2011), 12, DOE/EIA-0484(2011).

3. Energy Policy Institute of Canada, Guiding Principles, www.canadasenergy .ca/guiding-principles.

4. Jonathan Tirone, "Japan Nuclear Safety Plan Foresaw Quake, Underestimated Impact Of Tsunami," Bloomberg, March 15, 2011, http://www .bloomberg.com/news/2011–03–15/japan-nuclear-safety-plan-foresaw-quake-underestimated-tsunami.html.

5. Josh Wingrove, "Cheap and Dirty: Where Provinces Diverge on Energy Crossroads," *The Globe and Mail*, September 12, 2011.

6. Ibid.

7. International Energy Agency, U.S. Electrical Generation by Fuel, 2008.

8. Vivian Krause, "U.S. Foundations Against the Oil Sands: The Tides Foundation Has Spent $6 Million to Fund Green Lobbies," Financial Post, October 14, 2010, http://opinion.financialpost.com/2010/10/14/u-s-foundations-against-the-oil-sands/.

CH. 14. THE CHALLENGE OF GLOBAL WARNING

1. *IHS CERA, Oil Sands, Greenhouse Gases, and U.S. Oil Supply: Getting the Numbers Right*, Special report (Cambridge, MA: IHS CERA, September 2010).

2. Ibid.

3. James Burkhard, Samantha Gross, and Jackie Forrest, *Oil Sands, Greenhouse Gases, and European Oil Supply: Getting the Numbers Right*, Special report (Cambridge, MA: IHS CERA, April 25, 2011).

CH. 15. THE LEGENDARY TWO-JAWED FISH

1. Oakland Ross, "Oil Sands Threaten Our Survival, Al Gore Warns," *Toronto Star*, November 29, 2009, http://www.thestar.com/news/canada/article/729836—oil-sands-threaten-our-survival-al-gore-warns.

2. About.com, Trucks, SUV reviews and specs, http://trucks.about.com/cs/suvreviews/a/hummer_fue104.

3. Toyota, Prius 2012, www.toyota.ca/toyota/en/vehicles/prius/features-benefits/performance.

4. Erin N. Kelly, David W. Schindler, Peter V. Hodson, Jeffrey W. Short, Roseanna Radmanovick, and Charlene Nielsen, "Oil Sands Development

Contributes Elements Toxic at Low Concentrations to the Athabasca River and Its Tributaries," *Proceedings of the National Academy of Sciences of the United States of America*, 107, no. 37 (September 14, 2010), www.pnas.org/cgi/doi/10.1073/pnas.1008754107.

5. Vivian Krause, "Tarred by Science: How Green Groups Pursued Oil Sands Agenda," *Financial Post*, June 13, 2011, http://opinion.financialpost.com/2011/06/13/junk-science-week-tarred-by-science/.

6. Josh Wingrove, "Elevated Levels of Toxins Found in Athabasca River," *The Globe and Mail*, December 15, 2010, http://www.theglobeandmail.com/news/national/prairies/elevated-levels-of-toxins-found-in-athabasca-river/article1689578/.

7. Pierre Gosselin, Steve E. Hrudey, M. Anne Naeth, André Plourde, René Therrien, Glen Van Der Kraak, and Zhenghe Xu, *Environmental and Health Impacts of Canada's Oil Sands Industry* (Ottawa: Royal Society of Canada, December 2010), http://www.rsc.ca/documents/expert/RSC%20report%20complete%20secured%209Mb.pdf.

8. Carol Christian, "U of A Scientists Say Fish Caught in Lake Athabasca Doesn't Have Two Mouths," *Fort McMurray TODAY*, March 9, 2009.

9. Alberta Health Services, "Fort Chipewyan Cancer Study Findings Released," press release, February 6, 2009, www.albertahealthservices.ca/500.asp.

10. Elizabeth Kolbert, "The Catastrophist: NASA's Climate Expert Delivers the News No One Wants to Hear," *The New Yorker*, June 29, 2009, http://www.newyorker.com/reporting/2009/06/29/090629fa_fact_kolbert.

11. James E. Hansen, "Silence Is Deadly: An Appeal to Get Involved in Decisions Regarding the Tar Sands," June 3, 2011, www.columbia.edu/~jeh1/mailings.

12. Cassandra Szklarski, "James Cameron slams Alberta tar sands," *Toronto Star*, April 20, 2010.

13. Guy Adams, "James Cameron Labelled Climate Change 'Hypocrite,'" *The*

Independent (London), October 24, 2010, http://www.independent.co.uk /environment/climate-change/james-cameron-labelled-climate-change-hypocrite-2115151.html.

14. Glenn Whipp, "Is Avatar a Message Movie? Absolutely, Says James Cameron," *Los Angeles Times*, February 10, 2010, http://articles.latimes.com/2010/feb/10/news/la-en-cameron10–2010feb10.

CH. 16. THE PROMISE OF ALTERNATIVE FUELS

1. Canadian Wind Energy Association, "Canada On Track to Install More Than 1,500 MW of New Wind Energy Capacity in a Record Setting 2012," press release, April 17, 2012, http://www.canwea.ca/media/release /release_e.php?newsId=147.

2. Josh Wingrove, "Cheap and Dirty: Where Provinces Diverge on Energy Crossroads," *The Globe and Mail*, September 12, 2011. http://www.the-globeandmail.com/news/national/time-to-lead/cheap-and-dirty-where-provinces-diverge-on-energy-crossroads/article2162021/.

3. Len Coad and Marta Bristow, "Ethanol's Potential Contribution to Canada's Transportation Sector" (Ottawa: Conference Board of Canada, November 2011), http://www.growthenergy.org/images/reports/12–098 _EthanolContribution-RPTWeb_Final.pdf.

4. David Biello, "The False Promise of Biofuels," *Scientific American* (August 2011), 61.

5. Ibid., 60.

6. Brent D. Yacobucci and Randy Schnepf, *Ethanol and Biofuels: Agriculture, Infrastructure, and Market Constraints Related to Expanded Production*, Congressional Research Service Report for Congress, March 16, 2007, 8.

7. U.S. Department of Energy, Transportation Energy Data Book, Appendix B conversions, table B4, rates the energy content of ethanol at 21.2 megajoules per litre versus gasoline at 34.8 megajoules per litre.

8. Steve Brearton, "Power Hungry," *Report on Business Magazine* (October 2011), 9.

9. Ibid. Estimated at C$1.39 to 1, as of October 4, 2011.

10. James Kanter, "Fancy Batteries in Electric Cars Pose Recycling Challenges," *The New York Times*, August 30, 2011, http://www.nytimes.com/2011/08/31/business/energy-environment/fancy-batteries-in-electric-cars-pose-recycling-challenges.html?pagewanted=all.

11. Ibid.

12. Statistics Canada, "Electric Power Generation, Transmission and Distribution, 2007" (Ottawa: Minister of Industry, 2009), Catalogue no. 57–202-X, www.statcan.gc.ca/publications.

13. U.S. Energy Information Administration, "Electricity Explained: Electricity in the U.S.," www.eia.gov/energyexplained/index.cfm?page=electricity_in_the_united_states.

14. Living in Canada, "The Climate and Weather of Toronto, Ontario," www.livingin-canada.com/climate-toronto.html.

15. Living in Canada, "The Climate and Weather of Edmonton, Alberta," www.livingin-canada.com/climate-edmonton.html.

16. Potential Gas Committee, "Potential Gas Committee Reports Substantial Increase in Magnitude of U.S. Natural Gas Resource Base," press release, April 27, 2011, http://potentialgas.org/press-release.

CH. 18. A GREEN AND PLEASANT FUTURE

1. Afshin Honarvar, Jon Rozhon, Dinara Millington, Thorn Walden, and Carlos A. Murillo, *Economic Impacts of Staged Development of Oil Sands Projects in Alberta (2010–2035)*, study no. 125, section 1 (Calgary: Canadian Energy Research Institute, June 2011), xiii.

Index

Aamjiwnaang First Nation, 155

Abdullah, King, 16

Africa, 191, 222

Alberta
- climate, 38, 45–46, 152
- coal-fired power plants, 184
- environmental policy and enforcement, 69, 72, 149, 168, 252–53
- as petroleum producer, 78, 90
- royalties and taxes on oil, 39, 47, 147, 172, 176

Alberta Health Services, 214

Alberta Wilderness Association, 251

Algeria, 14

Angola, 14

Arab Spring (2011), 15, 16

Athabasca River, 1
- basin, 50, 152
- fish from, 211
- pollutants in, 207–08, 209
- use in oil sands production, 69, 71–72, 167–68, 209, 210, 212

Australia, 85–87, 190

automobile(s)
- electric, 21, 232–33, 234
- hybrid, 232, 233
- industry, 5–6, 167, 196, 233
- replacing petroleum-powered, 233–34

batteries, electric-powered vehicle, 232–33

Benson, Mel, 156–57, 258–59

biofuels, 200, 223, 226–30

bitumen, 2, 3, 35, 67–68, 207, 208, 211, 213

boreal forest, 1, 49, 67, 171

Boucher, Jim, 158

Bow River, 72

Brazil, 18, 21, 22, 145–46, 195–96

Brenneman, Ron, 99, 101, 102, 103, 104, 106, 107

Brush, CO, 131, 132

bucket wheels, 49–51, 52, 53, 61, 65, 256

Bush, George W., 18

Butts, Gerald, 66

Calgary, 72, 77, 78–79, 90, 108, 128

California, 199–202, 217

Cameron, James, 216–19

Campbell, Bob, 56, 59

Canada
- carbon dioxide emissions from, 192, 213

competitiveness in, 253–55

dependence on U.S. for sale of oil, 142–43, 144–45, 147, 148–50

importance of energy sector in, 144

National Energy Program (NEP), 40, 177

national energy strategy, need for, 177–79, 180, 182, 183, 188, 194, 202

national sovereignty of, 149–50, 187

productivity of, 253

royalties and taxes on oil, 39, 47, 76, 147, 148, 176

Canadian Energy Research Institute (CERI), 147, 251–52

Canadian Women's Foundation, 247

carbon dioxide emissions. *See also* carbon tax; greenhouse gases (GHG)

from coal-fired power plants, 184–85, 186

from oil sands, 215–16, 251

from transportation sector, 182, 192, 194, 196, 200

carbon tax, 181–82, 183, 198, 203

CARE (Clean Air Renewable Energy) Coalition, 224

cars. *See* automobiles

CBC, 207, 208, 212fn, 217

cellphone charges, 253–54

CERI (Canadian Energy Research Institute), 147, 251–52

Chevrolet Volt, 232, 233

China, 21, 21fn, 22, 145, 180, 195–96

China National Petroleum Corporation, 117

Chip Manufacturing, 153

Chiquita, 244, 244fn

CIBC, 94

CIBC Wood Gundy, 58, 59

Clean Air Renewable Energy (CARE) Coalition, 224

climate change, 191, 193, 196, 223

coal, 20, 175, 180fn

coal-fired power plants, 183, 184, 185, 186, 192, 217, 234

Colorado, 88

Competition Bureau, 108

ConocoPhilips Canada, 224, 243

Conservative Party, 177–78

corn ethanol production, 226–30

Crown corporations, 98

CTV, 217

Cutting Edge Recycling, 153

David Suzuki Foundation, 189

Davis, William, 40, 63

DiCaprio, Leonardo, 142

Dion, Stéphane, 183

draglines, 50fn

Ducks Unlimited Canada, 251

Eaglespeaker, Casey, 259

E&P petroleum companies, 164–65

Economist, The, 83

Ecuador, 14, 16

Edmonton, 72, 235

Egypt, 15, 29

electric cars, 21, 232–33, 234

electric power, 234. *See also* coal-fired power plants; hydroelectric power; nuclear energy; solar energy; wind power

Enbridge, 143, 225

energy conservation, 194, 195, 202, 242, 251

Energy Policy Institute of Canada (EPIC), 178, 179

Energy Resources Conservation Board (ERCB), 252, 253

energy sources

alternative, 66, 75, 88, 165, 197, 222, 224–25, 226–30

timeline to switch, 20

engineers and engineering, 31, 32, 135

environmental groups, 13, 143, 189, 190, 191,
193, 197–98, 205–07, 222, 227
EPIC (Energy Policy Institute of Canada),
178, 179
Équiterre, 65
ERCB (Energy Resources Conservation
Board), 252, 253
ERP (enterprise resource planning), 112
ethanol, 200, 226–30
ExxonMobil, 3, 78, 118, 126, 156

Falconer, Dick, 59
Federation of Canadian Municipalities, 224
Ferguson, John, 99–100, 102, 103, 104,
105–06, 107, 109
First Nations, 1
    anti–oil sands protestors, 154–55
    and approval process for Suncor upgrader,
       253
    and Gateway pipeline, 144, 155
    historic use of bitumen, 2, 68
    language issues, 157
    in oil sands region, 155, 158, 163, 207
    oil sands workers and suppliers, 75–76,
       151–54, 155, 159, 163
    pipe ceremony, 259
Fort Chipweyan, 209, 214, 217
Fort Hills, 115, 122
Fort McKay, 158
Fort McKay First Nation, 152, 158
Fort McMurray, 152, 153, 158
fracking, 182, 236
France, 179
Friends of the Earth, 224

Gaddafi, Muammar, 15, 116, 118
Gallagher, John, 139
gasoline, 20
    GHG from oil sands–produced, 199–200

and hybrid vehicles, 232
prices, 13, 14–15
regulations regarding ethanol content, 228
regulations regarding lead and sulphur
    content, 203
Gateway pipeline, 143–44, 147, 150
GCOS (Great Canadian Oil Sands), 6,
    36–39, 40
George, Julie, 3, 4, 28, 29–30, 33–34, 78, 128,
    246–48, 259
George, Phil, 28
George, Rick
    on ambition, 134
    on American politics, 187, 188, 261
    and Canadian citizenship, 128, 259
    on Canadian reaction to American
      criticism, 187
    as CEO of Suncor, 3, 4–5, 8, 9–10, 44–45,
      53, 61–62, 66, 74, 79, 80, 85, 102, 106,
      135, 158, 166, 189, 196–97, 198, 223,
      239, 249, 256
    childhood, 131–32
    on "corporate soul," 125–26, 130
    on crisis management, 138–39
    on dealing with foreign regimes, 117–18
    on decision-making, 81–82, 83, 84, 87
    early career, 3–5, 27, 29–31, 32–34
    education, 28–29, 30–32
    on employees as company's most valuable
      asset, 85, 114, 134, 260, 261
    family, 3, 4, 5, 28, 33–34, 43, 78, 106–07,
      108–09, 128, 131, 189, 246–47
    First Nations pipe ceremony for, 259
    on fun in the workplace, 127–29
    on goals and strategies, 133–34
    on government's role in energy industry,
      180–81, 253
    on hiring and firing staff, 85, 113
    on investing, 62–63, 84

on labels and stereotypes, 190

on management skills, 83–84, 132, 137, 240, 247, 255, 261

on mergers, 111

move to Sun Oil in 1980, 34–35

as Officer of the Order of Canada, 260

on partnerships, 121, 123

pastimes, 131, 195, 256, 257

on public speaking, 129–30

retirement as CEO of Suncor, 257–58

on role of corporate board directors, 99

geothermal energy, 230

Germany, 230–31

GHG. *See* greenhouse gases

global economic crisis (2008), 104, 198

global poverty, 191, 222

global warming, 184, 191, 192, 195–96

Globe and Mail, The, 208

GM (General Motors), 232

Gore, Al, 206, 222

Great Barrier Reef, 87

Great Bear Rain Forest, 143

Great Canadian Oil Sands (GCOS), 6, 36–39, 40

greenhouse gases (GHG). *See also* carbon dioxide emissions; carbon tax
and ethanol, 228

from oil sands–produced gasoline, 199–200

reducing, 193–97, 198, 202, 210–11

wells-to-wheels measurement of, 191–92, 201

Greenpeace, 65, 189, 190, 191

Gretzky, Wayne, 83

Guilbeault, Steven, 65, 189

Gulf of Mexico, 229

Gull Lake, SK, 225

Hannah, Daryl, 212–14

Hansen, James, 215–16

Houston, 140

Hull Child and Family Services, 259

Hummer, 206

hydroelectric power, 20, 175, 178, 184, 235

IEA (International Energy Agency), 17–18, 22

IHS CERA, 145, 146

Imperial Oil, 36, 54, 78

India, 21, 21fn, 22, 195–96

Indonesia, 195–96

Inpex, 122

in situ processing, 68–69, 166, 171, 172, 211

International Energy Agency (IEA), 17–18, 22

International School Parents Forum, 246

Iran, 14, 257

Iraq, 14, 145

Jackman, Boris, 119

Japan, 179–80, 203, 235

Joslyn Mine, 121, 122

Juno House Foundation, 247

kerosene, 20

Keystone XL pipeline, 141–43, 212, 215

Kinder Morgan, 143

Kitimat, BC, 143, 150

Kuwait, 14, 176

Kyoto Protocol, 197

Lambert, Gord, 223, 224, 242

law, 31–32

LCA (life-cycle analysis) of fuel, 199–200

LCFS (Low-Carbon Fuel Standard), 199–202

Leduc oil field, 36, 39

Lee, Sue, 94, 114, 128–29
Liberal Party, 183
Libya, 14, 15, 18, 33, 116, 117–18, 119, 122, 257
Lickers, Michael, 259
lithium, 233
Little, Mark, 113–14
Low-Carbon Fuel Standard (LCFS), 199–202
Lundin Oil, 101

MacNeill, Brian, 99, 103, 104, 105, 106, 107
Malta, 33
Mansbridge, Peter, 217
Manwell, Gerry, 224
Markey, Edward, 185
McIntosh, Rob, 65
Merkel, Angela, 230–31
Métis, 75–76, 152, 153
Mexico, 146
MFT (mature fine tailings), 169
Middle East, 15, 16, 36, 82, 117, 176, 192
Mikisew Slings and Safety, 153
Millennium Mine, 80–84, 162, 169
Mississippi River, 229

National Energy Program (NEP), 40, 177
National Geographic, 143
natural gas, 20, 67, 140
    export of, 182–83
    fracking, 182, 236
    use in oil sands production, 171–72
    use in power plants, 236
Natural Resources Canada, 225
Natural Resources Defense Council (NRDC), 142
Nature Conservancy of Canada, 251
Nature of Things, The, 207
NEP (National Energy Program), 40, 177

Netherlands, The, 116
Nexen, 243
NGOs (non-governmental organizations), 181, 187–88, 189
Niagara River, 72fn
Nigeria, 14, 146, 162, 192
Norris, Mike, 59, 93, 101, 102
North Saskatchewan River, 72
North Sea, 4, 34, 45, 67, 100, 101, 115, 116
Norway, 17, 143, 176
NRDC (Natural Resources Defense Council), 142
nuclear energy, 20, 175, 179–80, 185, 230, 234–35

Obama, Barack, 142fn
O'Brien, Mike, 54, 55, 56, 57, 58–59, 94, 97, 251
Occidental Petroleum, 122
Ogilvie, Ken, 66
oil
    as commodity, 14, 24, 175, 244
    embargo, Middle Eastern, 29
    importance of, 19–20, 33, 165, 171, 175–76, 193–94, 222
    as political issue, 175
    prices, 7, 14, 17, 39, 80, 83–84, 172
    reserves in North America, 68
    royalties, 39, 47, 76, 147, 148, 176
    search for new deposits of, 18, 22–23, 44, 74, 80, 226
    spills, 80, 139–40, 141
    timeline to reduce consumption of, 231
    worldwide consumption of, 18, 19–20, 22, 177
oil industry
    American, 5, 145, 200–01
    Canadian, 39, 78, 83, 89, 109, 142–43, 144–45, 147, 162, 174, 202

competition in, 23–24, 121
international, 4, 14–17, 23, 118, 245
perceptions of, 13, 139, 176
retail side of, 61–62, 119–20
small companies in, 245–46, 258
women in, 23, 162
oil pipeline(s), 140
Gateway, 143–44, 147, 150
inspection of, 140–41
Keystone XL, 141–43
oil sands, 2–3, 67. *See also* Suncor oil sands
operation
and air quality, 210
American firms as suppliers to, 141
amount of bitumen in, 67, 68, 213
carbon contained in, 215
employment income provided by, 148,
152, 173
false, hypocritical or exaggerated
statements regarding, 48–49, 67, 167,
206–08, 211, 212–19, 223, 240
history of, 3, 6, 7, 35–38
impact of shutting down, 75–76, 165, 186,
192–93, 221
media's depiction of, 161, 162, 167,
212
size of, 2, 24, 67, 169
technology, 68, 71–72, 86, 137–38, 167,
171, 199, 204, 242, 243
and term *tar sands,* 2fn
water consumption, 69, 71–72, 167–69,
203, 209–10, 242, 250
workers, 75, 151–52, 159, 163, 219, 252
Oil Sands Developers Group (OSDG), 164
Oil Sands Leadership Initiative (OSLI),
242–43, 244
oil wells, offshore, 34
Oldman River, 72
Ontario, 78, 232

investment in Suncor, 6–7, 8, 40–41, 55,
56, 57, 58, 59, 60, 61, 63, 77
power plants, 184, 235
Ontario Teachers Pension Plan, 100
OPEC (Organization of Petroleum Exporting
Countries, 14–15, 16, 17, 18, 75
open-pit mining, 35, 48–49, 68, 69, 73, 161,
169. *See also* tailings ponds
Order of Canada, 260
Organization of Petroleum Exporting
Countries. *See* OPEC
OSLI (Oil Sands Leadership Initiative),
242–43, 244

Pacific Rim, as market for Canadian oil, 143,
147
Parallel Paths, 197, 223–24, 225, 226–27
Parkinson-Marcoux, Dee, 53
Pelosi, Nancy, 65, 183, 185, 186
Pembina Institute, 65, 224, 251
Petro-Canada, 7
board of directors, 101–02, 103–04, 105,
106, 107, 108
corporate culture, 92–93
as Crown corporation, 89–91
foreign assets, 100, 101
gasoline, 226
merger with Suncor. *See* Suncor takeover
of Petro-Canada
R&M (refining and marketing), 119, 120
share price, 91, 100, 101, 102, 104, 105
Petro-Canada Act, 94, 103, 108
petroleum industry. *See* oil industry
Pew, J. Howard, 36–37, 38
Pollution Probe, 66, 224
*Proceedings of the National Academy of Sciences
of the United States of America (PNAS),*
207–08, 211–12
public transit, 181, 182, 183, 194, 200

Quatar, 14
Quebec, 62, 178, 235

Rae, Bob, 63
RBC Capital Markets, 93, 101, 102
RBC Dominion Securities, 58, 59
Redford, Robert, 142
Roberts, Harry, 113–14
Rockefeller, John D., 3
Royal Bank, 23
Royal Society of Canada (RSC), 208–10,
    211–12, 213, 214

SAGD (steam-assisted gravity drainage),
    68–69, 171
Sarnia, ON, 155, 226
Saskatchewan, 18, 67, 225
Saskatchewan Environment and Resource
    Management (SERM), 225
Saudi Arabia, 14–16, 75, 145, 162
Schindler, David, 207, 208, 211, 212
Schwarzenegger, Arnold, 199
SERM (Saskatchewan Environment and
    Resource Management), 225
shale oil deposits, 18, 88
    Stuart project, 85–88
Shaw, JR, 85
Shell, 78, 118
Sierra Club, 65, 189, 208
Smith, Roger, 128
solar energy, 181, 235, 256
Southern Pacific Petroleum, 85
Standard Oil, 3
Stanford, Jim, 91, 93, 94, 95, 96, 97, 99
Statoil Canada, 243
Steepbank Mine, 81, 166
Stelmach, Ed, 217
Stewart, Barry, 53–54
Stuart shale oil project, 85–88, 190

Sunbridge, 225
Suncor, 6fn, 243. *See also* Sun Oil
    board of directors, 56, 104, 107, 108, 151,
        156–57
    capital from foreign sources, 187
    core purpose statement, 132–33
    corporate culture, 9, 46, 53, 77, 92, 112,
        113, 125–26
    and credit crisis of 2008, 102
    downstream assets, 43, 61–62, 119
    employee incentive plan, 134
    employee morale, 8, 9, 77
    ethanol facility, 226
    field operators, 79, 135
    and First Nations, 151, 156–59
    growth of (1991–2011), 10, 23, 63, 240,
        241. *See also* Suncor takeover of
        Petro-Canada
    head office relocation, 77–79, 127–28
    investment in alternative energy sources,
        66, 75, 88, 197, 223–27, 230, 256
    management system, 112–13
    merger with Petro-Canada. *See* Suncor
        takeover of Petro-Canada
    name change, 88, 223
    refineries, 115, 155
    revenue, 240, 241
    royalties paid to government by, 148
    service stations, 62, 119–20
    share price, 105, 106, 138
    size of workforce, 23, 148
    and Southern Pacific Petroleum, 86
    taking company public, 55–61, 62–63
    technological breakthroughs, 170, 251, 255
    Total partnership agreement with, 121–23
    as unique petroleum company, 54–55,
        125, 132–33
    value system, 74, 113, 130, 133
Suncor Energy. *See* Suncor